The
EVERYTHING®
Success Book

Dear Reader:

When I was a nineteen-year-old college student, studying the art of business from dry textbooks, I opted to sample the real thing. Along with a partner, I purchased a small pet food and supplies shop called "Pet Nosh" in the New York City borough of Queens. Our initial investment was $7,000—everything both of us had.

When the business got rolling in the autumn of 1979, I resolved to succeed. I set goals all along the way. In 1996, Pet Nosh—not just one neighborhood shop by this time, but eight superstores—was sold to the retail giant Petco for $19 million. I was financially secure at the age of thirty-six.

In *The Everything® Success Book*, I unveil many of the key ingredients that define genuine success in life, from career to family to anything in between. I'm certain that the particulars of your vision of success are quite different from mine. Nevertheless, success has what we might call a common ground—a basic state of personal satisfaction—that all of us seek, and that's where this title firmly pitches its tent.

Always believe that it is possible to realize authentic and lasting successes in life. I wish you as much success in your quest for success as I've had in mine.

Joseph Nigro

The EVERYTHING® Series

Editorial

Publishing Director	Gary M. Krebs
Managing Editor	Kate McBride
Copy Chief	Laura MacLaughlin
Acquisitions Editor	Bethany Brown
Development Editor	Patrycja Pasek-Gradziuk
Production Editor	Jamie Wielgus

Production

Production Director	Susan Beale
Production Manager	Michelle Roy Kelly
Series Designers	Daria Perreault
	Colleen Cunningham
Cover Design	Paul Beatrice
	Frank Rivera
Layout and Graphics	Colleen Cunningham
	Rachael Eiben
	Michelle Roy Kelly
	Daria Perreault
	Erin Ring
Series Cover Artist	Barry Littmann

Visit the entire Everything® Series at everything.com

THE
EVERYTHING®
SUCCESS
BOOK

Reach your goals, shape your
dreams, and achieve fulfillment—
in business and at home

Joseph Nigro & Nicholas Nigro

Adams Media
Avon, Massachusetts

An Everything® Series Book.
Everything® and everything.com® are registered trademarks of F+W Publications, Inc.

Published by Adams Media, an F+W Publications Company
57 Littlefield Street, Avon, MA 02322 U.S.A.
www.adamsmedia.com

ISBN: 1-58062-975-X
Printed in the United States of America.

J   I   H   G   F   E   D   C   B   A

Library of Congress Cataloging-in-Publication Data
Nigro, Joseph.
The everything success book / Joseph Nigro and Nicholas Nigro.
     p.   cm.   (An everything series book)
ISBN 1-58062-975-X
1. Success in business–Handbooks, manuals, etc.
2. Business planning–Handbooks, manuals, etc.
3. Success–Handbooks, manuals, etc.
4. Self-management (Psychology)–Handbooks, manuals, etc.
5. Goal(Psychology)–Handbooks, manuals, etc. I. Nigro, Nicholas J.
II. Title. III. Series: Everything series.

HF5386.N47 2003
650.1–dc21

2003014834

This publication is designed to provide accurate and authoritative information with
regard to the subject matter covered. It is sold with the understanding that the pub-
lisher is not engaged in rendering legal, accounting, or other professional advice.
If legal advice or other expert assistance is required, the services of a competent
professional person should be sought.
        —From a *Declaration of Principles* jointly adopted by a Committee of the
American Bar Association and a Committee of Publishers and Associations

Many of the designations used by manufacturers and sellers to distinguish their
products are claimed as trademarks. Where those designations appear in this book
and Adams Media was aware of a trademark claim, the designations have been
printed with initial capital letters.

This book is available at quantity discounts for bulk purchases.
For information, call 1-800-872-5627.

Contents

Acknowledgments

First and foremost, we thank our editor Bethany Brown, who made this and past projects both possible and pleasurable. And, we are eternally grateful to Larry Troisi for his time, wisdom, and a fine meal on top of that. Much thanks also to Martha Shaffer for her insight, support, and unique expertise on the ABCs of writing mission statements. Last but not least, we owe a debt of gratitude to Rich Covello, who took a chance in partnering in a business with a nineteen-year-old kid.

Top Ten Attributes
of a Successful Individual

1. Practices the art of self-actualization: converting potential into reality.

2. Utilizes self-awareness to appreciate both possibilities and limitations.

3. Accepts setbacks as part of life and always moves forward.

4. Shares successes and good fortune with others.

5. Scrupulously attends to both physical and spiritual health and wellness.

6. Actively seeks out positive relationships, both personally and professionally.

7. Financially plans for the future, but lives in the present.

8. Views all learning as a never-ending story.

9. Smoothly adapts to change.

10. Maintains positive self-esteem in good times as well as bad times.

Introduction

▶ WHAT IS SUCCESS? You aren't likely to find a satisfactory answer to this question in your dictionary. Definitions of the word itself are usually quite broad, and they tend to leave ample room for interpretation and exploration. Most dictionaries define "success" something like this: "A favorable or desired outcome." But we all know that success consists of much more than a lifeless, impersonal description. We know this because each and every one of us desires to become a "success," even if we don't quite have all the particulars in order.

From our individual perspectives, each one of us maintains a specific notion of what constitutes success. Computer visionary and educator Alan Kay said, "The best way to predict the future is to invent it." What that means to each of us, individually, is that if we want to make things happen, we must chart our own course. We all want to realize certain things in life, reach certain plateaus, and live lives of genuine fulfillment. Whether it's financial security, peace of mind, sound physical and spiritual health, healthy relationships, more leisure time, or a combination of all these things, we see success in terms of the betterment of our lives. Although the particular goals and dreams vary from person to person, overall success is rooted in the same rich earth.

The Everything® Success Book explores many of the roads you can explore on your quest for real and lasting successes in life. On this rather extensive and sometimes circuitous expedition, the book addresses subject matter that ranges far and wide. It provides a mother lode of helpful techniques to aid you in achieving the ultimate goal—success and personal fulfillment in all aspects of your life.

While the specific meaning of success is the subject of many debates—and always will be—certain special mindsets and life accomplishments are nevertheless the marks of the truly successful. Success awaits those who are genuinely committed to realizing it, from maintaining positive self-esteem and an open mind, to showcasing an ability to persevere through life's obstacles, to understanding how to maximize time and establish a proper balance between career and family. In other words, success doesn't ordinarily come knocking on our doors—opportunities do, however!—nor does it fall out of the sky into our laps. We must consciously seek out success and follow it to the ends of the earth—metaphorically speaking—if necessary.

After you've read *The Everything® Success Book*, you'll be more aware of the myriad ingredients that infuse the life of countless men and women who enjoy the trappings of success. And you'll understand that in the big picture, the choices you make are what inevitably determine whether you get what you want out of life. You'll also come to appreciate that it's never too late to grab the success baton and run with it. It's also never too late to climb out of life's deepest ravines.

First and foremost, you must determine exactly what success means to you. You must decide what you want out of life and how you are going to achieve these things. Once you visualize what success is, set your life goals, and make plans, the odds are good that positive things will happen in your life. There are no guarantees, and failures are a part of the success journey. If there is one personality trait found in all successful people, it's that they endure—they don't give up.

The Everything® Success Book is a user-friendly guide that is designed to assist you on your quest for success. Of course, no single book is going to make you a success in life. Success is a process that unfolds incrementally over time. Keep in mind that success in life is really a must. We only go around once on this earthly plane, and taking the trip as a success is a whole lot more fun than the alternative.

Chapter 1

The Essential Foundation of Success

The true meaning of the word "success" has been the subject of long debate and much reflection. The particulars of what constitutes success vary from person to person. Nevertheless, everyone can agree that there are universal attitudes and behaviors associated with success. There is no argument from any quarter: Genuine and lasting successes in life are built on rock-solid foundations.

The Ground Floor: Positive Self-Esteem

Never underestimate the all-encompassing power of believing in yourself. Positive self-esteem is the fuel that drives us to genuine success. Without some healthy self-esteem sitting in your personality's driver seat, no forward movement in life is possible. And without such positive momentum, real and durable successes are unattainable.

You can undertake certain specific actions to enhance your overall self-esteem. You might very well need to do a major overhaul of an entrenched negative mindset. More likely, though, you'll require nothing so dramatic, and a little tweaking of your core personality will put your self-esteem on the positive side of the ledger.

Positive Personality Makeovers

Any personality makeover—big or small—is a task. Let's just say that working on improving your personality is a little bit more involved than putting on your socks in the morning. For a positive personality change or attitude adjustment of any magnitude, four essential ingredients must come together in perfect harmony:

1. Awareness that a positive life change is necessary.
2. Conscious and committed decision to make the change.
3. Heightened self-awareness of precisely what needs to be accomplished.
4. Dedicated effort to see things through to an optimum conclusion.

Ralph Waldo Emerson once wrote, "We are what we think about all day long." The talented poet and writer of yesteryear hit the bull's-eye with this simple declarative sentence. The true measures of who we are can be found in what we think about, how we cope with life's inevitable obstacles, and the way we interact with the people in our inner circles. Our daily thoughts and everyday behaviors are regular displays of how we feel about ourselves.

Your Self-Esteem Quotient

Many of us are under the misconception that negative self-esteem is cast, like a cement mold, in an individual's personality at birth. Self-esteem is not predetermined, however, nor is it a foregone conclusion that a rough-and-tumble upbringing produces boys or girls—later men and women—of low self-esteem. With a sincere and tenacious effort, a negative of any variety, anywhere and of any degree, can always be converted into a positive.

Why not start your success engine by honestly assessing your own self-esteem? If you find that it is difficult to candidly investigate this essential facet of your personality, you have a self-esteem issue on your plate. You might consider yourself a person whose self-esteem measures miles high. But if you answer "yes" to any one of the following questions, a little work on bolstering your self-esteem profile is in order. Carefully consider these queries:

- Do you see your proverbial glass as half empty—accenting the negative—as opposed to half full—focusing on the positive?
- Do you constantly criticize yourself?
- Do you second-guess yourself with lots of "I should have done this or should have done that" recriminations?
- Do you feel helpless on many occasions?
- Do you bear grudges, cling to the past, and encounter difficulties forgiving others?
- Do you feel that you must do everything perfectly or not at all?

If you answered "yes" to one or more of these questions, you have ample room to better your personality and make yourself a more viable candidate for success in winning life's gold medal. It's important to keep in mind that there's nothing wrong with that. The quest for success asks us to improve ourselves around the clock: twenty-four hours a day, seven days a week, three hundred and sixty-five days a year. Our journey also requires us to continually learn from our mistakes and shortcomings.

The Power of Positive Thinking

It is important for us to investigate the difference between the glass half-full and glass half-empty mindsets. When you approach each one of life's moments and interpersonal encounters from the best possible angle, you are seeing your glass as half full. You are accenting the positive!

FACT

By always putting positive spins on the situations in your life—on all those events that happen around you—you can't help but feel better about yourself, what you are doing, and where you are going.

Replace Criticism with Encouragement

Self-criticism. Is it a good thing? It's enough to say that it's best to leave the critics where they thrive: in the movie section of the newspapers or on Amazon.com, critiquing books and DVDs. Self-criticism and positive self-esteem do not amicably coexist.

Replace criticism of yourself with encouragement. Let's say you made a mistake. You fell down and scraped your knee. The thing to do is learn from your mistake. The way to learn is to pick yourself up and patch up your knee—not further browbeat yourself. This is self-improvement at work. It stands in stark contrast to regressive self-criticism.

No Monday-Morning Quarterbacking

Second-guessing yourself is also incompatible with your positive self-esteem. Self-doubt drains us of positive energy and halts all forward motion in our lives. Don't wallow in guilt or shame, either. These kinds of negative behaviors are always counterproductive, and they can sometimes be so debilitating that they lead to physical and psychological illnesses.

Accepting Life's Limitations

The feeling of helplessness in the face of life's many troubles is commonplace for a lot of people. But here's where that personality makeover we previously touched upon can make all the difference in the world. Yes, there are certain things in life that you can't do—you do have limitations. There are things, too, that you have absolutely no control over. Accept these facts of life, cruel as they sometimes are. Focus on feeling good about yourself, the things you can do, and the places you can go with your special talents and your determination to succeed.

In your never-ending quest for success, it's important for you to recognize your potential and also your limitations. Totally eliminate the things that are out of your control from your decision-making process, and concentrate solely on the things that are in your hands and at your disposal. Accept that there are sometimes boundaries in life.

Living in the Present

Never lose sight of the fact, either, that an individual with positive self-esteem is always a forward-looking person. You can't live in the past, bear grudges, and carry a sack full of grievances on your shoulders morning, noon, and night. These aren't the marks of a positive person. Forgiveness is a positive action that is essential to elevating self-esteem. If you can't find it in yourself to come to terms with—and let go of—the negative stumbling blocks from your past, you'll be incapable of fully embracing the many opportunities available to you in the present.

Perfection: An Unrealistic Goal

Some of us confuse positive self-esteem—and, indeed, the ability to achieve success in life—with perfection or, at the very least, with seeking absolute perfection. Perfection certainly is a goal that many individuals set for themselves. But why set such unrealistic goals?

If you haven't yet noticed, there isn't a person walking this green earth who is perfect. Let's say you have noticed. Why not set your goals and dream your dreams under the bright lights of reality? Extract all you can from your talents. Always give your best, and explore life's many possibilities. You have plenty to keep you busy without worrying about mastering the impossible—perfection!

FACT

In many instances, success comes after many failed attempts: business ventures, for instance, or interpersonal relationships. Mistakes—big and small—are both a big and small part of life. Success demands not perfection but our willingness to learn valuable lessons from our misadventures and to keep our sense of our life's direction.

Locating Your Talents

People who are clearly successful are just as clearly able to tap into their unique abilities and use them without reservation. They forge careers, found businesses, and follow their dreams by letting their unparalleled talents and insights find their true expression. Remember, though, that each and every one of us is a true original. And the key to unlocking our potentials—and availing ourselves of many of life's infinite possibilities—is very often found under the mats at our front doors, not in some faraway land.

Expressing Your Unique Talents

Do you know what separates you from the rest of the human pack? Are you accomplished in a particular technical field? Are you a people person? Do you have a distinct artistic gift? What are your extracurricular interests and hobbies? What makes you truly happy?

Ponder these questions. Their answers go straight to the heart of who you are and what makes you an exceptional human being. Their answers also play definitive roles in defining whether or not you will sample the sweet taste of success in this life.

It's Never Too Early

It's no big mystery that children are starting school earlier these days than they did twenty or thirty years ago. No longer do youngsters simplystart kindergarten at the age of five. Instead, it's common to find two- and three-year-olds enrolled in preschool, developing their singular talents and interests soon after they take their first steps.

When you experience success along life's highways and byways, you'll witness the best aspects of your personality assuming center stage. You'll see that your singular talents and interests are no longer latent and hidden away from the wider world. Too often in life, talented people with a great many gifts never grab the opportunity to reveal themselves. Note the active verb there: grab. It's entirely up to you to make things happen.

ALERT!

Achieving success often means taking risks. Risk-taking builds confidence. When you're thinking about taking a risk, define what you expect to gain. Carefully review the anticipated benefits versus the potential losses. Risk-taking doesn't mean taking dangerous chances. You should take a careful look at all risks before you take them.

One of life's more depressing realities is that a lot of us get caught up in the same old rat race, or we get hopelessly entangled in a morass of responsibilities. Sometimes it's the age-old fear of the unknown and an understandable aversion to risk that pens us in. Moving outside of the box—outside of societal expectations—is not always easy. But then, nobody ever said that life was easy. Achieving success is not a simple affair. Rather, it is a quest, and a noble one. It requires a great capacity for understanding, determination, and confidence as you progress through its many stages.

Self-Actualization: Converting Potential into Reality

Exactly how do you discover your special talents, which you may always have kept private, and apply them to your public life out in the world? You do it by following a process known as self-actualization—that's how. Self-actualization helps us express the deep-down, meat-and-potatoes essence of who we are and what we can accomplish to bring us true personal fulfillment (that is, measurable success in life). Self-actualization means becoming in actuality what, as human beings, we are in potential.

Let It Begin with You

How many times have you mused about someone close to you who had such "unfulfilled potential"? Maybe it was a sibling wasting his or her talent in a dead-end job; maybe you had a close friend who preferred nightclubs and excessive drinking to ambition and personal growth. If so, consider this. We very often transfer our own inner feelings, fears, and insecurities—the way we feel about ourselves—onto others and their actions.

We should use our curiosity to probe the area where knowledge can truly do us good—ourselves. We should worry about our own self-actualization before we concern ourselves with others' unrealized potential. It is difficult enough to motivate ourselves into performing the positive, sustained actions that lead to success; forget about motivating family, friends, and acquaintances. Attempting to transform others into the ideal images we see for them is a fool's mission. Leave such transformations to Jerry Springer and Ricki Lake.

Okay, let's now consider your own self-actualization. There are some key characteristics that all self-actualizing individuals share in order to be able to convert their potential into reality. The primary personality trait of a self-actualizing person is self-acceptance.

Acceptance of who you are is a ground-floor personality trademark that you will build upon as you strive for success. It is the catalyst that starts the reaction that will eventually unlock your real potential and possibility.

Self-Acceptance

Without any question, you must be comfortable in your own skin to fully unlock your potential as a human being. This is heightened self-esteem. You cannot travel life's circuitous roads crippled with self-doubt, guilt, and shame. When you accept yourself as an imperfect personality, one who will make mistakes now and again, you can stop wallowing in regret and making apologies.

Making the Complex Simple

Self-actualizing individuals are usually very simple souls. Right now, you are probably wondering, "Doesn't that contradict everything that's been said up to this point?" We are not talking about a Forrest Gump version of simple here. This isn't about how "Life is like a box of chocolates." By "simple," we merely mean that people who realize their true potential often break free from the many societal restraints and conventions. They permit their quests for success to move forward unhindered—simply, as it were.

This rather advanced mentality takes something that is very complex—life itself—and places it in a simple and straightforward mold. A wise man once said, "To be simplistic is easy, but to be simple is hard." Those who are successful in their self-actualization embrace simplicity, but in practice, they are the antithesis of simplistic individuals. By committing themselves to a dedicated mission, with success as the goal, they are at once realistic, sincere, and spontaneous—all forward-moving personality traits.

What does this all mean to you? It means that you must release all your inhibitions and move unfettered while seeking out the areas in life where you want to succeed. You must never permit others' expectations of you to impede your progress in achieving the most with your unique talents. You must not allow your distinctly personal vision of success to ever lose its sharpness.

FACT

Examples of self-actualization include the talented writer who needs to write, the accomplished artist who needs to paint, and the gifted musician who needs to make music, all in order to maximize self-fulfillment in their lives. This list is infinite. It includes the seasoned accountant who relishes crunching numbers as well as the truck driver who loves the open road.

Serenity in Motion

You've embraced self-acceptance and simplicity as your *modus operandi* on your merry way to self-actualization and, eventually, to success. Let's now add a third ingredient to the pot and create an exemplary threesome. In going from Point A to Point B in life, serenity in motion is a powerfully beneficial way to behave.

When you are attempting to rise to the surface of your true potential, it is wise to concentrate on that effort—to focus on it in such a way so as to leave you in complete and utter serenity. If you are a chronic worrier, perpetually riddled with anxiety, and always sweating over trivial matters, then you won't likely see your self-actualization through to its optimum conclusion.

If you carefully map all the positive attitudes and behaviors, you'll see that it's not only possible to find out who you really are and what you can truly accomplish in life—it's probable. Where there is positive self-esteem and self-actualization, there is great potential for success.

The Complementary Career

We've talked about tapping into your talents and the process of self-actualization—turning your potential into reality. Now it's time to discuss applying your abilities to the working world. But how do you really know that you have a knack for business?

First things first. The only way you can know anything about yourself is if you explore the possibilities, and that means you have to try. The questions that were posed earlier in the chapter about your abilities and interests were designed to measure your personality and talent quotient in a very preliminary way. For once you understand and appreciate who your true self is, where your talents lie, and what gives you real pleasure and satisfaction in life, you must take it from there.

The Necessity of Perseverance

If you are pursuing a job or career that complements your talents, you simultaneously set the stage for both personal satisfaction and genuine success in life. Successful businesspeople often start small, and many of them fail a time or two or three on the way up. But the key to their success—and their satisfaction—is that they aren't deterred along the way. The successful among us are not easily discouraged. They remain confident at the foot of their mistakes and in the wake of their failures, too.

Successful people view business acumen as their special talent, and they delight in the entrepreneurial game. They don't abandon their quests for success in midfield. That's because they derive pleasure and excitement from what they are doing, even when they aren't quite realizing the successes they are after. They are patient and persistent.

Patience and persistence are two personality traits that are regularly found in successful people. Since success is not something that happens overnight, patience is a necessity. The people who ultimately sample the fruits of success are those who persist through good and bad times without getting sidetracked or discouraged.

This is just as true for those musicians, for instance, who tap into their abilities and forge ahead. Music is a competitive career field, and those who persevere are those who make it. The fact is that many—dare we say, most—people do not perfect self-actualization. Instead, they settle for second-rate life careers and unhappy relationships that do not personally fulfill them as human beings.

You Like It, It Likes You

When you know what you like doing, and what gives you pleasure, it is a worthwhile option to consider pursuing a career in a related field. If you thoroughly enjoy your volunteer work with underprivileged children— giving something back to society—maybe a life of social work is right for you. If you have a green thumb in the garden, and you love being under the sun and working with the earth, perhaps a gardening and landscaping business would be your dream come true. If you love cooking, you might give real thought to signing on with a restaurant school.

Rewarding Yourself

It is prudent to regularly note milestones—that is, your accomplishments—all throughout your quest for success. Celebrate your achievements, big and small. Treat yourself to a night on the town. Buy yourself something special, or, at the bare minimum, give yourself a well-earned pat on the back when you see progress.

Don't ever lose sight of the fact that your pursuit of success and personal satisfaction is a long-term commitment. You are striving to reach a goal by building upon a series of small successes. As we've seen throughout this chapter, success is a very complex state of being. It brings together countless aspects of our personalities. Sometimes it asks a lot of us. Because of these demands, it is essential that we reward ourselves every step of the way.

Let's imagine that you've committed yourself to making a positive change in the way you deal with your employees at work. In the past, a problem might have thrown you into a tantrum. Now, however, you may find you can handle it with calm resolve and move on, releasing your negative feelings at the source. If ever there was one, this is a celebratory moment on your road to success. A seemingly small accomplishment can be of key importance as you develop into a better human being, one who is more apt to realize success.

You should note and applaud every small success you achieve (and certainly the large ones). You will know when these moments occur and what their significance is in the big picture—the one you've painted for yourself.

Optimism: Dynamic and Empowering

One of the most crucial ingredients in achieving success is something called optimism. Time and again we witness how successful people are optimistic in both the face of obstacles and the face of failures. They believe in themselves and what they've set out to accomplish. When we believe in ourselves, we are at once confident and optimistic.

Optimism is a dynamic, empowering, invaluable attitude to have. In contrast to pessimism, its evil twin, optimism focuses on possibilities and opportunities and never surrenders. Thus, an optimistic mindset forges the optimal environment for success.

Optimistic people suffer setbacks in life without wavering because optimism is like a magic spell. It enables people to attribute the problems that naturally arise in their lives to external causes. This allows the optimistic person to view any and all such problems as temporary and fixable. Life's obstacles and curve balls are, therefore, removed from the optimistic person's burden. This is the power of optimism at work.

FACT

A psychological analysis of Wolfgang Amadeus Mozart (1756–1791), conducted through his correspondence, revealed him to be an irrepressibly optimistic person. Even after the death of four children, his own serious illness, and professional and financial disasters cluttering his path, he remained exuberant, self-confident, and productive until his own death at the age of thirty-five.

Try to embrace all of the positive personality aspects laid out in this chapter. If you do, your quest for success will be more productive. If you maintain a positive self-esteem, practice self-actualization, and sport an optimistic spirit in life, success most assuredly is in your grasp.

Subsequent chapters will pick up on many of the important themes raised in this introductory chapter and flesh them in greater detail. But you must never lose sight of the fact that a strong foundation is essential to realizing success in life. Ignore the foundation—the fundamentals—at your own peril.

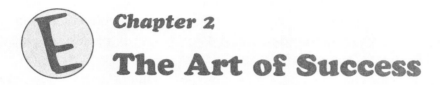

Chapter 2

The Art of Success

The realization of genuine success is not a cold science. It is an art form. Lasting successes flourish over time and through dedicated effort. The journey to success is quite often more significant than the final destination. For in the enriching quest for success, human character is repeatedly tested and stretched to its most productive limits.

Success: An Art, Not a Science

The words "art" and "science" are frequently used interchangeably in today's society. Some motivational gurus speak of success in terms of science, as if it's somehow a set of proven laws and time-tested principles. In the tough quest for success, however, we can derive no hard-and-fast rules that come with any kind of guaranteed outcome attached. As we've already indicated—and in no uncertain terms—many successes in life are accomplished only after a run of mistakes, failures, and painful lessons learned.

Exactly what does this "no guarantee" business mean for you and your own success mission? Should you feel discouraged? On the contrary. You should continue to work diligently. Lay the proper foundation for success, and set out on your personal journey—committed as ever and with abundant confidence. If you follow this path, the odds are that you will encounter measurable success at various points along the way.

Success and the Artist's Canvas

You are fortunate enough to have a supremely talented artist painting for you, in intricate and rich detail. The artist's subject is a very personalized picture of your success. The identity of this gifted artist is none other than you. Your conception of success—the goals you set for yourself—can be revised and improved upon as necessary to adapt to changing circumstances in your life, as well as to those unforeseen problems upon which you have no control. This is clearly art at work, and not science.

In your overall pilgrimage to the Promised Land of success, it is important that you fully appreciate and accept that life is sometimes unfair and always unpredictable. Even if you follow your carefully prepared success script to the letter, your performance might not turn out quite the way you planned.

Exactly why are there no "take it to the bank" guarantees in achieving success? Because we all know from our life experiences how easily laughter and joy can turn to tragedy and despair. But, by the same token, we've witnessed darkness and gloom lift in a heartbeat.

This reality check should not disillusion you. Rather, it should help you see clearly that success is not a dry science. Instead, it is a malleable art form. You must stay focused on it and always remain vigilant to its slings and arrows. A success story is always a work in progress.

The World Stage

The legendary playwright William Shakespeare wrote, "All the world's a stage, and all the men and women merely players." As usual, the Bard hammered the nail on the head. Life's stage is where each one of us performs. It is where we dream our dreams, fashion our hopes, set our goals, and then valiantly strive to make them happen.

On this sprawling life stage, there are events and assorted complications that we cannot possibly foresee. Thus, we can never be certain that our plans will run smoothly or that we will reach our goals when we want to, if at all. But on this very same stage, we can nevertheless master our performance—that is, we can master the art form of success. When we master that which is in our control, we can counterbalance, and sometimes even negate, the problems and obstacles that are outside of our purview.

Character Is Destiny Is Success

The Greek philosopher Heraclitus long ago stated that "Character is destiny." By this, he probably meant that our characters—our particular talents and personal values—are largely responsible for dictating which roads we choose to travel during our lives. Indeed, our characters are the repositories of all our values and virtues. There are many people who are financially successful but who we otherwise might not regard very highly. Why? Because we don't approve of their methods or the ground they've scorched on the way to their riches.

If success is performance art, then it's the performance that counts above all else—not the proverbial box-office numbers. It all comes back to giving the journey as much or more importance than the destination itself. We cannot merely select a destination, call it our ideal of successfulness, and then steamroll our way there. If we followed that path, we would create negative consequences for others as we fulfilled our desires. This treacherous road can hardly be classified a legitimate way of reaching the heights of success.

FACT

Society regularly equates success with wealth, power, and fame. However, it is goodness, and not greatness, that is the true measure of success. You can certainly be wealthy, powerful, and famous and still measure up. Just remember the "goodness" part of the equation on the way to your fame and fortune.

The Five Brushstrokes of Success

In the art of success, there are five indispensable qualities—call them brushstrokes—that we can highlight to reveal both the color and depth of the masterpiece that success makes of our lives. They are the following:

1. Virtue
2. Confidence
3. Dedication
4. Consistency
5. Happiness

Virtues Matter Most

We are subject to endless chatter about the importance of "values" in life. The New Age has brought us value clarification guidebooks, and armies of self-helpers talk the talk on the same theme. What are your values? Do you need them in your quest for success?

The great irony is that every living person has values of some kind. The worst human beings have them—they're just not very positive, uplifting values. Philandering spouses value many things—fidelity not among them.

Embezzlers in companies also flaunt their values—with personal enrichment and greed leading the way.

It is plain to see that values in the success safari vary widely from individual to individual. Just as obviously, some values are more legitimate than others. Some are virtuous, while others are deserving of contempt. We need our values to reflect our virtues.

Virtue is what we should value—no pun intended—above all else as we seek out success in life. The chief reason we keep referring to the importance of the journey to success, as opposed to success's end results, is because the actions taken along the way are of such great consequence.

Along with the actions we take as we strive for success, virtuous decision-making ensures that we can hold our heads high and sleep well at night. Our virtues reassure us, too, that our successes are well earned and worthy of celebrating and duplicating. When we know that in all our successes, the only ingredients are our aboveboard, virtuous efforts, we are personally fulfilled and inspired to replicate them.

What Is Virtue?

Virtue is a positive attitude or behavior applied to any number of life circumstances. You've no doubt heard the expression, "Patience is a virtue." Well, it sure is! However, other vital virtues play big roles in our lives, particularly in our quests to succeed in life. Here are some essential virtues that nobly assist us in achieving self-fulfillment and success:

- Honesty
- Generosity
- Courage
- Compassion
- Fairness
- Self-control

By combing through this short list of virtues (by no means comprehensive), you immediately see the differences between values and virtues. We choose the things we value. Our values, in other words, can be seen in the things we hold dear to our hearts. These are not personality characteristics but judgment calls. Virtues, on the other hand, are ingrained in our persons.

We are not born with ready-made virtues. Virtues are mostly learned, then practiced and finely honed over time. This is precisely why families, schools, churches and synagogues, and civic associations perform critical roles in society. Good parenting, for instance, instills virtuous behavior in children from the get-go.

FACT

The philosopher Aristotle discoursed on the importance of virtue in an individual's life—in ancient times, no less. He suggested that self-discipline was the key to the virtuous life, with virtue representing success. The alternative, he suggested, was the excessive self-indulgence that corrupted a person's character. Aristotle married virtue and ethics with true success in life.

Honesty, the Best Policy

Honesty tops the list of virtues for good reason. When we are upfront and truthful in life, we automatically gain the respect of others—at least those whose respect we value. Honesty really is the best policy. Throughout your journey to success, honest actions will open up doors and reward you in ways that you never dreamed possible. If you travel through life with integrity always in the vanguard, you'll—as the saying goes—"go places."

Generosity of Spirit

Generosity is a virtue. Share your successes and good fortune with others. Life is too short not to.

This doesn't mean that you have to write out checks to friends and family members when you achieve financial security. Generosity of spirit is more to the point. (See Chapter 12 for a full overview of this important success characteristic.) True, this may include giving others money. More important, though, it entails giving of your time and know-how—giving of yourself. Successful people who share their positive thoughts, special skills, and learned life lessons add to their own success portfolios in the process.

Being generous all across the board enables you to feel better about yourself. Successful people network throughout their lives, consciously and unconsciously. They make friends and positive associations en route to success with honesty and generosity in the forefront. They give of themselves, and they see the benefits of their positive attitudes and behaviors time and time again.

The Courage Umbrella

Throughout this book, you will encounter a heaping helping of advice on the importance of attitudes such as perseverance, risk-taking, forward motion, positive momentum, and confidence. We can place all of these personality attributes and actions under one vast umbrella and call them courage. Courage is a virtue.

ALERT!

Courage is one of life's virtues and a key to unlocking success in life. However, courage doesn't mean climbing into a lion's den or swimming in shark-infested waters. Don't ever confuse courage with stupidity—which is not a virtue, by the way. Courage is always admirable and wise.

Compassion: More Than a Word

Compassion is a virtue that is oftentimes given short shrift, particularly in discussions of the meaning of success. Many overviews of success focus on the successful person's pursuit of financial fortune. Surely something's missing here.

A compassionate individual feels for other people. In the quest for success, compassion is enriching in and of itself. It places the quest in a distinctly positive, unselfish light. Nobody can do it alone. Our family, friends, and coworkers—even total strangers—all play central roles in our lives, regardless of whether we feel personally satisfied and successful.

Compassion flows from the heart. It signals to others that we feel and care for them in their time of need or sorrow. It also demonstrates our understanding that success—while it is the goal of our personal journeys—still depends on the other players on life's extended stage.

Fair Is Positive

Fairness is a virtue worth holding onto, though that isn't always easy. We've noted that life is often unfair. However, this doesn't mean you should compound the problem with unfair behaviors of your own.

In both your personal and professional life, consciously strive to be fair. To accomplish this task you must accept the personalities around you. Treat them with respect; they are individuals, as you are, with goals and hopes and dreams of their own. Do not place undue expectations on others. Do not expect others to think and act like you do.

FACT

The question of fairness, or the lack of it, regularly rears its head in both family settings and work situations. Children accuse parents of being unfair all the time, such as when parents are perceived to prefer one child over the others. Bosses are regularly accused of playing favorites and of violating fairness principles.

If you work hard at applying an even hand in all aspects of your life, you'll succeed at being fair. This positive behavior will help you achieve success because you will gain the respect of others. Fair-minded people stand out from the crowd and distinguish themselves.

The Best Control Is Self-Control

Let's call this the all-encompassing virtue. Self-control covers a whole lot of ground. Successful people generally master self-control. They know what they want and what they don't want. They also know the difference between right and wrong.

Life is chock-full of temptations and shortcuts. Self-control is what permits us to remain focused and to move forward. Without self-control, we have trouble making progress—and sometimes we get stopped for good.

For illustration purposes, let's put you on a diet. At this very minute, people all over the country are doing just that. They are making plans that determine how much and what they should eat, what kind of exercise they will enjoy, and so on. To these many people, success is defined by the number of pounds they lose.

Let's say that you want to drop twenty pounds. You know what you have to do—you have to make changes in what you eat, exercise regularly, and generally pay attention to how your actions influence your size and self-image. Here's where you really need that self-control. If you lose it, and night after night you raid the fridge for a midnight snack of soda pop, chocolate cake, and potato chips, you will totally sabotage your own diet. Self-control is what makes a diet—or any other great endeavor—work. Tempering excesses, making reasoned decisions, and keeping destructive temptations at bay are all-important actions on the road to success.

This isn't to suggest that you will always come out on top in your attempt to perfect your self-control. Nevertheless, it is in your best interest to learn and understand what self-control entails. You should be acutely aware of the moments in your life when the need for self-control matters, particularly when those moments relate to your ability to achieve success.

Freedom from Uncertainty

If you want to know genuine success, you have to feel confident. You must not only believe that success is possible, you must also have confidence that you know what it takes to reach your goals. Having faith in your abilities is a key brushstroke in the art of success. This cannot be overstated. It is vital, as you strive for success, that you are confident that you have what it takes to see things through to a positive conclusion.

Successful people are confident people. They are self-assured and have set themselves free from one of life's most stubborn road-blocks—uncertainty. Uncertainty breeds hesitation, and hesitation often initiates backpedaling. On the journey to success, as with any other kind of journey, backpedaling means moving away from your goal—not toward it.

The Confidence Shadow

"Confidence" is another word we toss around without thinking much about what it truly means. Confidence-building seminars, tapes, books—you name it—abound. But we are much more likely to build confidence in our everyday lives than we are to pick it up from the pages of a book. Events or situations that enable us to exhibit a talent, whether intellectual or physical, are the pre-eminent confidence-building laboratories.

Maybe your coworkers are hotly debating some important issue of the day. If you jump in and hold your own in the discussion, maybe convincing a few others to share your point of view, your confidence gets a big boost. If you paint your house and maybe do a little remodeling in the process, and your neighbor—the handyman king—comes over especially to compliment your work, you're going to feel a lot more confident about your next home improvement project. If you successfully complete a crossword puzzle in the newspaper, it's a confidence booster for sure.

Confidence plays a part in everything we do. It's a matter of faith. When we have confidence, we believe in our abilities, and that means we believe that we will come out on top in a variety of life circumstances. That's pretty powerful stuff.

Dedication: Start to Finish

The art of success demands dedication. How many times have you found yourself losing interest in a goal or project that you set out to accomplish? How many times have you lost your concentration or desire to complete a job or task? This happens to everybody sometimes, and you can probably point to plenty of examples throughout your life. In almost every case, it's a lack of dedication that derails us.

Why the lack of dedication? Well, it can be hard to remain dedicated to an effort that won't pay off until some point in the future. Sometimes it's easy to think we have better things to do. In terms of success, it is important to remember that dedication is an absolute necessity. You have to treat the journey toward your goal—that far-off point in the future—as though it is just important as the goal itself. That's dedication. Success is a reward for the dedicated.

ALERT!

You've heard the expression, "He's going nowhere fast." Without dedication as a guide, the efforts we make in life usually end up doing just that. In your quest for success, it is critical that your efforts be firmly grounded in undeniable dedication. Dedication requires you to be both concentrated and serious—a winning combination.

Dedicate yourself to success. When you set goals and plan your course, be sure you remain focused on what you want to accomplish. Don't fall prey to boredom, and don't let yourself run out of energy or enthusiasm. It is all too common to start out gung-ho, dedicated, and determined, and then quickly fall by the wayside as actual obstacles present themselves that block the way. A dedicated effort is a true effort. Without dedication, a so-called effort is merely uninspired activity—actions leading to nowhere special.

Consistency: A to Z

The best artists in the world are consistent across the board. They develop their own individual styles, and all of their creations display that style. This is precisely why we can identify individual artists' works so easily, even when the subject matter widely varies. The palette of colors, the distinctive brushstrokes or subject matter, all these things are consistent from one work to the next. They are the artists' signatures.

You, too, must strive to be consistent throughout your quest for success. Consistency is the mark of an individual who has his or her life in the proper focus and on the right track. The telltale indications of a person in trouble are inconsistency and an exhibition of erratic behavior.

Don't Worry, Be Happy

It sounds almost trite to link happiness with success. It's obvious, isn't it, to say that happiness and success go together like bacon and eggs. Yet countless people seem to be surrounded by all the trappings of success, but happiness is nowhere to be found in their lives.

Despite what we seem to see, it is safe to say that success and happiness really do go hand in hand. Successful people are, by and large, happy people. They have to be. It is ludicrous to brand someone a success who is depressed and angry most of the time, even if he is lounging around his ornate Beverly Hills swimming pool or sailing the Florida Keys on her seventy-five-foot yacht.

The notion of personal fulfillment that we keep raising on these pages is the sum and substance of all true success. Unhappiness and displeasure continually accompany wealth and power, but they don't accompany success. This reality confuses the people who view success only in terms of fame and fortune.

The Illusion of Happiness

During the gold rush of the 1840s and 1850s, many miners confused a mineral called iron pyrite with the real thing—gold. The trouble was that iron pyrite—which glittered just like gold—was worthless. It subsequently became known as fool's gold.

QUESTION?

Can success exist without happiness?
Genuine success is inextricably linked with happiness. You cannot truly stake a claim to success without feeling good about yourself and your life circumstances—without being happy to be alive, as it were.

And so it is with happiness. We often confuse the mirage of happiness with the real thing. People who descend into drug and alcohol use are, for example, substituting artificial and harmful means for genuine happiness in their lives. This may be a simplification, but it is fundamentally accurate.

There's just no substitute for happiness. Success must come with a happiness component. If it doesn't, it cannot be categorized as real, lasting success. This isn't to imply that success requires you to be happy every waking hour of every day—a near impossibility. Happiness that belongs to the center of your life, that is part of your core personality, is what we have in mind.

Self-Affirmation: Words to the Wise

In the art of success, self-affirmation plays a productive role. Self-affirmation is the process of giving yourself compliments and encouraging words from time to time. We might recite these self-affirmations out loud, let them rattle around our minds, or we can write them down on paper or cards—it doesn't matter. What matters is that we believe in what we are saying to ourselves about ourselves.

Self-affirmations—the repetitions of positive phrases and sayings—are popularly prescribed elixirs in the current self-help age. By repeating phrases like "I am somebody," "I can succeed," or "I will like myself," it is believed that a self-fulfilling prophecy will be set in motion. Self-affirmations are common sense. The logic behind them is simple and straightforward. What it all boils down to is believing in yourself and never letting yourself forget it.

However, self-affirming slogans repeated in front of the mirror, in your inner monologue, or scribbled on index cards are close to meaningless unless they are built on a solid foundation. Many people buy into the belief that self-affirmation alone will carry them away into bliss they've never known before. Often, though, it's more harmful than helpful to mouth plati-tudes without the proper support behind them. Self-affirmations without cor-responding positive, forward moving attitudes are empty vessels that sometimes confuse those uttering them into thinking that they are pro-gressing in life.

Self-Affirmations: Examples

For self-affirmations to do any good, they must work in concert with the positive attitudes and actions that are the preludes to success. Here's a sampling of some common self-affirmations, which you can tweak to fit your own circumstances and your goals. They are divided into the three common classifications:

- **The "I am" self-affirmations:** I am intelligent; I am talented; I am beautiful; I am strong.
- **The "I can" self-affirmations:** I can solve my problems; I can be assertive; I can pass the test; I can lose weight.
- **The "I will" self-affirmations:** I will stretch my limits today; I will be positive; I will praise my children today; and I will succeed.

As you can see, each one of these affirmations accents a positive. They offer encouragement and hope. They also reinforce what you need to believe about yourself and your abilities if you are to find success in life.

The Big Mo: Positive Momentum

Self-affirmations, used to fuel your journey to success, play a part in sustaining positive momentum. Building and sustaining positive momentum in your quest for success is a must. You do this by adopting the positive attitudes and behaviors that are often the precursors of success in life, taking them along with you on your journey, and replicating them over and over.

Indeed, achieving success means more than hitting a run of good luck. It's the right attitudes and behaviors that usher in success. Positive actions produce positive results, and this builds confidence and inspires more of the same. This "Big Mo," as it's affectionately known, is hard to stop. On the quest for success, you always want the Big Mo on your side. (E)

Chapter 3

The Right Relationships Are Everything

Success is contagious. This is something that we all want to catch. We cannot afford to quarantine ourselves from successful people. Rather, it's in our best interests to befriend and associate with positive thinking people, supreme achievers, solid role models, and wise teachers and mentors. It is likewise in our interests to steer clear of those purveyors of negative thinking.

Positive Relationships Matter

The timeless expression, "You can judge a person by the company he or she keeps," says a mouthful. The interpersonal relationships that distinguish all of our lives are often forged between and among like-minded individuals. The bully in the schoolyard surrounds himself with other bullies and assorted flunkeys. The honor student, on the other hand, keeps the company of fellow honor students and intellectual peers. So it goes throughout adulthood, too.

Granted, many of our associations in life are not so easily categorized and explained. Each one of us, after all, is a member of a unique family. As a general rule of thumb, we tend to prize our associations with blood relatives. Blood is thicker than water, isn't it?

Some cult-like organizations urge their flocks to sever ties with "negative" people and "corrupt" influences in their lives, even if they happen to be spouses, brothers and sisters, moms and dads, and, yes, children, too—it doesn't much matter. Such a blanket dismissal of the relevant people in our lives is extreme, but it fits the cultist mindset. Cult groups need to keep tight control over their memberships or—let's face it—they'd be out of business.

The First Order of the Relationship Business

Our noble quest for success is the antithesis of these cultist endeavors. In seeking success, we set out on a journey that is reality based and uplifting from beginning to end. Naturally, we want to surround ourselves—as much as is humanly possible—with positive people. These friends and associates encourage us to feel good about ourselves and inspire us to live out our dreams. We want to be around people who appreciate our special talents, who compliment and complement us, and who value our insight and opinions. We want to learn from those with whom we associate.

Most people who have severed relationships with family members are not happy souls, nor are they successful individuals. There are some instances, of course, when keeping family ties intact is next to impossible and even unadvisable—but these are the rare exceptions. So, strive to fully open communications with all of your kin. This is your number-one job in getting your relationships in positive order as you pursue self-fulfillment and the success that comes with it.

Sometimes family dynamics work against the positive grain. If your family is dysfunctional in some way (and most are), work extra hard to strengthen your family relationships. Express your personal needs. Explain what you want and expect from family members one and all. Don't cut and run.

Positive Associations

Outside of the relationship we're simply handed in life (that is, the families that we are born into), we voluntarily enter into friendships, marriages, business partnerships, and so on. In this grand arena, we are empowered to choose our company and to actively seek out positive influences. We can surround ourselves with friends, soul mates, and other consequential life players who will encourage us to tap into our potentials.

Paradoxically, many travelers on the road to success skirt the all-important relationship ingredient. There are some people who view the company they keep as immaterial to what they want out of life. This attitude couldn't be more off the mark.

The people you choose as your associates are an apt reflection of your character. If you prefer to spend the preponderance of your time with negative people, it says, among many things, that you are unprepared to undertake the journey to success—unready to absorb all that the journey has to offer. If, on the other hand, you consistently keep company with positive, forward-thinking individuals, this is a mirror image of what you are all about and where you are headed in life.

One of the chief reasons the self-help industry has exploded onto the scene in recent years is that negative thinking and negative influences are so prevalent in today's society. Sometimes the negative reinforcement that we encounter in our daily lives is so subtle that it's barely noticeable. There are times, however, when it hits us over the head with the intensity of a jackhammer. Negativity is all around us, and it's insidious. Remember to stay particularly attentive to the defining role your various associations play in your life. Do these people create positive or negative influences?

ALERT!

It isn't just our associations that should concern us on the road to success. We must also be attentive to the powerful role of advertising. Often working in a sly, negative manner, this medium attempts to define the requirements of success as looking and thinking certain ways, using particular products, and so on.

The American Dream

To further illustrate how important our relationships are in determining whether we will tap into success's mother lode of riches, let us briefly analyze a dream—the American dream. The American dream is most often affiliated with entrepreneurial achievements. Many of us dream of starting a business of our own. We want to be our own bosses. More than anything else, we would like to succeed in the most satisfying fashion—leading the charge and staying in complete control of our lives.

Unfortunately, the cold facts of life are that new businesses fall by the wayside faster than a high-speed Internet connection. There are numerous reasons for this high failure rate. A huge one is that the associations in the lives of many fledgling businesspeople are unhealthy and decidedly negative. Many people commence businesses in an atmosphere of pessimism, disdain, and even ridicule. Such a barrage of negativity is hard to overcome.

It's very common for the inner circle of family and friends to scorn new entrepreneurs who embark on their business ventures. You know how this commentary goes: Why leave a safe and secure job with all those perks and benefits for a risky business undertaking? The power of such negative field forces should never be underestimated. If you start a business, or switch careers, it matters a great deal when you are simultaneously greeted with negative energy from your support network.

To fully embrace success in life, you have to be properly conditioned and trained to grab hold of it—to seize opportunities when they come your way. If all, or most, of your interpersonal relationships are pulling against you, you are going to have a tough time yanking in the opposite direction.

Successful People: The Giveaways

You now know, beyond even the shadow of a doubt, that if you want to be successful yourself, it's in your best interest to hobnob with successful people. You wouldn't be reading this book if you didn't covet success in life. So what do you do? Put an ad in the newspaper: "Wanted. Successful person or people to be friends—and maybe more?"

This approach is a little excessive and is unnecessary for our purposes. You don't have to advertise for successful people to fill up your inner circle. Instead, what you need to do is vet all of your associations very carefully.

If you want to locate successful people—and really get to know them—go where they go. That is, join their clubs and organizations, frequent their after-hour haunts, play their games (such as golf), read what they read, and so on. In other words, become a part of the culture of success.

Consciously seek out positive, uplifting relationships to fill up your life from morning to night. An important area to consider is your love life. Don't leap headfirst into any serious romantic relationships until you've established utter compatibility, including mutual agreement on the meaning of success. As for friends, mentors, and such, keep an eye out for the unmistakable signs of success, which you will recognize via the characteristics that typify successful people. These are the people you want in your company.

The Qualities of the Successful

Successful individuals reveal many shared personality traits. Actively seek, and you will find them. Learn from them. Pattern yourself after them.

Find inspiration in their powers-of-example. Here are some specific personality traits found in successful people:

- Integrity
- Positive attitude
- Decisiveness
- Discipline
- Supportiveness

Integrity tops the list because it encompasses an untold number of virtues. Above all else, you want to consort with honest people. There is no doubt, for instance, that you need to keep company with people who are trustworthy and reliable.

FACT

Perseverance is an admirable characteristic found in successful people. Ray Kroc, founder of the McDonald's hamburger chain, was rejected eight times when applying for a loan to start his franchise business. He persevered—the ninth time being the charm—got the loan, and the formerly hungry world has never been the same.

As for a positive attitude, this one is a no-brainer. Negative attitudes are toxic. They bring negative results—end of story. You, as an individual, don't want to go through life with a poor attitude, so don't keep company with those who sport destructive attitudes. A negative plus a negative equals a negative in any kind of math, particularly in the mathematics of success.

Risk-Taking and Problem-Solving

Successful people are decisive people. Be vigilant in searching for decisive individuals as friends and associates. The ability to make good decisions is a personality quality to greatly admire. Decisive actions in life often separate the successful from the unsuccessful and the winners from the losers.

The positive feature of decisiveness also brings into its tent both risk-taking and problem-solving. As we've already seen, risk-taking is one of the marks of a successful person. Little is gained without risk—sticking our necks out, so to speak, in key life moments.

Problem-solving abilities are an offshoot of decisiveness. Successful individuals confront their problems head on. They do what it takes to dispense with their problems, even if it means looking to others for help, and then they move forward. The successful mind is a confident mind. What that means for successful people is that they have no fear of looking to others for helping hands when necessary. They don't feel threatened by others' talents and know-how.

Disciplinary Actions

Successful people are also disciplined people. They know what they want, and they set out after it. They know how to set realistic goals, and they monitor every step of their progress along the way to realizing them. Discipline is a personality trait worth having in your own arsenal. It is all about remaining focused—keeping your eyes on the prize—and it often requires hard work.

The importance of discipline, both at home and in school, is often stressed to children and young adults. Many students, for example, are instructed to be self-directed, to set goals, and to hunger for knowledge, in contrast to leaving their futures to the whims of fate and chance. In other words, they are taught to be disciplined.

The Backbone of Relationships

A final personality trait for us to consider in this section is support-iveness. Naturally, you want your inner circle to be a supportive bunch. You want your friends, significant others, and business partners to encourage you all the time. They should see you as a distinct human being with special needs and aspirations.

Always seek out supportive people to call your friends, and support them in return. Mutually supportive relationships fuel success in any venue. Don't miss any opportunity to fill up your tank with support and get moving.

Negativity: Success's Third Rail

We've made reference many times to negative people, negative energy, negative thinking, and to how you should avoid all three. You don't want to spend your time with negative people. You don't want to get consumed by negative energy, and you certainly don't want to become hostage to your own negative thinking.

Up to this point, you've been inundated with many of the finer points of personality—the characteristics that define successful individuals. You've been introduced to everything from the vast powers of positive self-esteem to the absolute necessity of discipline in establishing goals in life and seeing them through.

But you should also be made aware of the revealing indicators of the negative person and the personality foibles that cry out: "Stay away!" For in your heroic crusade to associate with only positive-thinking and forward-moving individuals, you should also know what to look out for on the negative side of the human ledger.

FACT

Life is full of negative souls. Many times these individuals mask themselves as positive animals—wolves in sheep's clothing. This makes your task of sorting out the right relationships from the wrong all the more difficult—and all the more important!

Beware the Negative Personality

Negative individuals are those who see their life glasses as half empty. They take a pessimistic view of life in general. They see bad motives lurking in the recesses of their relationships with families, friends, and acquaintances. They are cynical sorts who live their lives in restrictive boxes, rarely venturing beyond tight parameters. On the far side of the negative gamut, there are "the climbers." These people have escaped that restrictive box but who view their own life quests as the only ones that matter.

You've already been furnished with a roster of positive personality traits. What we're describing here is the flip side—the underbelly—of that list. These are the traits found in your fellow travelers that you don't want to rub off on you. Here's a list of these toxic traits:

- Deceitfulness
- Negative attitude
- Self-absorption
- Anger
- Paranoia

The No-Trust Account

Just as integrity topped the list of positive personality attributes, a lack of honesty—deceitfulness—leads the charge on the negative side. In life, you will repeatedly encounter untrustworthy individuals. These are people to watch out for: Trust is the most essential ingredient in any relationship, from a marriage to a business partnership to anything in between. When the bonds of trust are nonexistent, or if they are breached in any way, relationships disintegrate.

ALERT!

Honesty and trust are the cornerstones of any kind of relationship. Trustworthy individuals manifest integrity in all life situations. A philandering spouse, for example, is unlikely to be a person of trust in other aspects of his or her life. The same is true for the dishonest businessperson. Dishonesty, just like honesty, runs true to form.

Some people have a knack for coming across as upright individuals when in fact they are nothing of the kind. There wouldn't be so many successful scams around if this weren't the case. There wouldn't be so many disreputable people reaching positions of power in politics and business.

Fortunately, though, most people are bad actors. This means that we can get their "numbers" pretty quickly. One big lie, or a serious breach of trust, should be enough to tell you who somebody really is. Avoid liars and untruthful people at all costs on your journey to success.

The Negative-Attitude Poison

People who are psychologically motionless—rigid—are negative attitude carriers. By the same token, people who are active dream-busters are also carriers of negative attitudes. What are the giveaways that people are carrying around such negatively charged and destructive attitudes?

People with poor attitudes generally have singular worldviews. They see things one way, with no deviation in their thinking. When others in their presence dare to be different, they treat these people as fools.

Needless to say, you don't want to keep company with people like this. They will hold you back. Negative people shoot down new ideas and scoff at innovation. They look at the world through a pinhole. In essence, they are unhappy at their core, and they resent the forward movement and success of others.

Resentment, or bitterness, trickles down into the recesses of the psyche and spills over into the wider world. Your relationships matter precisely because these kinds of people are out there, waiting to latch onto someone just like you. Yes, search for success stories and successful people to be a part of your life, but also be cognizant of the flip side.

Looking Out for Number One

Negative people are self-absorbed. They are not interested in you or what you are doing unless, of course, you are doing things of which they disapprove. In the relationship arena, we want to establish positive associations with people who are very much interested in our well being.

We may have negative people in our lives who may, in fact, care for our physical well being. That is, they don't wish us dead or anything so final. They may even love us. But real, genuine caring runs much deeper. It entails caring for our interior needs.

Dream-busters are ubiquitous. The key defense mechanism to use against this bunch is distance. Simply put, keep your distance. Don't ever permit the self-absorbed to take you down to their level, and don't be disappointed if the self-absorbed don't accept your offer of a ride on up.

There's nothing wrong with looking out for Number One—you. Your personal journey to success puts a premium on you and your talents, your goals, and your particular vision of success. But, as we've seen in examples, the journey is not a solitary one. It can't be. This chapter, chronicling the important role our relationships play in the success quest, underscores this point so worthy of consideration.

Looking out for Ol' Number One is perfectly acceptable, positive behavior, but only if you also look out for numbers two and three. The road to success is both a very personal journey and one highly dependent on our relationships with others.

Anger: It's Big . . . Really Big

You are doubtless aware of the sprawling "Hollywood" sign in the hills of that famous city. Travelers in that part of southern California certainly know when they are on the edge of Tinseltown, courtesy of the humongous letters that spell out H-O-L-L-Y-W-O-O-D. What's this travelogue leading up to? A-N-G-E-R.

Consider anger to be like the Hollywood sign, a sure sign that you're headed in a certain direction. In this case, anger relates directly to negativity. While anger is a perfectly legitimate emotion that all of us exhibit on occasion, it is not something that we should be carrying around with us from dawn until dusk, from January to December. When we encounter angry people—the people who are angry, it seem, morning, noon, and night—we should run for the hills.

Associating with perpetually angry people is the equivalent of smoking four or more packs of cigarettes a day. Sooner or later, health problems surface. With smoking, it starts with coughing, then shortness of breath, then gets serious with heart disease or cancer. Being in the regular company of angry people initiates all sorts of health problems, too.

These problems may be emotional or they may manifest themselves in physical symptoms. The worst consequence, though, is probably the change an angry person can make in your character. An angry person makes you angry. If you resist responding in kind, you easily become sullen and introverted, building a defensive shell around yourself for protection and relief.

Paranoia Will Destroy You

Negative people are quite often paranoid. That is, they see the world and its many inhabitants as being out to get them in some way. This brand of negativism takes skepticism to its most destructive, regressive level.

FACT

When asked how he could sign an arms control agreement with his old nemesis, the Soviet Union, President Ronald Reagan quoted a popular Russian saying, "Trust, but verify." Trust, but verify, is also sound advice in the relationship business—anywhere and at any time.

There are, of course, degrees of paranoia. There is clinical mental illness, which we will leave to the medical specialists. We are concerned with the everyday negative individuals who believe that all butchers have their thumbs on the scale, all supermarkets have their cash registers set to overcharge, and, most importantly, that all good deeds by others are backed up by dark, ulterior motives.

We encounter this brand of negativity all the time. Paranoid individuals offer us advice on the ways of the world. Their mantra is "Don't trust anybody, anywhere, anytime." They see every man, woman, and child as being out for himself or herself—without exception. It's wise to be skeptical on life's journey. Just leave paranoia out of the equation. It's just as good to keep clear of individuals who see no honesty and decency in the world.

Lasting Positive Relationships

Without healthy and positive relationships in our lives, can we truly call ourselves successful? The answer is plainly "No!" Throughout this chapter, we've tackled the key issue of identifying positive people. We've examined the importance of positive associations in all aspects of our lives, both personal and professional. We've also addressed the negative half of this important equation in our quest for success.

Now that we know who and what to look for in all of our many life associations, we should also know how to maintain and improve our relationships. Our relationships are integral chapters in the story of our success. Unless we bestow our energy and take care to keep our relationships strong and healthy, success often comes only in rare and fleeting momentary happy bursts.

High Maintenance

Maintaining solid relationships both at home and on the job requires absolute commitment. We must remain aware of their consequence and long-term value. Relationships don't start and then just switch over to some kind of automatic pilot. You must sustain them, and that means you'll weather a few storms along the way. Nothing in life is maintenance free. Here are several relationship tips to keep foremost in your mind as you strive for success:

1. Always pay attention to the value of strong relationships.
2. Regularly show appreciation to those in your "Inner Circle" (that is, your nearest and most trusted family members, friends, and colleagues).
3. Always respect the individuality of those you know.
4. Follow the Golden Rule.
5. Never permit relationships to grow stale.

Let's briefly explore each one of these five maintenance points.

Value of Strong Relationships

Understanding and appreciating the value of strong relationships is the natural starting point. When you are acutely aware of the role that solid associations play in your quest for success, you automatically work harder to keep the relationships strong and oriented toward the future.

When you start your own family, you should plan for your financial future, your children's college education, medical emergencies, and so on. By taking this thorough route, you are strengthening both your present and future relationships and increasing your chances of success in life.

Showing Appreciation and Respect

The next relationship maintenance point involves consistently showing appreciation to those in your life. At work, let your business partner know that you value her as part of your life, and that she plays the leading role in your quest for success. At home, make sure your spouse understands that he is critical to your success and how much you appreciate his contributions.

Don't let relationship maintenance end in the home. Business associations, in particular, are often not properly maintained. If you are involved in any kind of partnership, or if you work closely with a coworker on the job, repeatedly show how much you value the relationship. Verbal and other recognition of the relationship's importance goes a long way in cementing established bonds and keeping them forward moving.

Mutual respect in relationships is an all-important *equalizer.* Strong relationships are firmly grounded in such respect. Those seeking real and lasting success fashion and attend to such relationships throughout their journey. They are acutely sensitive to telltale behaviors that indicate a lack of respect, superiority and condescension chief among them.

Maintenance in relationships also demands mutual respect: parent to child, husband to wife, coworker to coworker, pupil to teacher, and partner to partner in any kind of relationship. Without mutual respect of the individual personalities, there is no healthy, forward movement. Keep the need for respect foremost on your agenda.

The Golden Rule

Perhaps the one relationship maintenance point that distinguishes itself above all others is the Golden Rule: Do unto others as you wish to be done unto you. In our quests for success, we now and then lose sight of the impact our actions have on others in our circle of family, friends, and business associates. We may, on occasion, say and do things to others that we would find offensive and unprofessional, if the very same things were said or done to us.

Keep the Golden Rule in mind around the clock. Use it to evaluate your actions, and see to it that you are, in fact, measuring up. Self-awareness and real success are linked in so many ways. When you know who you are, and what you are capable of, you simultaneously know the consequence your actions will have on others. That makes you more keenly aware of the dynamics involved in all of your relationships.

The Freshness Factor

A final maintenance point to consider in the relationship province revolves around the importance of keeping your interactions fresh and interesting. In other words, try not to get bogged down in dull routine. Life has so much to offer. You needn't do the same things over and over again, day in and day out.

You don't have to go to the same restaurant all the time. You don't have to vacation in the same spot or stay in the same motel. You don't have to do the same tasks in your business, while your partner does hers.

You just don't want to go stale. You know the difference between the taste of a stale piece of cake and a fresh one. It's often the difference between inedible and edible. Keep your relationships edible. They'll be stronger and more successful if you do. It's really a piece of cake. If you focus on maintaining your relationships by keeping them active and pointed in a positive direction, you can't go wrong. Ⓔ

Chapter 4

Know Thyself and Know Success

Success beckons to those who truly know themselves. Knowing our strengths, as well as our weaknesses, permits us to plow ahead. We are aware of what we want and what we can do, and that makes us fully prepared to meet and greet life's challenges and opportunities.

Intuition and the Road to Success

Have you ever noticed that some people are more intuitive than others? They seem to be able to get a feel for another person or a particular situation—one that is right on the mark—before anybody else does. Keen self-awareness helps foster intuition, that hard-to-define sense that we can use to make an honest assessment of all that is happening in our lives in the here and now.

QUESTION?

What does intuition have to do with success?
Intuition enables us to carefully read life's many situations and, thus, identify genuine opportunities. It plays a defining role in the way we enter into successful personal relationships, locate the right careers, and attain overall happiness and personal satisfaction.

Intuition is not about picking winners at the racetrack or finding the next Microsoft buried somewhere on the NASDAQ. Rather, it's about feelings that we can trust, even though we don't know why; it can also tell us things about ourselves, both good and bad. Intuition on the road to success is a trusty friend and a faithful companion. It separates the wheat from the chaff in those countless life opportunity moments. Among its many benefits, intuition assists us in finding true love, reliable friendships, the right kind of job, and the best place to live and raise a family.

Have you ever rued the day that you moved from the peaceful countryside to the loud, obnoxious city? Have you felt, perhaps, that you weren't attentive enough to a partner in a past relationship? Maybe you're sorry you left your last job for your present, higher-paying position, which is proving to be something other than what you anticipated. These are instances in which self-awareness plus intuition could have spared you a ton of heartache, pain, and—yes—regret.

Valuable Life Lessons

We all have regrets in life. After all, being only human, we are loaded with imperfections. Some self-help gurus would have us heave all of our accumulated regrets into one communal bonfire and let them burn away. This may or may not be sound advice. It all depends on what we do with our regrets.

If regret over things that you said or did in the past—or didn't say or do—are holding you back, then you should toss them promptly into that flickering blaze. If, on the other hand, you are extracting meaningful life lessons from your regrets, you are building your future by learning from your past. When you absorb valuable lessons from your mistakes of yesteryear, you automatically transform these past blunders and missed opportunities into both a healthier present and better tomorrow.

ALERT!

Life's regrets are often diamonds in the rough. If you view your regrets—be they over interpersonal relationships, career moves, or anything else—as important life lessons, you convert negative experiences into positive possibilities. Such conversions portend success.

Jack Be Nimble

Like so many others before and after him, Jack's first marriage ended unhappily. His relationships with his three teenaged children, too, were very distant and even acrimonious at times. The main reason for the big chill in his relations with his kids was that he was an absentee father—a workaholic. Even when he came home from the office, his job responsibilities took precedence over quality time with his family.

All along, Jack rationalized that he was doing right by his family. He believed that the sole reason he was laboring so long and hard was to provide for them. After all, his children didn't need a thing. In fact, each one of them was destined to go to the best college or university that money could buy. Jack's high-paying job also provided his brood with the nicest clothes, state-of-the-art computers, elite summer camp enrollments, European vacations, and so on. Surely they had it all . . . or did they? Jack's wife ultimately separated from him, taking the kids to live with her. She cited his inattention to both her and the children as the reason for the breakup. He was married to his work, she said—an all-too-common refrain in divorce proceedings.

As the years passed, Jack got on with his life. He remarried. The second time around, however—and with a mound of regrets—Jack vowed to behave differently. He placed his life and his notion of success in an entirely new perspective. In the future, he would carefully balance work with his home life. Jack now understood that it was entirely possible to be at once a reliable provider and a good husband and father.

Many of our regrets revolve around things that we didn't do, rather than things we wish we had done differently. In other words, it's those missed opportunities that most of us regret. Keep this reality foremost in your mind when present opportunities come your way!

In effect, Jack converted his numerous past regrets into priceless life lessons. He wasn't about to travel down the same littered path of his first marriage. He now saw clearly—heightened self-awareness on his part— where he went wrong, and exactly what he needed to do to avoid repeating his past mistakes. Jack's eyes were opened to what he once deemed "success." He plainly grasped that it was not success at all, but a perverted version of it.

The Creative Impulse

Know yourself, and tap into your creative impulses. There isn't a living being among us who is not creative in some particular way. Creativity lurks in every man, woman, and child. Even if they appear as bland ciphers on the surface, there's always something beneath the facade. We know that not everybody practices self-actualization—the process of turning potential into reality. Thus, many creative impulses remain dormant.

Self-awareness permits you to see yourself and your talents in an honest light. It enables you to develop the things you love to do and that you do well. The best teachers, mentors, and motivators reach their students in ways that inspire them to detect their creative inclinations.

When you start mining this wealth, you are setting the table for the feast of success.

Consider the individuals who are successful in life. Each one is a creative person in some very distinct way. A successful small businessperson doesn't just sign a lease, throw open the door, and start counting his money. Instead, a successful business is a creative endeavor run by a creative person or people.

FACT

A mom-and-pop pet food store ran an advertisement: "Have your pet's picture taken with Santa Claus." Pet owners and their beloved pets lined up for more than a city block for the free holiday snapshot. This creative marketing idea spawned a tradition, beginning in that one small store—and the brainchild of two businessmen—that was subsequently imitated by the big pet-related superstores.

Successful parents with strong family bonds are, likewise, creative. They work hard at doing all the right things. They know that what works for one child may not work for another. These parents tap their creative impulses by knowing both themselves and their children.

Leading the Way

Strong leaders are rare birds. Whether on the grade-school playground, atop the family tree, on the sports field, or ruling the roost in the confines of the office, successful leaders stand out from the crowd. People are drawn to them and respond to them.

Leadership and success are intertwined. Fear not! This doesn't mean you have to become the boss at work, start a business of your own, or be president of the PTA to inhale the bouquet of success. It does, however, mean that you must be the leader of your own life. The very same leadership qualities that typically define top managers in companies, respected parents, or team captains in sports are the same attributes that each one of us needs to master in our own individual quest for success.

It Begins with Self-Awareness

Many people attain leadership positions at some point in their lives, and it's no stretch to say that a healthy percentage of them fail miserably in doing the leading. The most frequent failures are those who come up short in the "know thyself" department. If you don't know yourself, it's highly unlikely that you are going to know others. It is this awareness deficit that causes more problems at home, in the classroom, on the sports field, and on the job than any other.

The infamous "Peter principle," famous in many workplaces, says that managers are often promoted to the level of their incompetence. That is, they move up to the very plateau at which their knowledge and skills are ill-matched with their job responsibilities. "Knowing thyself," however, stands the Peter principle on its head every single time.

When you cut to the chase and figure out exactly who you are, you locate your true strengths. Then—and only then—can you realistically expect to lead others. However, you must first be capable of leading yourself. There's nothing more unbecoming than an individual in some kind of leadership role who lacks any semblance of authority. This might be a parent, a Little League coach, or a corporate manager—it doesn't matter which.

When we are wholly self-aware, we know two things: We have strengths, and we have weaknesses. We accept, therefore, that we are imperfect human beings, and that we do not lord over the rest of humanity. Strong, effective leadership is always grounded in the two R's: respect and reciprocity.

Are You a Natural Leader?

Successful individuals are ordinarily leadership material. Positive leadership is a trait that is highly prized in society, whether that's at home, in leisure activities, in government, or in business. People are always searching for leaders to improve their lives and help them succeed.

We've just described exactly how self-awareness is the precursor of leadership. We noted that leadership in guiding our own lives in a responsible, forward-moving direction is at the top of the agenda. The next step is leading others to do the same.

Let's now explore the personality traits that are found in successful leaders. Consider yourself a leader in training, and see if you can identify with them. Positive leaders do the following:

- Aim for the future
- Embrace challenges
- Exhibit mental toughness
- Accept responsibility
- Have a practical nature
- Command respect

Future Orientation

Naturally, leaders must be future oriented. This makes perfect sense because leading means that there is a destination—a forward destination—unless, of course, you are a lemming. If you live in the past, or are a slave to the status quo, you won't make a good leader.

Welcoming Challenges and Mental Toughness

Leaders not only welcome challenges, they relish the opportunity to go places where no one has gone before. If you want to be an effective leader, you have to show your followers that you are not afraid to tackle any problems or obstacles that come your way. You must also demonstrate that you welcome the chance to do so with open arms.

Mental toughness and leadership go together like peanut butter and jelly. The reason is simple: Leaders encounter criticism all the time. It's the nature of the business, in business and out. You can't buckle under to it. You must accept criticism as part of the job of being a leader and part of life's big picture, too. When criticism spawns discouragement, backpedaling occurs. Leaders don't backpedal! Hence, they can't afford to get discouraged.

Responsibility and Practicality

Responsibility and leadership are blood brothers for obvious reasons. Leadership is a tremendous responsibility, in and of itself. When you are in charge of other people, whether at home, in school, or on the job, you have a lot on your plate. You're dealing with fellow human beings and influencing their lives with the decisions that you make. Therefore, you must weigh each decision carefully. Never shoot from the hip or take your responsibilities lightly.

Respect Is Key

The last and most important element elevating leadership is that thing called respect. Without respect firmly in place, leadership cannot happen. If your children, your pupils, your ball players, the members of the town committee you are in charge of, or your team at the office does not respect you, you are not going to get what you want out of them. Your decisions will be second-guessed, ridiculed, or ignored.

ALERT!

Respect is always a two-way street, so you also have to respect those whom you lead. Always remember that respect is built on a foundation of integrity and, of course, competence.

Self-Awareness: It Awes and Humbles Us

Self-awareness empowers us to unearth our potential leadership skills because it both awes and humbles us. You stand in awe of what you can do and what you can accomplish. But you also appreciate your humanity and your limitations, too.

The tyrannical blowhard, in a leadership position, may achieve results. For example, the father who hits his kids may keep them in line, but their obedience comes out of fear, not out of respect for him and good behavior. A self-aware parent, on the other hand, would find less harsh alternatives to accomplishing the same results. Instilling virtue in kids through the power of example is self-aware parental leadership at its best.

You can see this situation within the business scene. Their names are legion—the callous taskmasters who make their employees' lives holy hells. They browbeat their underlings and demean them from nine to six (or longer). Sometimes they exact the productivity they want. But this managerial approach cannot be measured with an "ends justifies the means" ruler. Many employees respond to cruel managers because, among other things, they need jobs and money to pay their bills. Fear takes some people to very high levels of performance.

True self-awareness and managerial monsters are as far apart as the North and South Poles. The road to self-awareness cuts a swath across conscience. Severe, uncaring individuals in leadership roles—whether parents, teachers, managers, or coaches—do not let their consciences speak to them; they do not let their consciences set them straight.

When Conscience Talks

When you sit down and appraise yourself—take your own inventory, as it were—what are you actually doing? You're seeing who you are, warts and all, and attempting to make sense of your place in life. Above all else, though, you are letting your conscience do the talking.

FACT

Self-awareness works in concert with your conscience. By its very definition, self-awareness is a plainly positive thing. An individual, for instance, might conclude that she is a bad person and has done rotten things. As a result, her self-awareness empowers her to correct the bad behavior and move forward in life. Self-awareness always has a welcome mat out for redemption.

Your conscience will either permit you to reach out for life's successes, or it will tie you up in knots and hold you back. You have a couple of options. Maybe you choose to allow your conscience to evaluate the good and the bad in you, knowing that eventually you will come down on the good side. Or you might let your conscience weigh you down with so much negative baggage that you'll be prostrate for the remainder of your life. And prostrate people never achieve success!

Unfortunately, many people are not self-aware, and they don't take that all-important inventory of themselves. Because of this interior neglect, they don't ever wrestle with their consciences. Our quests for success are deeply rooted in the decisions that we make; these are decisions with real consequences, not only for ourselves, but also for others. In making our myriad life decisions, we confront moral and ethical dilemmas all the time. This is precisely why self-awareness is so essential in seeing us through to authentic and sustained successes.

Self-Awareness Strengthens Relationships

You've already been exposed to the central role that relationships play in your quest for success. Positive associations all along the road to success are mandatory, simply because nobody can walk life's marathon in isolation. There are close to 300 million people in the United States alone and over 6 billion in the world. You might as well prepare yourself for dealing intimately with an infinitesimal fraction of them.

Exactly how does self-awareness strengthen your interpersonal relationships? Well, let's think about it. The more that you know about yourself, the more you see and understand how your demeanor and conduct impacts others. Self-awareness transcends the self. This transcendentalism is a powerful relationship booster and, logically, a success booster as well.

The Human Wall

Have you ever noticed how some people—and you may very well be one of them—have an invisible wall around them? It feels like a kind of personality force field. They limit personal revelations about themselves, keep their private lives very private, and have territorial boundaries that outsiders dare not cross. In simple terms, these are private people who expect others to respect their privacy.

The personality boundaries that people define for themselves vary in size and intensity. Some are quiet souls who don't ask others personal questions, and they expect reciprocal behavior in return. Others are more gregarious sorts, but they confine their banter to mostly current events, the weather, and sports. Still others may talk up a blue streak while managing to keep particular areas of their lives completely private: family relations, sex lives, occupations, and so on.

ALERT!

On the road to success, it is imperative that you respect other people's boundaries. Never invade their privacy with prying questions. Achieving success means encountering and working with a large, diverse lot of people. By knowing yourself and respecting others, you will automatically go places that you wouldn't if your behaviors were careless and impolite.

Why is it that so many salespeople are held in such low regard? Because many of them are boundary busters. They are offensive because they try to ingratiate themselves to their clients without caring to know or respect them as individual human beings.

The best salespeople are self-aware and intuitive. They chalk up both high sales and garner the respect of their peers by carefully navigating the personality boundaries of their customers. They don't come on too strong, nor do they treat everybody the same way. They understand human nature and accept that it is complex and layered with individuality. They succeed because they treat their customers as unique people on a one-to-one basis. In other words, they respect their customers' boundaries.

You Are a Salesperson

You are always a salesperson on your quest for success. You are selling yourself, your special talents, and your insights all along the way. You are selling a totally unique product. As you seek out successes in life, keep yourself in the selling mode—the positive selling mode. Following is a sampling of some sales you might make on your trip to success:

- When you go out on a date, you want to make a good impression. You are selling yourself as a solid person.
- You want to find Mr. or Ms. Right at some point in time, so you search and sell yourself as a good match for some lucky person.
- You hope that you'll get the job you applied for, so you put your best foot forward in the job interview.
- When you start the business of your dreams, you want customers to patronize it, so you welcome them with open arms into your store.
- You want your children to respect you and listen to your advice, so you set a good example for them.

Sell yourself in a sincere, self-aware style. Respect others while doing so. You'll encounter success this way, more so than if you crash others' parties and trash their personal boundaries.

You're selling yourself in all of these instances. In fact, you have to sell yourself to others throughout your entire life. You'll only find your soul mate if you look hard and present yourself in the best possible light. People will patronize your business if you give them a product that they want, and if you show that they can trust you to back your product and your word. Your kids will respect you because of your consistently honest actions, not because they're constantly told to respect their elders.

A Potent Team: Self-Awareness and Positive Attitude

To some cynical sorts, the mere notion of self-awareness comes with a troublesome worry. These people might argue that it is possible to know too much about ourselves and what's really going on in our cold and dangerous world. You've no doubt heard these doomsayers infer that the truly happy souls in the world are shallow individuals, because if they were intelligent, they'd be gloomy and pessimistic. This line of reasoning concludes that because they are in touch with the harsh realities of life, truly self-aware people must be unhappy and must sport negative attitudes.

Finite Living Means a Lot of Living

Don't believe this attempt to tarnish the positive benefits of self-awareness in your quest for success. Certain realities of life are difficult to swallow. Eventually, we will all shuffle off this mortal coil, and this isn't a particularly comforting thought. Nevertheless, this fact alone infuses the finite living that we do have with a sense of purpose. We have no choice but to make our limited time on this earth a self-fulfilling and largely successful one.

It is self-awareness that opens up so many avenues into our souls. Why is it that we are captivated by the allure of oceans, mountains, and rolling plains? If life is so mean and ugly, why do we get a rush at watching the sunset or coming upon a meadow of wildflowers?

Truly successful people are self-aware on many different levels. One of the most important focuses on appreciating the so-called "little things" in life, such as the beauty and mystique of nature. Sure, there are countless tough breaks in the game of life, and a ton of heartache and pain. But there's also so much that is uplifting. Success lies here, on life's upside.

A Couple of Successes

Ralph and Helen worked their entire married lives in two separate midtown Manhattan office buildings. They vacationed every summer on Cape Cod, hoping to retire there when they were both eligible for Social Security. When their retirement drew near, the couple purchased a cozy home in earshot of the roaring Atlantic Ocean.

Throughout their working lives, Ralph and Helen exemplified self-awareness. They both found jobs that complemented their talents and ambitions. They were emotionally and financially satisfied working in their careers. Although a very close couple, they set goals individually as to where they each wanted to be in five, ten, twenty years, and upon retirement. In addition, the pair set combined goals and planned for their future as a married couple.

Ralph and Helen maintained a positive attitude all throughout their lives. When their retirement years greeted them, they were poised to enjoy themselves. The fruits of their success placed them by the seashore they loved. They now spend every single day walking along sandy beaches and breathing in salty air. Not too shabby!

FACT

Psychologist Carl Jung said, "Your vision will become clear only when you can look into your own heart. Who looks outside, dreams; who looks inside, awakes." Looking at self-awareness from a somewhat different angle, Ann Landers once opined: "Know yourself. Don't accept your dog's admiration as conclusive evidence that you are wonderful."

Ralph and Helen's keen self-awareness equipped them with the tools to appreciate all that life has to offer. Their view of life as a whole is one of mystery and magnificence, not death and destruction. Self-awareness needn't conjure up violent images (although we should always be mindful in this day and age of rightful causes for worry). It need not weigh us down with concerns about contracting a serious illness (although we should scrupulously tend to our health and wellness). Nor should self-awareness riddle us with fears of dying (there's nothing we can do about that—it's a given).

Rather, your self-awareness should unlock doors for you. By knowing yourself, you can tap into the many things in life that really give you pleasure and satisfaction. Don't obscure your quest for success under the darkest cloud of all—a negative attitude. Life's too short and too great for that!

Chapter 5
Personal Satisfaction

The bottom line of success is quite unlike a large corporation's bottom line. Success is not about numbers in a ledger or zeroes on a bank statement. Rather, the success bottom line is called personal satisfaction. When you are genuinely satisfied with your life as a whole—at home and at work—you are successful.

What Exactly Is It?

In previous chapters, we've made numerous references to personal satisfaction, or personal fulfillment. When you can honestly say to yourself that you are content with your lot in life—in areas ranging from your interpersonal relationships, to your job and career, to good health and your faith in a bright tomorrow—you can truly lay claim to being a success.

As we've repeatedly emphasized, success amounts to different strokes for different folks. It's an art form, and for that reason its exact definition can be very hard to put a finger on. Success's leading indicator, however, is always personal satisfaction.

Farm Fresh Success

Here's an intriguing case study of personal satisfaction and success and how they meet in the strangest of places. Marie is happily married and lives in a bucolic town in the lush Lehigh Valley of Pennsylvania. Her husband Tony is a farmer. On Marie and Tony's farm live some Holstein cattle, pigs, chickens, and row upon row of corn. The couple live in a very modest house, just a stone's throw from a silo stacked with dry corn for their farm animals. Marie and Tony's two boys are also involved in working the family farm, and they intend to keep it in the family for at least another generation, or longer.

Marie and Tony are a happy pair. They wouldn't trade their lifestyle for any other, even though their way of life is not always easy. Marie is involved in all kinds of community activities and local politics. And while their financial situation, after so many years of hard work and struggle, may signal to some folks that Marie and Tony are hardly successful—don't tell that to them!

In this example, personal satisfaction is deeply rooted in rich soil. Marie and Tony are living where they want to be living, and they are doing what they want to be doing. Their kids value the same life that their parents do. They want to carry on the family business and—more importantly—the family traditions. Yet Marie and Tony are, in fact, just "getting by." They are not getting rich by any stretch of the imagination.

However, this doesn't trouble them in the least because their life goals are not focused on building monetary wealth.

There's nothing wrong with setting financial goals and desiring financial security. In fact, it's highly recommended that you carefully plan for your financial future! (See Chapter 16 for a full discussion on the financial planning that's right for you.) However, high income and monetary wealth don't have to be driving your success agenda.

FACT

If you require additional proof of the success mystique, consider what the notion of success is to a young Amish farmer in Lancaster, Pennsylvania. Contrast that to the vision of a wealthy doctor's child, one studying at the Harvard University business school. It's a pretty safe bet that these two individuals see success in two very distinct lights.

It's a Personal Thing

Again, personal satisfaction is a deeply personal thing. Farm families want to get the best prices for their crops, milk, beef, pork, and eggs. They want to have good years. They want to be able to put something away for a rainy day because those rainy days will pour down on them time and again. But they also understand that their businesses aren't going to make them rich, even if they string together several banner years in a row. They live with this reality, with success defined in their singular parameters.

Personal Satisfaction and Career Planning

In high schools and colleges everywhere, guidance and career counselors are as plentiful as ants at a picnic. Their jobs are to get young adults to start thinking about their futures and visualizing lives of success. If, for instance, you want to study engineering in college, you have to secure good grades in key high school courses, such as physics and calculus.

Charting Our Futures

Throughout our lives, we have to plan and make the decisions that will chart our futures. Some school kids have their prospective careers all mapped out upon high school graduation and even before that, but usually it's their parents who are leading the charge. At that age, most of us have very few clues as to what we want do with our lives.

ALERT!

All of us want to be successful, but this doesn't mean that our work lives are all preordained in high school and college. In fact, our jobs and career paths need not be etched in stone at any point in our lives.

Life's Curveballs

Life throws us lots of curveballs. Your ideal of the perfect job or career may look quite different at the age of eighteen or twenty-two than it does at thirty or forty. There's no reason that you should ever feel trapped in a particular job or profession. In fact, there are ample reasons why you should feel free to switch jobs or career paths at any given moment in your life. Here are some common reasons for considering a change in jobs or re-evaluating your career choice:

- Your knowledge and skills grow and take you beyond your current job or particular profession.
- The kind of work you are doing is personally unfulfilling, be it in job responsibilities, compensation, growth opportunities, interpersonal relationships, or a combination of things.
- Technology negatively affects your field, downsizing your job or perhaps eliminating it altogether.
- Economic conditions result in upheavals in your particular profession, making you rethink the future stability of your chosen industry or career path.
- Unforeseen personal responsibilities make your present job or career difficult to sustain due to long hours, inadequate pay, or travel obligations.

We can put it simply: Life is highly unpredictable. Thus, your notion of the perfect career and your personal satisfaction threshold will likely change with time. For some people, the change can be a dramatic one. The stockbroker who leaves her job to become a forest ranger is making a big time life change. The editor in a big publishing house, on the other hand, who leaves his position to work for a top advertising agency remains in the same corporate milieu, albeit with different responsibilities.

The Job That's Right for You

Finding work that's right for you—personally satisfying—is an integral part of the success formula. The other primary ingredient of success is healthy, enduring relationships. But the reality is that personal satisfaction at work and at home is often one and the same. It has to be! In most instances, you can't have one without the other.

The right job or career is key to your personal satisfaction. The duplicate key is the right interpersonal relationships. These two keys open the very same door. Fulfillment in career and fulfillment at home do not usually exist apart from one another. Personal satisfaction in one is hard to come by without the other.

Job and Career Questions

Let's focus on finding you the work that'll bring you genuine satisfaction and provide you with real and lasting successes. First, carefully consider what you really want out of a job or a career. Consider what work responsibilities and compensation will satisfy you. Consider where the job or career will take you in the years to come. Consider where you will be living and if you want to be there. Here's a list of pertinent job and career questions to ponder:

1. Do you want a job or career where you can work by yourself?
2. Do you want a job or career that's very people-oriented?
3. Do you want a job or career with advancement possibilities?
4. Do you want a job or career with high income potential?
5. Do you want a job or career that is secure over the long term?
6. Do you want a job or career that is interesting and exciting?
7. Do you want a job or career that entails helping other people?
8. Do you want a job or career that affords you ample leisure time?

Prioritize

It's a safe bet that you will answer "yes" to more than one of these job and career questions. If so, it's a good idea to prioritize your "yes" responses. What is most important to you in your job or career? If, for instance, you want to work independently, you might contemplate starting a business of your own. If you are skilled in a particular trade, becoming an independent contractor might be just what the doctor ordered.

If high income and fast wealth accumulation are on the top of your list, then you don't want to work for the government. If job security is more important to you, though, why not look into a civil service career? If, on the other hand, you want increased growth opportunities on the job, avoid the bureaucracy like quicksand. Again, it all boils down to your priorities and what you view as success.

ALERT!

In the twenty-first century, also known as the Information Age, computer programmers and software developers are highly prized. If you relish buzzing around cyberspace and know the ABCs of RAM and megabytes, a career in this dynamic field could be right for you—both intellectually stimulating and financially rewarding.

Typecasting: Personality Types

Before taking this discussion any further, let's find out whether you are a Type A or Type B personality. This little letter distinction assumes great importance when you're considering the type of job or career that's right for you.

If you are a Type A personality, you are openly aggressive and highly competitive. You sport an unrelenting drive and desire to do things—lots of things. You are probably very impatient and quick to anger, too. Conversely, if you are a Type B personality, you are more relaxed, with an undeniably placid temperament. You are more apt to roll with life's punches, even the ones that hit you in the gut and take your breath away.

For obvious reasons, Type B is the preferred personality. Too much aggression, anger, and impatience create stress, which then leads to all kinds of health problems and sometimes prematurely summons the Grim Reaper to our front doors. At the same time, we need Type A personalities to fill lots of jobs. The beauty of life is that even if you perceive yourself as more Type A than Type B, you can modify your attitude and behaviors for your own benefit.

For instance, you can convert your combative tendencies into forward-moving, attentive ambition. You can turn your zealous competitive spirit into a strict discipline leading to sustained success. You can convert arrogance into confidence and leadership.

FACT

Type A personalities often find themselves in high-pressure occupations and professions, such as the law or the military. It is Type A personalities who generally make the best stockbrokers and investment bankers, for they thrive in the rough-and-tumble atmosphere of financial services. Type B personalities, on the other hand, are well suited in jobs as teachers and counselors.

Career Match Game

Okay, you have a fix on who you are as a person and the kinds of things that you want out of your work life. Now let's play a little match game. If you want to make big bucks fast, then you should explore investment-related jobs. Financial analysts and others who deal with big money usually make big money. There are also marketing and sales positions to consider. If you are an assertive person who is ready and willing to sell—and who can stand a little rejection—there are high-paying jobs just waiting for your special talent.

Are you looking for adventure in a career, perhaps even with a hint of danger? Consider becoming a police officer or firefighter. In this day and age, law enforcement agencies—whether local or federal, such as the FBI—are clamoring for more than a few good men and women. In these particular professions, you live with the unexpected while simultaneously serving your fellow citizens and your country. Police, firefighting, and other law-enforcement jobs are pressure-filled, but the interior rewards—the personal satisfaction—often compensates for this downside.

Maybe you are a people person who wants to be in the company of others while you work. Perhaps you're considering giving something back to the society. Why not explore teaching or some kind of social work? Another people-intensive job choice might be hotel management. How about working as a waiter or a waitress? Good wait staff make good money!

Counseling careers come in many variations, too, from helping students to guiding problem drinkers; from offering a hand to women in distress to working with troubled married couples. We live in an age of counseling, and counselors of all stripes are in great demand.

If you are a talented craftsperson, you should consider putting your genius to work. For people who are good at building things, there are carpentry careers to look into. If you fancy yourself adept in the kitchen—and enjoy cooking—there are restaurant jobs aplenty crying out for capable chefs and cooks. As you can see, the sky's the limit in finding the work or the profession that's right for you. And when the sky's the limit, it's time to reach for the sky.

Priority One

Finding the right kind of work should be your top priority, whether you're twenty-two, forty-two, or sixty-two. Job and career should never be taken lightly. The answers to the job and career questions previously posed should act as your guide for success throughout your life. If you bypass the right kind of work for your particular personality and unique talents, you are not going to experience profound and lasting success. Instead, you'll end up resentful of what might or could have been.

Consider the person who labored his or her entire adult life in the post office. This is a perfectly fine place to work (with good pay, benefits, and job security), but not if you abhor your job hours and duties, and not if you always wanted to do something else with your life. Many people do jobs that don't satisfy them, but they nevertheless get corralled into them for years and even decades.

ALERT!

Life's got a funny habit of tying us down. You should be conscious of this onerous reality at all times as you pursue the job and career that's right for you. Personal satisfaction—from financial to intellectual and everything in between—should be your ultimate job and career litmus test.

Work and careers are funny things. There are untold people who are ridiculously mismatched with their jobs or professions. Walk into a retail store, and you may encounter a surly owner who seems to detest the mere sight of human beings—her customers, no less. Stroll around any big city and look at the faces of the office workers streaming onto the sidewalks at lunchtime. A portion of them appear highly charged, raring to go, and happy with their lot in life! They seem exhilarated with what they are doing for a living. Meanwhile, there are others who sport hangdog looks and seem totally deflated and sucked dry of all of life's critical juices. You can't spend half your waking day in a shadow of gloom and claim that you're happy with the state of your life.

Be All That You Can Be

The U.S. Army's popular advertising slogan is "Be All That You Can Be." The campaign boasts that by joining this revered branch of the armed services, individuals can acquire a mass of skills that will serve them well in life. In essence, the army is saying that they will assist their enlistees in tapping into their unique potentials and seeing their self-actualization through. Indeed, for many people, army life is a godsend—a career that they come to love and value for teaching them so much about life and responsibility, not to mention all sorts of priceless technical skills.

But it's your individual personality that matters most here. Some of us, for example, bristle at authority and rules. We would not appreciate reveille call at five o'clock in the morning, nor would we value the experience of having an obnoxious drill sergeant getting in our faces. This is precisely why you must know your personality and interests—know thyself!—and match your unique character with work that'll fulfill you not only today, but also tomorrow, and the tomorrow after that.

Job and Career Sources

There are plenty of valuable job and career Web sites, books, counselors, and other resources you can turn to for information and advice. Remember that in selecting the job or career that's right for you, it's important that you consider many factors. The factor that's most important is your very own personal satisfaction. Your career is not a game of roulette. It's too valuable to be left to chance.

Trying your hand at different jobs in different professions often works for some people, and trial-and-error is an important part of career vetting. For instance, if you think you might be nurse material, try volunteer work in a hospital first before enrolling in nursing school. Then, if you faint at the sight of blood, you can effortlessly move on to another career possibility.

Career Counselor

The twenty-first century is home to lots of counselors, sometimes known as coaches. Coaches were once confined to athletics, with the titles dispensed only to guys and gals with whistles around their necks and booming voices. But it's a New Age, with new coaches. Career coaching is readily available, and you don't have to be a school kid to access it.

If you opt for career counseling, a competent counselor or coach can assist you in putting together the pieces of your life puzzle so that it spells out S-U-C-C-E-S-S. Above all else, such career counseling enables you to be heard. By vocalizing what you deem important to a trained career coach, you can get good solid help in finding the best possible career paths—the ones that will bring you the utmost in personal satisfaction.

Trained career coaches view success as your inalienable right. They treat all of their clients with dignity, regardless of their backgrounds, goals, or dreams. They view their clients as individuals with unique talents who require jobs and careers that complement—rather than contradict—their personalities.

Life Isn't One-Dimensional

Let's face it. Sometimes we just don't know what we want out of life. We are often conditioned through our upbringing, education, and media sources to see life as one-dimensional. That is, we don't fully understand or appreciate that there are many options available to us. We needn't settle for second best when it comes to our working lives, our associates, and where we live.

Some valuable Web sites for job seekers include ✍ *www.careerbuilder.com*, ✍ *www.bestjobsusa.com*, and ✍ *www.monster.com*. Post your resume, search for specific types of jobs in particular locations, and join in on career discussions. By merely combing through available jobs and their descriptions, you can often find new things that catch your fancy and jibe with your interests and dreams.

Some behavioral scientists suggest that, in general, we use only a tiny fraction of our potential. For this reason, counseling and coaching really do help a lot of people, particularly in regard to their careers. If you are in the dark about what you want out of life, and what you see as success, a competent coach can help you find your way. (See Chapter 19 for a complete discussion on the important role of coaching in today's society.)

Home Sweet Home

Every year, *Money* magazine conducts surveys on the best places to live and raise a family. Here are some of the key factors evaluated in determining the preferred locations:

- Cost of living
- Quality of schools
- Average commute time
- Job market
- Future growth rate

Where you live matters a lot in relation to success. You can't separate your personal satisfaction from the city or town you call home, your particular neighborhood, or your relations with your neighbors. Some people love the fast pace and excitement of a big city and find country or suburban living excruciatingly boring. Others find the peace and serenity of non-city life meditative, and they loathe the hustle and bustle of urban living.

Consider your job and career in unison with its location. Many people leave locations in which they are completely happy to take higher-paying jobs in places they abhor. Depending on who you are and your special life circumstances (single, married, children, and so on), where you live counts for an awful lot as it relates to personal satisfaction.

Best Places to Live

Consider those surveys conducted by *Money* magazine that list the best places to live. They often note the average cost of a home. In Portland, Oregon, a place recommended for its high quality of life, the average home price is $165,700. In Providence, Rhode Island—also a winning locale—the average price of a home is $128,900. What's the cost in your city? How much did you pay for your humble abode?

Other survey results list the student/teacher ratio. In Chicago, Illinois, it's 17.6; in Salt Lake City, Utah, it's 21.2. Both of these very different cities made the cut as being among the best places to live. What's the student/teacher ratio in your neck of the woods? Do you have any clue?

FACT

Some cities and towns that have made "Best Places to Live and Raise Families" lists include: Winston-Salem, North Carolina; Huntsville, Alabama; Tempe, Arizona; Billings, Montana; Minneapolis, Minnesota; Ames, Iowa; Sacramento, California; Cambridge, Massachusetts; Richmond, Virginia; Columbus, Ohio; Ann Arbor, Michigan; Sarasota, Florida; Salt Lake City, Utah; Chicago, Illinois; Portland, Oregon; Athens, Georgia; Raleigh-Durham/Chapel Hill, North Carolina; Madison, Wisconsin; and Fort Collins, Colorado.

You see, there's quite a lot to look into. A job or career is more than a paycheck. You have to be living someplace in order to perform your job. When the workday is done, you go home, patronize local businesses, send your kids to local schools, and join in community activities.

America is a vast place. You don't have to live in a high-crime city if you don't want to. You don't have to live through brutally cold winters or devilishly hot and humid summers. Personal satisfaction covers a lot of square miles. Obviously, for you to be a true success in life, you have to be where you want to be, physically as well as emotionally.

Hi, Neighbor

Personal satisfaction with your life sprouts its tentacles in all sorts of directions. We've just established how important it is to live in a city or town that makes you proud to call it home. It's just as essential that you peacefully coexist with your neighbors.

It's not unusual to see neighbors bickering over something silly and resolvable. Maybe it's one neighbor's cat converting another neighbor's lawn into its personal privy. Perhaps it's a trivial boundary dispute, a barking dog in the next apartment, loud music in the wee hours, or obnoxious kids. You get the picture.

Neighbors make neighborhoods. You could be in the most beautiful city in the country, in a great job, and still dread going home at night because of your less-than-neighborly neighbors. You must add a little extra due diligence to your search for the right place to work and live. This means getting a real feel for your home surroundings, including your prospective neighbors.

The moral of the story is that you should never downplay anything in your quest for success. This is particularly true for the big-ticket items, like what you do, where you live, and who you live with and around, including neighbors. Neighbors, after all, quite often become your best friends. On the other hand, neighbors can be the worst of enemies.

Frustration and Boredom

Boredom and frustration are often invisible enemies. You might think that you are contented with your work and life in general, but then you find yourself coming home from the job worn out and lifeless, tired of going to the same shops in town, and sick of eating in the same dull restaurants. Maybe you've had your fill of the same narrow-minded disputes on the job. This list could go on and on.

Boredom and frustration along your life journey impedes your realization of success. It pays to keep an eye out for signs of the dastardly duo. Never forget that it is always in your power to make things right— to infuse your life circumstances with the perfect antidote to boredom and frustration.

What's that, you ask? Only you know the answer to the question. It's your life. You know what makes you happy. You know what your dreams are. You set your goals. You know what success and personal satisfaction are to you.

Chapter 6

The Success Goalpost

Success is primarily the byproduct of careful planning—not mere happenstance. This is precisely why it is so vital to establish ambitious but realistic life goals in your quest for success. When you set goals for yourself, establish timetables for achieving them. If you persevere through the bad times that always come with the good, you will find that more often than not it is success that awaits you at the other end of the tunnel.

Not Leaving Success to Chance

Success is not something you can leave to chance. If you sit back and wait for your lottery numbers to come in, or for your can't-miss penny stock to swell into the next IBM, you more than likely have a very long wait on your hands! If you dream of meeting Mr. Right, you are not going to find him while lounging in an easy chair in your living room and watching sitcom reruns.

An important key to unlocking the door to success entails setting goals for yourself and then doing what it takes to make them reality. Indeed, actions always speak louder than words. Enunciating your goals is merely the first step, albeit a very important one. Scrupulously mapping out the ways you intend to achieve your goals is more involved, and is ultimately what will enable them to see the light of day.

Where There's a Goal, There's a Way

The first leg in the goal-setting marathon is identifying whether there's a genuine desire on your part to achieve the goal. Is the prospect of seeing your goal through stirring your insides with anticipation and excitement? Some people choose goals that don't jibe with their genuine wants and particular circumstances. Their goals are based on what they think others expect of them or on what they think society demands. Sometimes the goals are even media-driven.

Many people set goals in direct response to media and advertising. They are bamboozled into believing that wearing certain clothes is what constitutes success, or driving certain cars, working in certain places, and behaving in certain ways. Movies, television, and advertising add a perverse and corrosive dimension to goal-setting, which often produces unrealistic and shallow goals.

Your goals, however, are very personal. They must be deeply rooted in what you want out of life—in what you deem success. As soon as you set your goals, you must have a powerful desire to achieve them. This desire cannot be a fleeting one. You must fully understand and appreciate the positive benefits of achieving your goals.

Setting Goals

For starters, it is an excellent idea to write down your life goals on a piece of paper or type them up on a computer. When writing your goals, don't just scribble or type one line, as in, "I intend to have better relations with my family," or "I want to make a million dollars." First things first. Identify and catalog the benefits that you see accruing upon the realization of your goals. List as many of the advantages that you can think of. By the time you are reaching for that second and third sheet of paper, you'll know that your goals are not only right for you. More than that, you'll see clearly that it's in your absolute best interests to make them happen.

Timing Is Everything

Once you've established goals that complement you, your life circumstances, and your vision of success, your next step requires you to become a fortune-teller of sorts. You must decide the point at which you anticipate turning your goals from goals into actions—done deals, no less. Establishing your goals within exact time parameters is essential. You should avoid at all costs saddling yourself with long inventories of open-ended goals.

QUESTION?

Should you set deadlines for accomplishing your goals?
Yes! Establish time frames for realizing your goals. An open-ended proclamation like, "My goal is to take a trip around the world before I die," often finds the goal-maker meeting his maker before ever realizing his goals.

Set a specific deadline for every goal on your plate. Don't fix unreasonable time frames. If your goal is to earn $100,000 a year, and you are presently pulling in $16,500, don't place the goal's completion time in a six-month window. You'll probably be disappointed if you do.

Always be ambitious, but stay realistic. Have a cogent plan for reaching every one of your goals. Nothing is more deflating than failing to achieve the goals that you set for yourself. Make the time frames for your goals practical, with enough leeway for you to reach them. By the same token, avoid an overly extended time period. You'll find that too much time lapsing between the start and finish lines takes the edge—the sharpness—off your goals. You always want to work with a sense of immediacy as it relates to your life goals—that's because immediacy translates into a sense of purpose.

Work Your Plan

Naturally, when you set goals in life, you must also have correspon- ding plans on how you are going to achieve them. Goals aren't wishes. Get out that pencil and paper (or sit down at the computer) and start jotting them down. In your planning, first identify the poten- tial obstacles that you envision hindering you as you reach for your goals.

Remember that neither success nor realization of your goals is guaranteed. However, when you are completely honest about what you are up against, you automatically make more reasoned decisions and wiser choices. To illustrate, let's return for a moment to your goal of making $100,000 per year. How are you going to do it? What are the obstacles in your way? What exactly can you do to remove those obstacles? These are the kinds of questions to ask as you set your plans in motion. You should make sure you answer your own questions with a thoroughness befitting Perry Mason as well as a sense of urgency.

Helping Hands

After noting the rough roads you might have to travel to attain your goals, your next step involves recognizing the people whose help you're going to need along the way. Can you realize your goals without assistance from anyone else? In most instances, achieving your personal goals will be dependent on various outside forces. Acquiring knowledge or new skills, for example, is not ordinarily done in isolation. Working alongside others, joining organizations, or taking risks in your career all involve lots of interpersonal contact.

When setting goals for yourself, never neglect the help you'll need from others in seeing them through. Most of our goals are partially dependent on outside forces that we cannot afford to ignore. Goals regularly revolve around things like attitude improvements, earning more money, or acquiring new skills, and these often require the helping hands of others.

Let's just say that goal fulfillment is rarely a solo act. Sure, there are goals that you can pretty much accomplish all by your lonesome, such as teaching yourself how to speak French by using a set of cassette tapes, or how to play the guitar by reading a book. Indeed, these are valid self-improvement goals that do fall under the general category of success. However, in the big picture, there is a thread of interdependence that you just cannot ignore.

The Complete Goal Plan

You've completed Stage One of your goal-setting plan. So far, that means the following:

1. You have a heartfelt desire to see your goals through to their optimum conclusions.
2. You've written your goals down on a piece of paper and have established actual contracts with yourself.
3. You've defined reasonable time frames for reaching your goals.
4. You've identified the outside obstacles as well as resources—like people, organizations, and so on—that will play key roles in deciding whether you achieve your goals.

After you've completed these preliminaries, it is time to develop comprehensive plans on how to move forward from here. At the end of the line, your goals will either be met or not met. Between Stage One and the end of the line are the specific actions you will take to meet your goals. These actions will make or break your goals, so carefully consider your planning. Never lose sight of what you are trying to accomplish.

Take the Controls

When you set ambitious goals for yourself, you should carefully reconnoiter your playing field. That is, you should recognize the outside factors that will have an impact on the outcomes of your goals—the people and the various other ingredients at play. At the same time, this is not to suggest that you should surrender control of your destiny in any way, shape, or form to forces outside of your control.

When you start enumerating the specifics of your plan, carefully consider your degree of control in reaching them. Keep in mind that you have to be the pilot of your own ship, and that means it is up to you to exact as much control as is humanly possible on your actions and their outcomes. For your goals are unique to you and intrinsic to your success.

Performance versus Outcome

The plans that you implement in setting out after your goals are essentially your performances on life's sprawling stage. It benefits you to put your focus primarily on these performances and less on the outcomes, which are your stated goals. For your performances, or actions, will determine the outcomes. If you concentrate on precisely what you have to do to see your goals become reality, the outcomes will invariably be positive.

There is a school of thought that differentiates between two kinds of goals: performance goals and outcome goals. In this line of thinking, it becomes clear that one kind of goal—the outcome goal—depends on factors outside the individual's area of influence. Other competitors, for instance, or market conditions have the power to determine whether you achieve an outcome goal. A performance goal, on the other hand, is focused on achieving a certain level of performance, without any reference to any kind of outcome that may result.

In our approach to achieving success, setting and paying attention to performance goals is a far more sensible rationale. Performance goals are more in your control than are outcome goals, which are more susceptible to outside influences. Consider this scenario. You set as your goal a job promotion to supervisor, but somebody else gets the position because of a quota policy. Had you set as a performance goal getting a good performance review, instead of the promotion, you could live with the unfair and unethical policy that passed you over.

You could then rightfully claim that you achieved your goal of being supervisor caliber. What your superiors do with that fact, then, would be up to them. This way, the ball is in your court. For one, you could look elsewhere for a job, in a place that values merit and productivity over jellybean counting.

ALERT!

Establish your goals with absolute confidence in their positive outcomes. Fully concentrate on your performance—your decisions and actions—in your quest to make them reality. That is, don't get stuck in the muck worrying about outcomes. Solid performances will ensure solid outcomes.

Goal Fundamentals

It's important to treat your life goals with a degree of reverence. Don't take them for granted. Keep them positive and realistic. Prioritize your goals, and then plan on realizing them. Let's now chronicle and review the fundamentals of goal-setting, starting with accenting the positive.

Positive Goals

You are probably saying right now that you've heard this one before. You know—be positive and all that jazz. And you have. While mentioning the vast power of positive thinking may sound rather trite, in practice it's anything but. Your goals should accent the positive and not the negative.

For instance, your goals should stress your future accomplishments. You don't want your goals enunciated in negative terms or language that demeans you. Some people beat themselves up when setting their goals. They say: "I won't be a jerk on my upcoming dates." "I won't make the same stupid mistakes on the job." "I won't be living in this stinking house a year from now."

These same goals can be presented in positive veins. "I will be sophisticated and agreeable on my future dates." "I will better prepare myself for my job responsibilities." "I will be living in a new home and location in one year's time." Positively framing goals is not some semantics game. Success is about forward movement and optimism. It's not about wallowing in past mistakes or present predicaments.

Goals Without Contradiction

There are dreams, and there are goals. Sometimes dreams become goals, and many times goals become reality. Accordingly, dreams do become reality on many occasions. This is what success in life rests on. However, you must make certain that your goals don't contradict one another or cross the boundaries out of your slice of reality. Your goals must be integrated and come together as a neatly completed puzzle.

FACT

When establishing goals for yourself, there are six areas for you to explore: home and family life; job and career; morals and ethics; health and wellness; social life; and intellectual betterment. Working with a variety of goals in all aspects of your life strikes an important balance that is very important to realizing genuine success in life.

For instance, if you are married with children, and you put a premium on your relations with your family, you can't reasonably set a goal to go on an ocean voyage with your drinking buddies, can you? This wouldn't integrate very well with your particular reality. And if your goal is to take your current income of $15,000 and double it, you don't want to set a corresponding goal to own a Jaguar as your next car. A $30,000 salary and a Jaguar don't exactly meld, to put it mildly.

When you establish goals that come together like a Gershwin tune, you are hitting all the right notes in your quest for success. Those who sample life's successes are people who understand what they really want—what personally satisfies them. But they simultaneously know what is attainable every step of the way on life's circuitous journey. That is, you won't be buying a Jaguar on a $30,000 income; but maybe—just maybe—at $130,000.

The Angel Is in the Details

What we've talked about thus far are general, simply worded goals, and the many benefits that would be yours when you achieve them. However, when setting goals for yourself, you don't have to keep them so simple. In fact, you should take each goal in your arsenal and flesh it out. That is, you should be very specific and define your goals in detail.

Okay, you want that Jaguar, and now you're making enough money to afford it. Congratulations! Well, why not set as your goal a British racing green XJ-6 convertible loaded with all the options you can think of. When you visualize your goals in such rich detail, it spurs the subconscious mind on by making everything more real.

It's akin to punching information into a computer. The more reliable the data that goes in, the more reliable answers you will get back. Simple logic. A detective has a better chance of solving a case with clues at his disposal—the more the merrier. The same direct reasoning applies to goal-setting. The more your mind and body have to play with, the more you will get back in return in the form of confidence, discipline, drive, and results.

Meat on the Bone

By adding meat to the bone of your goals, you are more apt to visualize and achieve them because they are more real to you. If your goal is to own a home in earshot of the Pacific Ocean, visualize it.

Picture what you will see outside of your bay window. Conjure up the kinds of chairs and lounges that you'll sit in on your deck. Don't forget about the barbecue grill!

Take these detailed images a step further and bring in all of your five senses (sight, hearing, taste, smell, and touch). Listen to the seagull chorus. Taste your grilled tuna. Inhale the sea air billowing in on a blanket of fog, and touch the smooth sand in your backyard as you sift it through your hands.

Keep in mind, though, that goals need be more than pipe dreams. Before setting all of these finer points in motion, determine that you can have that ocean home, for instance. You can't have your goals contingent on a long-lost relative leaving you a fortune. Live in reality, set your goals in reality, but understand that your reality is pliable and a work in progress.

When Sharing Is Wrong

In our earliest memories, we can probably remember Mom lecturing us on the virtues of sharing and our schoolteachers harping on the same thing. Share your toys. Share your candy. Share your good fortune.

ALERT!

You should keep your goals to yourself, except for sharing with those whom you implicitly trust to encourage and sustain you. Telling family, friends, neighbors, and coworkers about your goals all too often engenders skepticism and ridicule. This can be very deflating.

This is all sound-as-a-dollar advice. However, there are always exceptions to every rule, even to the nobility of sharing, and we've come across a big one in the sharing of your goals. This is not a clarion call to be greedy with the largesse that you will realize when you achieve your goals. On the contrary, you should always share your good fortune with others. What we have in mind right now is sharing your goals in their fledgling state—that is, revealing to others just what your goals are.

You're the only one who knows who deserves to share your goals and who will give you unconditional support in return. Generally speaking, we live in a world that does not always encourage independence and or the determination to convert dreams into goals into reality into success. People who set high but realistic goals succeed most often when—as a certain ad campaign boasts—they "Just do it!" Establish your goals. Write them down, being sure to list the advantages of realizing them and plan how you are going to achieve them. Then go after them with unrestrained abandon. Avoid letting life's predictable naysayers in on what you are up to. Before you know it, you'll see your goals realized, your personal satisfaction maximized, and success looming large on your very bright horizon.

The Goal Formula

You've been encouraged to set ambitious goals and to be aggressive in believing in yourself and in what you can accomplish in life. You've simultaneously been instructed to be realistic in goal-setting. That is, you should avoid setting goals that are well-nigh impossible to achieve. Success may be about reaching for the stars—metaphorically speaking—but it's also about knowing thyself and what you can and cannot do.

Take stock of your progress toward your goals each and every day. When you wake up in the morning, read over your goals and visualize their coming to pass. Do the same thing before you retire to bed at night. Determine each day if you are closer or further from realizing your goals, and ask yourself, "Why?"

With this in mind, it is important that you follow the tried and true "goal formula" as you set each one of your life goals. When you use this simple formula in mapping out your goals, you'll give rise to goals that are in fact realistic—out of your present clutches, perhaps, but feasible in your short-term future.

The goal formula consists of these elements:

- Knowledge and skills
- Outside assistance and collaboration
- Resources
- Willingness to solve problems
- Commitment to clear thinking
- Choices

When you put all of these key elements into your goals' test tube, you should emerge with goals that are very much attainable.

Knowledge and Skills

To be successful, you must understand in detail the challenge that faces you. Undeniably, you need a degree of knowledge and a level of skill to achieve your goals. Of course, this knowledge and skills quotient is going to vary from person to person depending on what each individual desires out of life. Nevertheless, you must ask yourself if you have what it takes in this primary area. It's the all-important starting point.

Helping Hands and Resources

Next, think about the outside helping hands that'll you'll need in reaching your goals. Determine whether they are accessible—are they are ready, willing, and able to assist you? You must also consider the myriad resources that you'll need to make your goals become reality. Do you have all the vital components to reach your goals? For instance, if you are starting a business of your own, do you have the resources to sustain it beyond the set-up, such as the ability to replenish your inventory, meet unforeseen expenses, and so on?

Goal Evaluation

Finally, do you have what it takes to navigate the roads, often bumpy, that lead to making your goals into reality? You should also evaluate your goals and their timetables with a clear head. Are they feasible, or are you making overly optimistic assumptions? Your last act requires examining all of the choices available to you. What are the best routes to take in achieving your goals?

FACT

When you employ all of the elements that go into the goal formula—instead of casting your goals to the wind—you have a much better chance at seeing a happy ending. Goals are an inextricable part of success. Invariably, successful people work with goals. By and large, they follow the goal formula.

The Perseverance Complex

To tie a ribbon around this chapter, let us now address the importance of perseverance. When you set goals, it is imperative that you persevere on your mission to achieve them. What separates the men from the boys, and the women from the girls, is the willingness to persevere and see a goal through to its realization.

Sometime politician and self-made multimillionaire H. Ross Perot once said: "Most people give up just when they're about to achieve success. They quit on the one-yard line. They give up at the last minute of the game, one foot from the winning touchdown." You probably know from your own life experience how true this is. So often when we set out after life's bounty we see progress right away, but we let ourselves get sidetracked by an obstacle of some sort in our path. We then permit self-doubt to creep into our thinking and dismiss the progress we've made as insignificant.

Successful people know that perseverance is an indispensable trait. Goals become reality through perseverance. Success stands at the end of a long road of persevering through various glitches, some failures, and a lot of tough times.

A Lincoln Lesson

The great Abraham Lincoln said, "I am a slow walker, but I never walk backwards." In other words, you don't have to accomplish everything you want out of life today. Just keep moving forward undeterred.

Lincoln was tested time and again in his life. He lost elections. He lost his children to disease. He confronted supreme heartbreak and failure in the early years of the Civil War, witnessing thousands of his soldiers die in a cause that looked almost lost.

Lincoln remained, however, steadfast in his belief—and true to his goal—of keeping the Union together, come what may. Many politicians wanted the president to throw in the towel and strike a deal to end the war. A deal like that would have destroyed our country, the United States of America, in the process. Over a century and a half later, all of us owe a debt of gratitude to this one man, who persevered and saw his goal of a unified nation with one flag—the Stars and Stripes—flying over it, come to pass. Ⓔ

Chapter 7

Overcoming Life's Obstacles en Route to Success

Success is not ordinarily handed around on silver platters. More often than not, we must earn it by overcoming the infinite obstacles that life tosses in our path. Those of us who keep trying to complete the course without throwing our hands up in resignation are the ones who achieve success.

Life's Obstacle Course

Life is full of obstacles to our happiness and success. These obstacles come in many guises—animate and inanimate, visible and invisible. We get socked with curious twists of fate when we least expect them. Routinely, we find ourselves confronting interior and emotional obstacles that now and again send us reeling.

This litany of life obstacles may sound rather ominous. But before you slam this book shut, reflect on all that the life journey has to offer. Sure, it's littered with stumbling blocks that run the gamut from financial to psychological to anything in between. Yes, I'm sure you would agree, there are certain givens in life. We have little choice but to swallow them whole.

However, as we've emphasized time and again, success is worth realizing—obstacles and all. That's why we set ambitious goals for self-improvement and plan for a better tomorrow. That's why we want to be successful. Lees and all, life's sweet wine dwarfs its bitter brew every time.

FACT

On August 9, 1974, with the clock ticking down on his presidency, Richard Nixon addressed the White House staff, telling them, "It's only a beginning—always—the young must know it; the old must know it; it must always sustain us." Despite leaving the office under a cloud of scandal, Nixon still offered words for all of us to heed on our journey through life.

Human beings are a resilient bunch. In most instances we can find joy and pleasure in what we accomplish, even after suffering great personal or other kinds of loss. In the game of life, every day is a beginning. This is the time-tested mantra that all of us must cling to as we walk the walk—make that "run the run"—to success. Obstacles popping up in our way needn't ever squash our dreams, torpedo our goals, or preclude us from attaining true success in life.

The Obstacle Called Fear

The greatest obstacle to success, hands down, is fear. You can't always see it or touch it, but it dwells in our hearts and minds on any number of occasions. As you know by now, the recipe for success calls for confidence, not fear. The quest for success is a forward-moving trek. Fear grinds this positive course to a halt, and it often reverses any gains you might have made.

If you want to play on a baseball team, you can't fear getting hit by a pitched or batted ball. If you want to manage a group of people in an office, you can't fear making decisions that will have unpleasant consequences for others. If you want to get married and raise a family, you can't fear commitment and intimacy. If you do fear any of these things, you'll likely be an unsuccessful ballplayer, office manager, or spouse/parent. You can take that one to the bank!

Fear in the Fast Lane

At a racecar driving school, a veteran instructor informed his class in no uncertain terms about what separates the successful students from the unsuccessful ones. He said that it all boils down to fear. Drivers who focus on *not* hitting fences and other roadside obstacles tend to hit the very things that they are trying to avoid. On the other hand, drivers who don't obsess on the various obstacles, and who concentrate instead on the road in front of them, tend to stay on that very road, which is what they are supposed to do.

In order to parry life's self-induced, mental obstacles—the most potent on the success journey, by the way—you must always concentrate on what you want, not on what you fear. When you do this, you neutralize your fears by placing the emphasis where it rightfully belongs: on your vision of success.

The experienced teacher added that without exception, a successful racecar driver is one who has mastered the ability to focus on the course, rather than giving in to the worrisome distraction of obstacles that must be avoided. This is an analogy for life and success. All of us must focus on staying on the road—the success road—by charting a steady course. We cannot allow life's inevitable obstacles to knock us off course and get the best of us.

He Could Have Been a Contender

Greg was in his early forties when he enrolled in night classes at a nearby law school. At the time, he was working as a clerk in a small pet food store in the borough of Queens in New York. He decided that it was high time to recharge his tedious, dispirited life. After all, he was a college graduate with a high IQ who had experienced early successes upon graduation. But his life subsequently drifted, and suddenly there he stood, with two decades post-college under his belt—balding, and with an expanding waistline—asking himself, "What just happened here?"

Greg vowed to resume the journey of success that he had jettisoned sometime in his twenties. Law school reinvigorated him. He talked again about his future. He set ambitious goals for himself. He would graduate, pass the bar exam, begin working as a lawyer, and make good money. He even had friends in the profession who offered him assistance. Greg felt that his life had a purpose again. Customers in the pet food store lauded him for what he was doing—working during the day and going to law school at night. Greg was an excellent example for a lot of people. He was living proof that it was never too late to start anew, to set goals, and to grab a hunk of success.

FACT

A most revelatory sign of the fear of success is a lack of motivation for achieving your life goals. Other fear of success indicators include feelings of guilt and anxiety when you do attain some measurable successes. The antidote to fear of success is a little bit of understanding. Understand that the fear is irrational and can be overcome.

He graduated from law school and diligently studied to pass the bar exam. By a whisker, he failed the first time. It discouraged him, but he vowed to pass it the second time—and he did. Greg had realized two of his three goals, with the biggest one still up in the air—a job in the law profession. Greg desperately wanted to earn big money. He believed that this financial shock would transform his life in so many positive ways—professionally, of course, but personally most of all. For too many years, Greg had felt diminished working a long string of uninspiring jobs.

Alas, this story doesn't have a happy ending. Greg, like so many people before and after him, didn't build upon his successes. He didn't put the star atop the Christmas tree of success. He didn't tap his more-than-willing contacts for a leg up and a law job. Instead, he went to work as a cab driver. He said that he planned to save up some money and then start looking for a job in his new profession. But that never happened. The enthusiasm that surrounded the possibility of life with a law degree fast dissipated. Greg succumbed to the most ubiquitous and insidious of all fears: the fear of success.

Fear of Success

If someone told you that you "fear success," you'd probably scoff at the notion. After all, why would anyone of sound mind and body fear such a wondrous, positive thing? Success is nothing to be afraid of, is it?

We shouldn't be afraid of achieving success, but many of us are. Why do you think there are so many self-help books and popular motivators sounding off on the subject? Of all life's varied obstacles, the fear of success looms largest. Fear encompasses many other human emotions. No matter who we are, we've all felt fear. It slices to the core of our humanity.

It's about Change

Success, first of all, is all about change. For many of us, change of any sort is a scary prospect. Think about it. Some of us can't imagine changing our hairstyles or our eyeglasses, let alone making seismic shifts in our overall lives. Some of us even eat the same thing every single day, rarely sampling anything new.

Life neatly sandwiched into a comfortable routine is exactly the way that many of us want it. It's certainly easier to live a banal, highly predictable life, but it's not necessarily better, nor is it very fulfilling. Changes usher in elements of the unknown. Yes, this is sometimes frightening, but at the same time change is always exciting and chock-full of possibility.

Fear Factors

Let's investigate the fear of success by exploring the key factors that make it such a formidable life obstacle. Here are some of the big ones:

1. The path of least resistance is the status quo, not success.
2. The higher expectations that surround success put more pressure on us.
3. We are expected to repeat and build upon our successes.
4. Success alters in considerable ways both our personal and professional lives.
5. Success makes demands on our time that weren't there before.
6. We make both new friends and new enemies when we encounter success.

By contemplating this list of six points, you can readily understand and appreciate why the fear of success is so omnipresent. When you strive for bigger and better things in life—whatever they may be—you are affecting change. There's no getting around it. Changes in lifestyle come packaged with success. There will be added pressures on you sometimes, along with modifications in your daily routine. And it's true, sadly, that some of your family and friends may be less than hospitable to the "new you."

To overcome the fear of success, you must make a thorough inventory of the various components of your life. Ask yourself what you want to happen in each area, be it in interpersonal relationships (marriage or family), your job and career, physical health, or emotional wellness. You can, of course, add classifications to this list that are unique to your life, from spiritual health to extracurricular activities and hobbies (sports, etc.), and anything else that you deem important to you. Then you are ready to mull over these queries:

- How do you envision success in each one of the key areas of your life?
- What do you see changing in your lifestyle if you achieve success in these areas?
- Is there any person or people who you think would be negatively impacted by your achieving the success that you envision?

- Would you in any way feel undeserving of accomplishing the success that you picture?
- What do you foresee as the biggest obstacles to realizing success in these key areas of your life?
- Do you think that you will feel unsatisfied in any way upon realization of this success?

Nothing to Fear but Fear Itself

What can you do to break the stranglehold known as the fear of success? In the depths of the Great Depression in 1933, President Franklin Delano Roosevelt attempted to reassure a panicked nation that all would one day be well. In his first inaugural address to the beleaguered citizenry, he uttered the now-famous words: "The only thing we have to fear is fear itself—nameless, unreasoning, unjustified terror which paralyzes needed efforts to convert retreat into advance." What the president meant by this statement was that our fears are often the forerunners of irrational actions, which have the propensity to snowball into new crises, compounding already difficult situations.

FACT

During the Great Depression, runs on banks were brought on by the fear that the banks themselves would run out of money. Of course, some financial institutions did run out of cash when thousands of their depositors descended on them to withdraw their savings.

Fear Busters

The fear of success is similarly an irrational fear. It's how you react to fear that will determine whether you vanquish its deleterious side effects or whether your fear will completely overwhelm you. You subdue the fear of success by confronting it with alacrity and determination. When you carefully evaluate what you want out of life—your definition of success—as well as the actions that you are taking to achieve your life goals, you come to one of two conclusions.

You either accept the fact that you want what success has to offer you, or you determine that it's not for you—not worth the struggle. If you "just say no" to success, you accept that your conventional, humdrum life—absent of challenges and responsibility—is what will most completely satisfy you today, tomorrow, and all the days of your life. When we are confronted with the reality of this stark life choice, we generally know the road to take. When we confidently stride down the right road, fear of success evaporates faster than a rain puddle on a hot, sunny midsummer afternoon.

The Responsibility Obstacle

From our discussion of the fear of success, we move logically to an exploration of the fear of responsibility. This is something of an outgrowth of the fear of success. The changes that are inherent in success tend to carry with them additional responsibilities. Success and responsibility, therefore, go together like cheese on a pizza.

More Goals, More Responsibilities

Consider the things you want out of life. Compare and contrast your life now with the way your life will be when your goals become reality. Do you have more responsibilities in the here-and-now than you will when your goals see the light of day? The answer, most probably, is that you'll have more responsibilities when you achieve your ambitious goals.

QUESTION?

Are you suffering from *hypegiaphobia*?
If you are suffering from a fear of responsibility, then you can diagnose yourself as being in the throes of this affliction. You are hardly alone. Hypegiaphobia is a common malady in today's society. To realize success in life, you have to conquer this phobia.

Indeed, the goals that we set for ourselves are commonly rooted in doing more of something and getting more back in return. Speaking of "more," this amounts to more responsibilities on our part. If you want a stronger marriage, for instance, you have to say and do different things than you are doing now, and you must allow yourself to be held strictly accountable for all of your actions. When you assume a higher-paying job, you have more responsibilities with the bigger check, and you are expected to deliver bigger and better results. Responsibility! You get more, but you must do more.

The Human Obstacle

Now that we've addressed the major obstacles that are within your power to handle at the source, it's time to move outside of the realm of your fears. We know that achieving success is not a one-person show. While you need the helping hands of others in your quest for success, you've also got to be on high alert for those whose hands are extended not to assist you, but to whack you down and throw you off course. In other words, you must keep an eye out for those people who don't want you to succeed.

The Human Comedy

How do so many of us succeed and achieve great things with all of the obstacles that litter our ways? When you look at the obstacles that are sometimes thrown in our paths—many, ironically, by those closest to us—it elevates our already lofty accomplishments. Many people who took personal and financial risks to start businesses of their own had to overcome serious human obstacles to achieve their success. The reality is that bold ideas and risk-taking are admired mostly in theory.

FACT

Not many individuals who start businesses, or who take career and other life risks, are encouraged by their inner circle of family, friends, and acquaintances. Entrepreneurial and career successes are more often applauded and admired from outsiders than they are from insiders.

Strange Family Values

People are a complex and contradictory bunch. Families, in particular, have a peculiar habit of championing the successes of other families, rather than their own. How often have you heard a relative speak of the accomplishments of someone outside the family in glowing terms? What if you had made the same achievements yourself—if the accomplishments were yours, would they be denounced in no uncertain terms? Here's an example: "Mrs. Jones's daughter, Suzy, took a sabbatical from work and flew a hot air balloon around the world—isn't that something? She's a real go-getter!"

Many highly successful people in life—particularly risk-taking entrepreneurs—were accused at some point of having their heads in the clouds or not having their feet firmly planted on the ground. Success, remember, doesn't ask that your feet be rendered immobile in Mother Earth—anywhere and at anytime. Quite the contrary!

Planning Obstacles

Much of success involves planning. As a matter of fact, we opened this chapter with the dictum that successes are not handed to us. Rather, we have to earn them with our toil, perseverance, and agility in dodging a whole range of life's obstacles.

When we set down our life goals, we need to marry them with compatible plans on specifically how we are going to achieve them. However, there's a flip side to planning, just as there is to everything else. To put it succinctly, there are good plans, and there are bad ones. Plans that are regressive in nature and impediments to success are bad for you.

Your plans should always be forward looking, but they should also be very flexible. In other words, you don't want to compose plans that script your life down to the last detail. Always be prepared to expand and adjust them to adapt to new circumstances in your life, or to change them altogether when and if they no longer complement your thinking.

No Social Security Plans

Some of us are so conditioned by our upbringing and sundry societal influences that we map out our lives with all the originality and panache of a dry-as-dust textbook. Just as we've entered the workforce, we are already thinking about collecting our Social Security checks. It's true that financial planning is wise. However, planning for your retirement is very different from basing today's important life decisions (especially if you are still relatively young) on the impact they will have on your retirement nest egg or on your capacity to live a rich life as a senior citizen.

Successful people live and plan, with the emphasis on the living part. They don't chart the course of their entire lives with those far-off Social Security checks at the top of the list. When you simultaneously live and plan in the here and now, you not only maximize your present, but your long-term future automatically shines brighter.

People who spend a lot of time now thinking about what their lives will be like way off in the future may be in for a rude awakening when they reach their ripe old age. They may look back with regret on the many years they let lapse, melancholy over the things they could or should have done but never did. Set your goals, and plan carefully, but accomplish what you can today. When you string your accomplishments together, your retirement will be a fitting culmination to a successful life.

No Guarantees

As everyone knows, and as we should state here once again, there is no way to guarantee success. Nothing is certain in life, and that includes our longevity. With this sober reality in mind, your planning takes on new meaning. This is precisely why you must view success as a work in progress. Concentrate on living life to the fullest today, but keep an eye on the future.

If you start fixating now on the size of your Social Security check, you will probably find when you retire that it's not nearly as big as your neighbor's check, who was focusing all along on more immediate concerns in his life. Your job and career selections should be grounded in your personal fulfillment now, not on the retirement check you hope to get thirty or forty years off in the future—a future that you are not guaranteed to even see.

Learning from Obstacles

It may sound like a timeworn cliché to suggest that we learn from our mistakes and that life's miscellaneous obstacles actually make us stronger. But it's all true. Successful people can invariably point to a past littered with mistakes and failures. Some of them can lay claim to overcoming some pretty nasty obstacles to get where they are today.

Take a close look at the most popular motivational gurus, be they writers or television personalities. From messed up personal lives to substance abuse to financial ruin, these motivators speak from experience; most of them learned their most valuable life lessons while wallowing in life's abyss. Hence, their redemption serves as a powerful example for us all.

FACT

Life's obstacles afford us many opportunities to learn and grow. Adversity challenges us to better ourselves. Obstacles to our success make us stronger by building in us a fighting spirit that nobly assists us as we set our goals, work our plans, and reach out for our success.

Of course, it's not a prerequisite for success that you first hit rock bottom. The majority of us who are valiantly striving for a taste of success are everyday, normal people. We lead normal lives, with no gruesome tales from the dark side to tell. Most of us just want an opportunity to take our lives up a peg, and then another peg after that, until we are personally fulfilled. We just want to be happy.

Nevertheless, all of us learn many lessons from our experiences. If you are wise, you learn from a bad first marriage, and your second go is more successful. If you are wise, you learn from bad investments, and the second time around you avoid putting your money into high-risk stocks. If you are wise, you learn from a drunk-driving conviction and never get behind the wheel of a car again with a hint of alcohol in your system. The list of learning from experience and obstacles is infinite and enriching.

Life's obstacles shouldn't frighten us in the least. In fact, they really can make us stronger—and in many instances, that's exactly what they have done. Without adversity in life, we lose our fighting spirit, which is so essential to the quest for success. Success demands that we carry a competitive edge and that we care enough to go the extra mile. We must make the effort to get the things we want out of life.

Chapter 8

Manage Your Time, Manage Your Success

There are twenty-four hours in a day and 168 hours in a week. It's one of those intractable life givens. What you do in this finite window of time determines whether or not you will achieve your life goals and realize your vision of success. Proper management of your time matters in all aspects of your life.

Your Most Precious Resource

Time is not only a primary resource, it is our most valuable one. Surprisingly, time is rarely treated with the solemnity that it so richly deserves, be it in time spent with our families, on the job, in recreational endeavors, or in navigating any one of our plans to reach our life goals. Nevertheless, the way we manage this priceless commodity pretty much determines whether we will be successful, less successful, or not successful at all.

Time Management Awareness

You've probably complained at some point in time that there's just not enough of them—hours in the day, that is, for you to do all the things that you want to do. By acquiring some rudimentary time management skills, you won't be able to lengthen the twenty-four-hour day, or pad the 168-hour week. However, you will be able to do more things and, thus, achieve more of your goals. By simply being aware of time, you can lengthen your days and weeks—metaphorically speaking—and cease and desist from grumbling about a shortage of hours in the day.

FACT

Those of us who are keenly aware of life's time constraints—and who employ time management fundamentals—seem more likely to be successful. It has been said that two weeks for a person who is self-aware is the equivalent of two months for a person who is not.

Time and Responsibility

In the previous chapter, we married success with change. And then we proceeded to wed this change with additional responsibilities. Well, now it's time for a third marriage. As our responsibilities grow, so too do the demands on our limited time.

There's really only one way that you can get a handle on what you are doing with your time. You must repeatedly measure what you are doing with it. Chart and evaluate all the activities and actions that fill in the blanks of your twenty-four-hour days and 168-hour weeks. You can commence this undertaking by keeping a scrupulous journal of your movements at home, on the job, and everywhere in between. Document the things you do and how long it takes you to do them.

As you secure more of your goals on the road to success, you naturally assume greater responsibilities and simultaneous demands on your time. Since there are only twenty-four hours in a day and 168 hours in a week, it's incumbent upon you to understand and practice conscientious time management.

Devise a simple time management chart to get you started. Record the number of hours that you spend each day going about your life business—morning, noon, and night—from the time you spend sleeping, eating, working, playing, and so on. Then multiply the hours by the appropriate number of days in the week. This should provide you with a neat blueprint of exactly what you are doing with yourself during the week, and your chart should identify where you could make adjustments to maximize your waking productivity.

Time Management Chart			
Sleep hours per night	_____	× 7	= _____
Grooming hours per day	_____	× 7	= _____
Meal hours per day (main/snacks)	_____	× 7	= _____
Travel hours to work per day	_____	× 5	= _____
Work hours per day	_____	× 5	= _____
Travel hours per day (weekend)	_____	× 2	= _____
Family hours per day	_____	× 7	= _____
Extracurricular activities hours per day (clubs, church, sports, and so on)	_____	× 7	= _____
Socializing/recreation hours per day (dates, family events, and so on)	_____	× 7	= _____
Chores/errands hours per day (laundry, food shopping, and so on)	_____	× 7	= _____

It's Prioritize Time!

You've filled in all the chart numbers, and now you have a good idea about precisely where your time goes. Now look closely at each one of the categories that characterize your daily life and the allotment of time given to them. Consider these questions:

1. Is the time spent in each category absolutely necessary?

2. If the answer is "no" in one or more, what can you do differently to free up some hours?

3. Are there actions or activities that are unnecessary in your life that you can totally remove from your regular schedule?

4. Are there actions or activities that can be combined in some way to clear the way for other things?

5. Are there particular activities that you'd like to add, or others that you'd just like to spend more time on?

Depending on your peculiar life circumstances—whether you're married versus single, your job status, and so on—what you do with the all-important conundrum of time management carries great weight. Obviously, if you have a wife and kids at home, you must spend ample quality time with them being both a good husband and father. On the other hand, if you are a swinging bachelor, your priorities are going to be a little different, as will your time management schedule.

The College Life Paradigm

Everybody benefits from solid time management. The grade school kid who comes home and plops in front of the television for four or five hours would be better off spending some of that time doing homework, reading books, or engaged in an educational hobby. College students, too, would be very wise to prioritize their time. The habit will prepare them nicely for what's ahead in that thing we affectionately call "real life."

College life is, in fact, a perfect laboratory for studying the ways and means of time management. That's because higher education embodies many of the competing demands upon our time but without the more stringent responsibilities of the adult working life. In college, for instance, we make most of our own decisions. What courses should we take? What should we major in? How much study time do we apportion each course? How much socializing versus studying can we afford to do?

In college, there are also assignment deadlines; appointments with teachers, counselors, and job recruiters; part-time work responsibilities; and all the complications that come with making hard choices. Priorities and the ability to use time management techniques are especially important in determining a student's overall success. In school, we set goals and make plans all the time. We want to succeed. Success in school ordinarily means good grades, which leads to graduation and from there to a good job in the outside world.

Time Management Battle Lines

The goals and plans for just those kinds of things often do battle with having a lot of fun. In college life—and, to some extent, in life in general—this is often where the battle lines are drawn. Most of our happy college memories aren't about taking tests and those "fascinating" courses that we loved attending. We remember the extracurricular stuff, the good times. And this thirst for the good times never really leaves our systems. Time management therefore assumes a key role in our lives. If we use our time well, we will have enough minutes to enjoy the good times and still be sure we've done the many things that we must do if we want to achieve lasting success.

Visiting Time's Wasteland

In any analysis of time management, it is particularly important to identify the biggest waste areas in your life. Vigorous time management requires that you not only recognize these patches of quicksand, but rope them off in a timely fashion. You only maximize your time when you put out the trash in your life.

Wasting time is a not a new phenomenon, and you've probably accused yourself of just that very thing on occasion. In the quest for success, however, the wasting of finite minutes, hours, and days is not recommended behavior. So why not cut to the chase and remove the behaviors and actions that are, in fact, wasting your time. Here is a selection of some common time wasters:

- Procrastination
- Attempting to do too much
- Lack of delegation
- Poor planning or none at all
- Interruptions
- Stress and exhaustion

QUESTION?

Can we really manage time?
The term "time management" is something of a misnomer. We can't literally manage time. What we can do is manage ourselves and how we use our time. Time management is essentially self-management.

Procrastination

Beyond the obvious time wasters, like the five minutes you have to wait for the ketchup at the diner to come out of the bottle and onto your hamburger, there are the big-ticket items like procrastination. There is no finer time thief than this scourge. In simple language, procrastination is putting off for tomorrow what you can do today. It is postponing decisions for another time.

Procrastination is a non-act at a time when action is called for. It is avoiding responsibility, the antithesis of seizing the day. So much of success in life is about timing. Successful people live and act in the moment because they know that their futures depend on it. There are so many individuals walking around in a funk, regretting their past procrastination and having let opportunity slip right by them. Don't join their ranks!

Procrastination, you see, is not a victimless crime. Its consequences extend beyond the procrastinator to the people in the procrastinator's path. On the job, a procrastinating boss on the job creates negative consequences for his staff. A procrastinating parent influences her children. Procrastination is an intentional act of delay. It bespeaks a lack of caring—not good in the home, on the job, or in interpersonal relationships of any kind.

FACT

Procrastination is an enemy of time management and success. It supplants decision making with delay. It makes future decisions all the more problematic and less likely to produce positive results. Procrastination amounts to the neglecting of responsibility. It is not forward-moving behavior and is an impediment to realizing success.

Attempting to Do Too Much

The flip side of procrastination is the feeling that you must do everything today—in the common parlance, "You have to get everything done yesterday." But the reality is there's not enough time in the day for you to do everything. When you attempt to do it all, you, in effect, do very little.

This is the perfect lead-in to the importance of delegation. Delegating is not something unique to job tasks in business environs. In the home, it is just as important to delegate. There are all sorts of tasks and responsibilities that should be delegated to others. If you feel that you must do everything because nobody else will do things "right," you are going to see your time eaten up by doing things that other people could and should be doing.

A Time Gobbler: Poor Planning or None At All

We've spent a lot of time in earlier chapters highlighting the need to plan. Set goals, and devise suitable plans to see them through—you need well-thought-out plans that account for all possible snafus that might meet and greet you on the road to success. Without solid planning, one of those aforementioned snafus could completely debilitate you.

Those who plan their work and then work their plans maximize their time. Those who "wing it," on the other hand, often find themselves in a proverbial leg trap. Time management requires good planning and devoted preparation to deal with life's many obstacles in a timely manner.

Interruptions

In business settings, in particular, interruptions to your work are commonplace—from the ringing telephone, to all sorts of people popping in unannounced, to meetings that sometimes go on too long and accomplish very little. Today, fortunately, we have voice mail and answering machines to keep you from having to answer the telephone all day long.

ALERT!

There are five words that are the bane of businesspeople everywhere trying to maximize their time spent on the job: "Have you got a minute?" Interruptions on the job (and at home, too) from uninvited visitors can consume a lot of your valuable time. Dispatch with uninvited visitors quickly, but politely.

As for people showing up uninvited for a chat, you have a working tongue that can effortlessly say, "I am very busy right now." Unproductive meetings, on the other hand, are a little more delicate. Depending on the particular situation, you might be able to bring some inconspicuous work with you or, at the very least, mentally work on other things unbeknownst to the other meeting attendees. Daydreaming, or falling asleep altogether, are bad options in the time management scheme of things.

Time out for Stress

Stress and exhaustion sometimes get the best of us, and this duo is a vaunted time stealer. Recall the moments in your life when you felt stressed out and bone weary. What was your emotional state? What was your physical state?

In all probability, you lost valuable time languishing in an exhausted state of mind and body. You may have lost your capacity to fully concentrate and make decisions. Perhaps your stressed and worn-out state led to a physical illness. No matter how you slice it, stress and exhaustion are emotional and physical bandits. So, just what do you do to fend off these life bullies?

You can battle stress and beat off the fatigue and high anxiety that accompanies it by staying in touch with your emotions. Many times in life we need to be "on the outside looking in" at ourselves. Here is an interior exercise in self-awareness that is very helpful when we are feeling stressed out.

What you need to do is take a step back and ask yourself just why you are feeling so worn out and downcast. Then consider all the things that you can do to improve your situation. Write them down on a piece of paper. There's no better elixir for what ails you than confronting your problems directly. When you boldly act, you will see your troubles diminish in magnitude, along with all of the stress and exhaustion that accompany them.

Find a nice quiet spot where you can practice basic breathing exercises for approximately five minutes a day. Relax, and breathe through your nose and mouth, with the tip of your tongue resting on your upper palate behind your front teeth. You'll soon experience a rising energy level as you gradually achieve a serene sense of balance.

The Little Things Add Up

There are many so-called "little things" that can really add up in maximizing your time management. For instance, learning to say "no" is key. You know from your life experiences that you've done many things that you wished you hadn't. That is, you wished that you had said "no" because your time would have been better spent doing something else.

Assertive, Not Aggressive

Saying "no" need not be an aggressive act on your part. You don't have to be curt in turning people down, be they at work, at home, in school, or wherever. There's a vast difference between being aggressive and being assertive. Being assertive is a personality trait that you will greatly value as you seek to get the most out of your limited time. So when Timmy calls and asks you to go out tonight for a few brews, when you had planned on finally painting your living room, just say "no," and tell him you have other plans.

Walking and Chewing Gum

What? You can't walk and chew gum at the same time? Perhaps this indignity has been hurled your way at some point in your life. Well, in the time management scheme of things, you have to be able to do both, because it'll free up some very valuable time.

Walking and chewing gum may be a mostly comical combination. Even speaking seriously, though the idea is still the same. You should always consider "layering" your activities whenever and wherever possible. When you are doing your laundry, for example, bring some kind of work to do while you are sitting around waiting for your drawers to dry. When you sit down to watch your favorite show, have the checkbook in hand and try paying your monthly bills.

Quality Time

Discussions of time management often focus solely on business and life in the office. Many time management tomes, for example, concentrate on the corporate milieu and the career individuals looking to increase their productivity and corresponding status as worker commodities. This is all good stuff for careerists in the business realm. However, there's another side to time management that requires an equally fair hearing.

Home and Family

Effective time management quite naturally increases the quality of home and family life because, as we've noted more than once, there are only twenty-four hours in the day. If you can cram more quality activities into the day, everybody in your inner circle benefits—whether family, friends, or coworkers. Your first responsibility, then, is to establish firm parameters on the hours you spend at work, including the work you bring home. If you have a family, you owe them quality hours every day.

A Lesson from the Cleavers

The Cleavers of syndicated television fame (Ward, June, Wally, and the Beaver) are excellent examples of good family time management. With very few exceptions, they share meals together as a family every single day. Follow the Cleaver model. Such firm and consistent get-togethers create a close, cohesive family unit. Family time offers every-body involved an opportunity to sound off about their day, talk about what successes they've had, and what's bugging them, too.

It's always enlightening to read about very busy and highly successful people and how they manage their time, particularly as it relates to home and family life. In many instances, you hear the familiar theme that, no matter what, the entire family comes together at dinnertime (or at some other point in the day) for a home-cooked repast or a bucket of chicken and the fixings from the Colonel. Beyond the important symbolism of such unity, making time for the events in your spouse and children's lives should always be a top time priority for you. Carve out the time, if you have to. Personal and professional lives can always coexist in perfect harmony with sensible time management.

You don't want to find yourself saddled with a sack full of regrets later in life. If you miss your kids' big moments, those are important times that you won't remember because you weren't there. But they were. To err is human, but to forgive (for some people) is not always possible. Keep that in mind.

The larger point is that you must build some sensible priorities into your time management system. Example of such priorities include the following:

- Recurring family routines
- Family events
- Health and wellness
- Friendships
- Acts of generosity

Build such priorities into the structure of your daily life, and place them on your time management pedestal. Success, remember, is always rooted in solid ground. Make your career work with your family life. They must complement one another. Insightful time management on your part facilitates this bonding.

There's No Time Like the Present

There is a classic *Twilight Zone* television episode entitled, "Time Enough At Last." The story chronicles the daily life of a mousy bookworm named Henry Bemis, whose only pleasure in life is reading books. This, naturally, makes him unpopular on the job, as his predilection for reading interferes with his work as a bank teller. This also puts him in the crosshairs of his shrewish wife, who feels he's a good-for-nothing husband, interested more in his books than in her and in ambition for the better things in life. This story takes a nasty turn when Planet Earth is obliterated. Reading in his bank's vault during his lunch hour, Mr. Bemis survives the apocalypse, and emerges from the rubble to find that he's the last man standing, as it were.

As he walks about the destruction, he comes upon mounds of books, the ruins of a nearby library. Bemis's despair quickly turns to excitement as he exclaims that there is "time enough at last" for him to read all the books he's long wanted to. There will be no more interruptions from his efficiency-minded boss at work, the customers, and, of course, his nagging wife.

Preparing for his read-a-thon, Bemis's eyeglasses slip off his nose, fall to the ground, and smash to pieces. This leaves him blind as a bat. And so, all the time in the world evaporates in this ironic twist of fate.

ALERT!

Life consists of time, and what we do with it determines our fate. There's no truer expression than "There's no time like the present." However, the present stands before us when we are ten, forty, or eighty. In other words, it's never too late to set goals, work plans, practice time management, and achieve success.

The moral of this story is that time is a mysterious thing. For much of our lives, it's a double-edged sword. Don't count on accomplishing your life goals tomorrow, when you can realize them today. Concerted time management, above all else, asks us to grab hold of that which is in our power—our twenty-four-hour days and 168-hour weeks—and faithfully manage them to maximize our levels of personal satisfaction and, of course, our successes. (E)

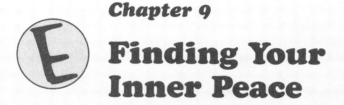

Chapter 9

Finding Your Inner Peace

Sometimes in life we are consumed by the pursuit of material pleasures, and we lose sight of the fact that what we are really after is peace and contentment. The ultimate in life is finding inner peace— what the Quakers call "peace at the center." Where there is inner peace, there is success.

It's What Happens Within You, Not to You

There is a highly regarded self-help technique that you would be wise to incorporate into your daily routine. Of course, as you might expect, this is easier said than done, for this technique is not something that you can turn on and off with the ease of your bathroom faucet. It'll take time and dedicated effort on your part to master it. This technique requires that you focus on what happens *within you,* rather than what happens *to you.* If you can do this regularly, you'll experience a positive sea change in your life.

Taking Events as They Come

Let's explore this rather grand and optimistic pronouncement, starting with first things first. You must take the myriad events in your life as they come—those that bring you great satisfaction and joy, as well as those that make you angry and sad. Now comes the hard part. You have to step back from these many and varied episodes in your life and contemplate your role in them.

Don't Dwell on the Minutia

You've essentially got to stand apart from the minutia of all that is said and done in your life. Instead, concentrate on how you are feeling about that which is swirling around you—even more important, figure out why you are feeling that way. If you go through life in this reflective posture, you will undoubtedly unearth some very important things about yourself that will make you a better and more successful person.

As events occur in your life and you struggle to understand them, use your discipline to ensure that the focal point is always an internal one (your feelings) and not external. This way, you won't ever get sidetracked by outside force.

When you attain a solid grip on what's happening in your insides, and you understand the reasons why, you'll find yourself gracefully moving forward in life rather than running the equivalent of a three-legged race to success (as so many of us do). This sensitive approach to living means you must cast aside your complaints about the past, your worries about the future, or your desire to wallow in constant anguish in the present—no more fighting the same battles over and over in your head.

Events Are Neutral

In any committed quest to attain inner peace, you must first acknowledge that the events in your life are neutral. It is your perception of these events that determines how you feel and, ultimately, how you react to them. You must be on guard never to permit one or several events in your life to define its entirety.

There are countless individuals living their lives in perpetual states of depression, remorse, bitterness, or some unhealthy combination of emotions, simply because they refuse to release past events in their lives. Life is perpetual motion. We have to move on—and keep moving on—if we want to find inner peace and know true success.

Moving on Up

Have you ever found yourself floored by something that was said to you—a put-down, perhaps, by a colleague at work? Does a cryptic comment made by a neighbor render you speechless as you try to figure out what exactly was meant by it? Do friends and family members hurt you beyond their mere words? If you answered "yes" to any of these questions, you are not alone. You are not addressing what's happening within you, but instead are letting what happens to you take on a debilitating life of its own.

FACT

A popular book on the subject of success and inner peace is *Ten Secrets for Success and Inner Peace,* by Dr. Wayne Dyer. This book reveals such secrets as "Knowing that you can't solve a problem with the same mind that created it"; "Treating yourself as if you already are what you'd like to become"; and "Understanding that there are no justified resentments in life."

Dead-End Street

His name is Walter, and his life and times fit smoothly into the subject matter we are covering right now. Walter, you see, permitted prior events in his life to grab hold of him and put him in a lifetime stranglehold. Nevertheless, he has always claimed that he was on a quest for success. Walter regularly broadcast how he was going to make it big as a photographer for the rich and famous. His quirky business card proclaimed, "I make people happy."

The problem—for starters—was that Walter didn't make himself happy. His longstanding psychological albatross was his conviction that his sisters had cheated him out of his late aunt's inheritance. Walter cited hanky-panky in the forty-year-old affair, charging his two older sisters with plying their elderly aunt with "spirits," which then caused her to change her will in their favor. In the final analysis, the aunt bequeathed the two sisters the tidy sums of $25,000 a piece, leaving the hapless Walter only $2,500.

Back then, Walter was newly married, and he desperately needed the money to kick off his new life on the right foot. He asked his two sisters to throw a few grand his way from their inheritances to even the score. Predictably, they declined, claiming that they needed every penny for themselves. Walter, then, devoted the rest of his life to besting his sisters. That is, he vowed to take his $2,500 inheritance and use it in some productive and entrepreneurial way to make oodles more than his two sisters' $25,000 apiece.

The phrase "what's done is done" assumes great meaning as you seek out inner peace. To truly achieve peace with yourself, you must not try to rewrite the history of your life. Instead, you have to focus on the future and what you can do—starting today—to ensure that it's a successful one.

Walter regularly cited this event in his life as his driving force—what motivated him to succeed. He never got over what happened to him, nor did he ever look into what happened within him. He never moved on. In reality, he based the preponderance of his adult life on seeking a revenge of sorts against his two sisters.

There's no surprise ending here. Walter didn't turn his $2,500 into the fortune that he long championed, nor did he end up successful and happy as a photographer for the glitterati (or for anybody else). Instead, his negative motivation served as the precursor for a steady stream of negative events in his life.

What You Need Is Not Everything

Another set of the keys to unlocking inner peace in life is the absolute recognition that you don't need to have everything. What you do need is a feeling of personal satisfaction—your very own. Consider then what you really do need to make you happy, satisfied, and at peace with yourself. Compare these needs with what you are presently doing with your life. Are the two in sync?

It's Your Life and Your Happiness

How is it that Carol is content to sit by a lake, soak up the scenery, and read a book for hours, while her husband Chris considers such things complete wastes of time? Carol's notion of peace and contentedness is felt in what most of us would call a placid setting. In reading, she is engaging in what the majority opinion would deem a relaxing pastime. Her husband, meanwhile, does not in the least appreciate the serenity of this picture, and regards it as "Dullsville." Indeed, Chris is completely unbearable in such calm settings. He'd rather be out on the road, on the go, visiting shopping malls and taking in movies.

In sharp contrast to his wife, Chris's inner peace is found among people—even a crowd—and he prefers his entertainment on a big screen, rather than on the pages of a book. Nothing in the world is going to make Chris extract personal satisfaction from what gives his wife, Carol, such peace and pleasure. It's just not the way it works. We've said it before: Different strokes for different folks.

The Things You Are Supposed to Do

There are many of us who spend our waking hours doing the things that we think we are supposed to be doing instead of things that we actually should be doing—the things that are necessary to our inner peace, personal satisfaction, and success in life. What are these "necessary things," and how are we supposed to distinguish between what's necessary and what's not?

FACT

Many individuals with identical achievements in life have quite varying opinions of them. Some consider themselves highly successful because of their achievements; others are less impressed with them; and still others view their lives, even though they have the same achievements, as failures.

We touched on this very subject earlier, when we addressed the power of the media, the pervasive nature of advertising, and the tendency of the status quo to establish itself as the "right" way to be. It is particularly important to watch out for this tendency in the people who share our inner circles. The stereotype that defines "proper living" is very powerful, and it can very easily determine what we think and believe. Similarly, there's also a stereotype that constitutes success.

The Things That Are Necessary

The things you are supposed to do in life are not necessarily the things that Aunt Mary or neighbor Jim think are appropriate. They are not the things your college professor says make for the only moral way to live a life. They are not what Madison Avenue wants you to believe, either. Nor do you need to take your cue from Dan, Tom, and Peter—or even a guy named Bill.

The elements that are necessary for your inner peace and success are all about you. If you are married with children, there are many actions on your part that are necessary. Marriage and family, for instance, are huge responsibilities. You have to attend to your family, be home with them as much as possible, and make certain that the kids are well fed, clothed, and—most importantly—educated in virtue and the ways of life. However, the ways and means to this end are innumerable!

You may think that you are supposed to do a whole host of things to be a good spouse and parent—things that drain your time and energy and leave you with the empty feeling that you are not living up to the image of the all-star family person. Inner peace is the antithesis of this empty feeling. If you are feeling drained and unfulfilled, pause and re-examine your priorities. Are you driven by what is necessary for your physical and emotional wellness, or are you driven by what you think you are supposed to do?

Take solace in the words of the great American philosopher Henry David Thoreau. He said, "Why should we be in such desperate haste to succeed in such desperate enterprises? If a man does not keep pace with his companions, perhaps it is because he hears a different drummer." Listening to a different drummer is a-okay!

It's Your Choice: Act or React?

When you finally do find some inner peace, or at least the semblance of it, you are in an enviable position to *act* rather than *react* to events in your life. This is where you want to be. Let us examine the lessons we've learned so far that have helped us reach this understanding of inner peace and our need for it:

1. Put the focus where it belongs: on what's happening within you, not to you.

2. Scrupulously view the events in your life as neutral.

3. Never permit one or more events to render you emotionally disabled for any portion of your life.

4. Do what is necessary in life to achieve success, not what you think you are supposed to do.

5. Act, don't react to events in your life, and manage your circumstances.

When you are comfortable in your own skin—that is, when you are at peace with yourself—you are ready to take on the world in your very own, distinct way. You don't allow events or circumstances in your life to dictate the paths you travel or the decisions you are going to make. By and large, when you act first, you establish control of your life's general course. This is what you both want and need in your quest for success.

A Business Model

Why are some of us successful in business, while others are not? There are many reasons for this difference. One of the chief reasons is preparation. Successful businesspeople act first and, thus, chart their business's courses. Less successful—or unsuccessful—businesspeople find themselves, more times than not, reacting to situations. They are unprepared or underprepared for unforeseen events. The businessperson who is always ready weathers all storms.

QUESTION?

Why is acting first so important, rather than just reacting to events?
You effectively determine the course of your life by the way you confront events. By acting swiftly and decisively, instead of always reacting to what happens around you, you stand a much better chance of knowing real inner peace and achieving success in your life.

Better Prepared

The well-prepared businessperson knows her situation—from the state of the economy to the state of the competition. The average person—that's us—who knows himself and his standing is thus prepared to deal with any and all eventualities in life.

The Golden Rules of Life

People who are at peace with themselves invariably abide by certain core principles. For starters, they adopt the Golden Rule in their everyday activities, which is the quintessential ethic of reciprocity. On your hunt for real and lasting success, it's essential that you follow the Golden Rule. When you conduct your life by treating others the same way that you wish to be treated, you can hold your head up high during the day and without regret put it down to sleep at night.

Beyond the Golden Rule, several other very fundamental principles can help you lead the good life and find inner peace. When you piece together all the lessons put forth in this book, you reach the natural conclusion that there is clearly such a thing as "right" and "wrong." The distinction is clear between what is moral and what is immoral, between good and evil. Successful people recognize these differences and come down on the right side. Inner peace is right, moral, and good.

Here is a guide, something we might call our "Inner Peace Principle Blueprint," to help you in your quest:

- Put love on your life's front burner.
- Make certain that your core values are virtuous.
- Accept responsibilities for your attitudes and actions—past and present.
- Be a truth teller every day and always.
- Expect and accept failures, but learn valuable lessons from them.
- Always move forward in your life, drawing lessons from the past, being self-aware in the present, and remaining confident about the future.
- Make sure that the company you keep is a positive bunch.
- Set life goals and go after them with gusto, conscious always of the Golden Rule.

Remember that our inherent natures are reflected in our beliefs and behaviors. The principles that we hold dear to our hearts matter a great deal; that's because success embodies the principles inherent in virtuous living. But there's no reason to fear! You aren't expected to achieve perfection or to be a model of virtue to qualify for success. All that is asked is that we continually seek to better ourselves. Committing an ethical lapse or two doesn't condemn us in perpetuity to any Hall of Shame.

FACT

The prolific and insightful Ralph Waldo Emerson tackled the Golden Rule when he wrote: "Every man takes care that his neighbor does not cheat him. But the day comes when he begins to care that he does not cheat his neighbor. Then all goes well."

If nothing else, in this chapter we are encouraged to tap into our feelings and move away from our "stuckness" on the events that cause them. This search for inner peace permits us tremendous latitude to learn from and understand all that's happening around us. But don't ever think that finding inner peace is a one-person job.

Inner Peace Networking

By now, you may very well see inner peace as a solitary journey: your solitary journey. Inner peace, however, sprouts many tentacles. Living a life of isolation is usually not the right path to inner peace, just as it isn't for success in life.

Inner Peace and the In Crowd

Sure, inner peace is about you. However, unless you live in a monastery, or as a hermit in a cave, there are people in your life who contribute to your happiness and, yes, to your troubles, too. You won't realize inner peace if you don't carefully tend to the whole of your life— and namely, that means the people close to you. Life and responsibilities go hand in glove. We all play different roles in other people's lives: husbands, wives, brothers, sisters, mothers, fathers, friends, coworkers, and neighbors. All of these are various and vital roles in our quest for inner peace. There's no getting around that!

Emotional Support

It is imperative that you strengthen all of your relationships—at home, at work, and at play. Among your many interpersonal relationships, you should aim to build at least one or two with people you can rely on for emotional support. If you are happily married, or living with a significant other, your main source of emotional support is obvious.

Often, though, valuable emotional support comes from a close friend—someone on the outside of your family circle. This is a person you can call on the telephone at any time of the day and talk about anything. A relationship like this means you have someone in your life who is "there" for you—in good times and bad times. When you know that a trusted friend, or a close family member, is ready to lend you an ear, you have something very valuable.

ALERT!

It is wise to have a support group in your life made up of trusted people who will be there for you when you need to get a problem off your chest; to share your fears, sorrows, and disappointments; and, of course, to help you celebrate all of your successes.

A support network is a cornerstone of inner peace. When you have someone in your life whom you can implicitly trust, and whom you feel completely comfortable with, you've struck pay dirt. Since the quest for success—and for inner peace, of course—is not always a smooth one, you genuinely need a sympathetic partner whom you can call on at a moment's notice.

Your support network should encourage listening all around. There should be no know-it-alls in the relationships, and advice should be dispensed only when requested. The knowledge that you have unconditional support from someone in your life goes a long way to helping you feel at peace with yourself. It's your inner peace, but you can always invite others to help you find it.

Chapter 10

Tending to Your Spiritual Health

Regardless of how we manifest it, our personal spirituality plays a key role in our lives. It helps us fathom the true meaning of life and provides us a glimpse of life's big picture. Healthy spiritual natures and successes in life nicely complement one another.

Your Spiritual Health: Why It Matters

It's an unwritten law that certain subjects of conversation are off limits in the cozy confines of the saloon. More precisely, it's talk of politics and religion that should be left outside the barroom doors. Yes, you heard it right: Religious debate and the spirits found in a bottle don't mix very well at all. That's because, generally speaking, we are very passionate about our spiritual beliefs—whatever they may be.

Since we are not lounging around a watering hole at the moment, we are completely free to take a bite of the forbidden fruit. So, without fear of heated arguments, fisticuffs, or drinks getting tossed in our faces, let's get started. What we have on our plates right now is not a discussion of religious dogmas but an examination of our spiritual natures. We are going to place our individual quests for success on a higher plane by exploring the very real spiritual element that each one of us shares. No matter where your spiritual leanings land—in a traditional, organized religion, a New Age alternative, or none of the above—you would probably say that your personal spirituality is very dear to you.

FACT

Each of us has a potent spiritual side that we must nurture if it is to mature and become a powerful influence in our lives. As a matter of fact, spirituality is interwoven in the fabric of who we are. We are spiritual beings. This is true if only because we want to make sense out of this finite life and find a greater purpose for our goal of achieving success.

There's More to Life Than Life

Why in a book about success is it so vital to investigate our spiritual sides? First of all, it is our spiritual temperaments that enable us to remove our lives from the daily grind of decisions and activities. It is this particular and potent niche in our inner selves that provides us with help and support in our times of need, despair, and heartbreak. Lastly, it is our spiritual natures that likewise supply us with enhanced appreciation of our accomplishments—our successes.

The Hollow Life versus Personal Fulfillment

Your personal spirituality reserve enables you, plain and simply, to succeed where you otherwise wouldn't. How often have you encountered individuals who appear to get little or no satisfaction from their accomplishments but who achieve things that impress you and that you view as remarkable successes? It happens every day.

Some individuals are indeed rising up life's ladder, but they will never find personal fulfillment on the top steps. Without some capacity for tapping into their personal spirituality reservoirs—and feeling a sense of their place in the universe—accomplishments can seem trivial and vacuous. Those individuals who feel no joy or sense of pride in their successes are often missing that critical spiritual center. They've got, metaphorically speaking, a black hole in their insides—no soul, as it were.

It's a Personal Thing

Your personal spirituality is, well, very personal. There's no single correct way to locate spiritual contentedness. Great numbers of us find it in churches or synagogues, in centuries-old religious traditions. Others forage around in the New Age for more unconventional avenues for exploration of their spiritual selves. There's also an at-home, do-it-yourself brand of spirituality.

QUESTION?

What are some common avenues to making a spiritual connection?
For one, appreciate life's many mysteries. View a newborn baby as a miracle. Relish the beauty of life in all its many glories, whether watching a sunset, surveying the fall foliage, or sitting by the ocean side. Read about your chosen form of spiritual expression, and talk to others who have had spiritual experiences.

In other words, you must find your own way in this ethereal arena. Your singular spiritual side requires a compatible form of expression. Rituals like Catholic mass or the countless other religious traditions may appeal to millions, but they are not for everybody. It's not important where you plug in your spiritual connection; it's just important that somehow, you do. Your spiritual health is too important to your overall health and well being—and quest for success—for you to give it short shrift.

Spirituality: Do You Have It?

Why is it that the definitions and displays of spirituality vary so greatly from person to person? Because, quite simply, each one of us is an uncommon individual—a one-of-a-kind creation. Our quests for success are distinct, and so are our spiritual sides and precise needs. There are, however, particular aspects of spirituality that are universal.

FACT

Your quest for success is not guaranteed to always run smoothly. You are, in all likelihood, going to experience periods when you are dispirited. It is precisely in these downcast moments when your spiritual reservoir must overflow.

For starters, your spiritual nature is ideally supposed to make you stronger and more capable of handling all that life can dish out. Let's now analyze your spiritual quotient by touching upon some of these key aspects. The series of questions to follow will help you take the pulse of your spiritual inner person:

1. Do you view life as more than a perpetual series of tasks to do and decisions to make?
2. What, if anything, do you do to broaden your spiritual side?
3. Do you carefully tend to all the relationships in your life, leaving none rancorous or unresolved?
4. Are you always true to yourself and your talents and abilities?
5. What do you do when you are feeling down and depressed?
6. Do you seek and need other people's approval before you can act in your life?
7. Do you forgive others who may have done you wrong?

8. Do you forgive yourself for regrettable things that you have done to others?

9. Do you feel energized about life and achieving success in it?

10. Do you often feel pleasure and happiness in your life?

Write down the answers to these questions. There's nothing quite like a writing exercise to make things more real. Be honest. The answers to these very broad and varied questions will clue you in on the intensity, or lack thereof, of your spiritual side. The questions are crafted to tap into your heart and soul. The health of your spiritual temperament will, in so many consequential ways, determine the paths your life will travel.

The Reverent Life

For many of us, spirituality conjures up images of conversing with a higher power and feeling a sense of peace and serenity that comes from making a connection with a celestial force larger than our teeny-weeny selves. Some of us, on the other hand, seek to find purpose and meaning in varying forms of meditation or other reflective endeavors. However, the bottom line is all the same. We desire happiness and success in the here and now, and sometimes the going gets a little tough.

As the saying has it, "When the going gets tough, the tough get going." It is during these rough life moments, in particular, when a powerful urge consumes us. We need to view life itself under a different light—a light that shines beyond the events and problems in our lives.

This is why that spiritual element that we all share encourages us to look at life with a degree of reverence, as a gift worth venerating. Surely, there are times when we view life in general as a monotonous grind. It is during these blue times that we focus on life's very unhappy, even tragic side.

It is fundamentally important that you continuously nurture your spiritual health. You want to be able to behold life with reverence, not regard it as a mere series of events and decisions, culminating in the great equalizer called death. Always insist that your life be about living. Live with purpose!

When the Going Gets Tough

When you are feeling down or depressed, the way you choose to lift yourself out of the dumps is very revealing. Spiritually healthy individuals demonstrate a great resilience. They don't flap around in their emotional down moments for very long—if at all—because they feel guided by an unseen but strongly felt energy that's a part of them.

We've repeated over and over on these pages how important it is to always move forward in life, as well as how the journey to success has little tolerance for backward movement—in fact, it's absolutely a one-way street. Of course, this doesn't mean that you won't fail or suffer setbacks in life as you strive for success. You will, from time to time. However, what it does mean is that you cannot ever lose your determination or your willingness, come what may, to pick yourself up.

The Spiritual Pick-Me-Up

The ultimate pick-me-up in life is our spirituality. Consider your own life, or the life of someone close to you. Think about how it's been impacted by the death of a loved one, or some other consequential event that occasioned a time of pain and anguish. Without a spiritual compass in your life, these rough times are often debilitating, and if you really want to be successful, happy, and at peace with yourself, you can't allow this to happen.

Acceptance

What a strong spiritual core gives you is a priceless strength called acceptance. You probably know some people or families (maybe your own) who have weathered their fair share of troubles and tragedies in life, and you wonder how they go on as well as they do. The answer is, very likely, that they have a recurring spiritual energy in their lives, be it a belief in a Supreme Being or something else that works for them in understanding the object of life. There are some parents, for instance, who lose young children to illness or accident. How do they go forward, when giving up would be the easier alternative and understandable, too?

They do so because they have to. More than ever, they need to make sense out of their lives and find a purpose in them. Terrible things happen to good people all the time.

Spiritual Strategies

Your personal spirituality will not evolve all by itself. You've got to tend it; you have to nurture it around the clock and in all situations in your life. You have to implement strategies that will give you a spiritual foundation you can rely on at a moment's notice.

As we have previously noted, many of us turn to our spiritual traditions for our spiritual sustenance. In times of crisis, or when we are feeling depressed, many of us look to our pastors or rabbis for helping hands and words of encouragement. In these situations, a spiritual strategy could entail you talking with a priest, minister, or rabbi when you are feeling low or embattled in one of life's crisis moments.

ALERT!

If you are a member of a church or synagogue, get to know your priest, minister, or rabbi. When you feel at ease in talking with these individuals, you establish a reliable outlet for your troubles. A compassionate, nonjudgmental ear in your times of need is worth its weight in gold.

For those of us who are not members of organized religious congregations, it is equally important to have contingency strategies on the spiritual side of the ledger to help us navigate through life's rugged times. Regardless of where you hang your hat spiritually, you should have spiritual safety valves for dealing with a sizeable personal loss or a big disappointment on your way to success. Being unprepared, with an underdeveloped or ignored spiritual side, often results in depression of one form or another; it often allows anger to run rampant and cause ever-increasing destruction in its wake.

Whatever your spiritual outlet, your goal is to be able to turn on that spigot when it's most needed. If going off by yourself and praying is what provides you comfort and peace of mind, then do it. If taking a long,

THE EVERYTHING SUCCESS BOOK

contemplative walk is where you find answers, don't hesitate to walk. Start conceptualizing spiritual strategies that will work for you.

Spiritual Readiness

It's very easy to get knocked off course on your way to success. Life is renowned for its perpetual, unexpected obstacles. When you are ready for these inevitable blows to fall, you can get back on the road with alacrity and with the same level of confidence as before. Here is where your spiritual nature can make a positive difference.

If you maintain a strong spiritual center, the nonspiritual aspects of life cannot keep you down. When you are spiritually whole, the things that you say and do in your daily routine—and all the problems and personal losses that confront you—are placed in a larger context, enabling you to always move forward.

We talked in Chapter 4 about intuition. It shouldn't come as a big surprise that a vibrant spiritual side enhances our intuition. We automatically make wiser decisions when we are spiritually complete. That's because we have a clearer sense of what's right and wrong, and we understand exactly what we want out of life. Success as seen from a spiritually healthy pair of eyes is more defined and thus more attainable. It also appears more permanent. In other words, with spirituality as a guiding force, success is not merely a quest for fame, money, or material things, but a richly layered journey of much nobler proportions.

Daily Nourishment

What can you do to nourish your spirit every day? Aside from the particular manifestations of your personal spirituality, such as daily prayers or spiritual meditations, there are also universal actions we can employ to become more spiritually healthy people, regardless of our individual predilections. Whether we are members of organized religions, alternative spiritual groups, or practicing spirituality on our own, we can enrich our spiritual selves by doing the following things:

- Learning to relax
- Exercising
- Appreciating our special talents
- Offering encouragement to others
- Working . . . and playing, too
- Laughing a lot

Relaxation and Exercise

Is there anything more important in life than relaxation? It's part of being spiritual. In order for you to pluck the most joy out of your life—and live the best success story—you have to free yourself of many tensions and stresses that regularly accompany life in the twenty-first century.

Walk into any bookstore, and you'll encounter copious titles dedicated to the "R" word: relaxation. You'll chance upon author-doctors of all stripes, with all sorts of letters after their names, preaching the benefits of relaxing the body and improving the mind in the process. It's an undeniable truth that both spiritual and physical health are uplifted by simple relaxation. So, set out to locate what truly relaxes you and . . . relax.

You've no doubt heard the expression: "Laugh, and the world laughs with you. Cry, and you cry alone." Well, the same sentiment applies to relaxation. Relax, and the world relaxes with you. Eschew relaxation, and you are an unhappy bundle of nerves all by your lonesome.

No matter your chronological age, you should marry relaxation with exercise in some way. Your spiritual side is supported when you are physically healthy. Your muscles should be stretched and put to use on a regular basis. This doesn't mean that you need to join a gym, lift weights, or run on a treadmill. It doesn't mean that you have to partake in a Richard Simmons style workout, either. At a minimum, all that is required is that you make a few simple changes in your routine to get your blood flowing, such as the following:

- Walk to nearby locations that you previously used your car to reach.
- Bypass elevators in favor of staircases.
- Ride a bicycle on a nice day.
- Stretch your muscles every morning with basic exercises.
- Do some elementary pushups every single day.

Work and Play, Too

Too often in today's fast-paced society, work is highlighted above all else as the true measure of a person's success. The notion of "play," on the other hand, is regarded as a waste of time; we consider playtime as nothing more than the moments that are spent not making a living. In addition, many people view play in its context of a spiritual component as contradictory, even silly.

Always remember that the things we do in our leisure moments are quite often the best barometers of who we are. Our hobbies and outside interests—the things that provide us our peaceful pleasures—are quite central to our spiritual sides.

It is vital on the journey to success that you find the things that really interest you, whatever and wherever they may be, and pursue them with abandon. Look at all the people who collect things. Collectors know there's an indescribable joy that comes with locating an addition to a collection, be it a baseball card, a piece of Depression glass, a stamp, or a bobbing head doll.

The reality is that what we do while at play is often very spiritual. Our spiritual core, after all, is about serenity, and that is regularly found while we are at play—in our leisure time activities.

Positive Inside and Outside

The greatest byproduct of a spiritual awakening is the positive light it shines on one and all. With a healthy spiritual side, you are empowered not only to be positive about your own abilities and possibilities, but you automatically exude a positive attitude to the wider world. That is, you encourage others to better themselves by complimenting them and recognizing their special talents and abilities.

Spiritually complete individuals are walking advertisements for the power of positive thinking and behavior. They radiate what's inside of them—a contentedness that runs deep. They exude what truly can be called success.

Laughter: The Best Spiritual Medicine

It is only fitting that we end a chapter on personal spirituality with a sense of humor, or, should we say, with a dose of the best spiritual medicine there is: a good laugh. Yes, laughter and humor are two faithful friends to bring along with you on your quest for success.

It has been said that in order to find true enlightenment in life, you have to lighten up. You must have a sense of humor concerning not only life in general, but about yourself, too. The success journey is better undertaken with a smile and usually is—there aren't too many dour successes!

FACT

One of the best indicators of spiritually whole and successful individuals is a self-deprecating sense of humor. The ability to laugh at yourself is a sure sign of confidence in your abilities and the vibrancy of your spiritual half. Spiritually healthy individuals acknowledge their basic humanity and all the imperfections that come with it, and they have no inhibitions about letting the world laugh with them.

Don't ever permit yourself to lose your sense of the absurd, because life is often quite absurd. Don't confuse spirituality with bland piousness, either. They are not one and the same. Lastly, don't view your quest for success as a completely sober and serious endeavor. Ⓔ

Chapter 11

There's No Success Without Good Health

In order for us to truly maximize our successes in life, we have to feel good, not only about ourselves, but physically as well. We have to be both emotionally and physically healthy. Our health and wellness can't ever be isolated from our respective quests for success.

If You Have Your Health, You Have Everything

You've no doubt heard the expression, "If you have your health, you have everything." Of course, an argument could be made that this isn't always so, and that it all depends on the meaning of "everything." Nevertheless, there's much truth in the sentiment.

Consider how you feel when you've caught a flu bug. You are constantly blowing your nose. Your throat is sore. You are burning up with fever, and your body aches from head to toe. In fact, when we find ourselves in such sickly straits, we have a penchant for waxing nostalgic—that is, of recalling the glory days when we were clear-headed, full of pep, and pain free. When we are suffering, we often vow to appreciate and value good health as never before.

However, when the flu symptoms subside and we feel better again, we fast forget what it was like to be under the weather. We quickly lapse back into our regular routine, fit as usual, and never expecting to be laid low again with the next bout of whatever bug is making its rounds.

Celebrate Your Good Health

The moral of the story is quite simple. Don't neglect your health, and do not take your ordinary good health for granted. We are inclined to see ourselves as indestructible, particularly when we are young, and we often don't envision growing old and suffering from the many infirmities that accompany the golden years. In the same vein, we don't envision a day when we can no longer do so many of the things that we do today.

Since it is not within our mortal powers to turn back the clock and arrest the aging process, we have to do the next best thing. Contrary to numerous books on the subject that claim otherwise, nobody has discovered the fountain of youth or defeated Father Time. However, many fine doctors, nutritionists, and dieticians have greatly advanced the science of health and wellness. Their cogent counsel on what we should eat and not eat can extend our lives and make them more productive, too. And that's really what success is all about—a productive life.

Positive-thinking people with high self-esteem seem better equipped at fending off illnesses throughout their lives. They are more resistant to all kinds of diseases, from common colds to life-threatening cancers. Be positive and forward-thinking, and increase your chances at both a healthier and longer life.

Pack of Trouble

Try to imagine success apart from your overall health. Let's say that you smoke four packs of cigarettes a day in your quest for success. Something's amiss here. You're not supposed to be gasping for breath on the journey. The facts speak for themselves—or wheeze for themselves, in this instance.

Smoking is hazardous to your health. It is the forerunner of every kind of illness imaginable, from cancer to heart disease to emphysema. Smoking makes your common colds last longer and appear more frequently. Smoking wrinkles your skin faster, turns your teeth yellow, and makes your breath smell foul. Jeez, do these things fit into your picture of success? If you are a smoker, you should not feel picked upon; you should, however, consider how on earth you manage to fit such a habit into your conception of health and success.

We Are What We Eat

At various points throughout this book, we've noted how the particulars of success can vary dramatically from individual to individual. There are, however, common threads running through the success journey that are important to each and every one of us. One such concern involves what we put in our mouths, swallow, and digest every single day. Since we all have to eat, there's no dancing around the fact that our nutritional habits assume vital roles in our success stories.

Your health is one of the keys to unlocking your success potential. What you eat largely determines the state of your health today. It is also a factor in how healthy you'll be tomorrow and the day after. So, why don't we set the table and lay out several fundamental nutritional principles for you to adopt as your own:

1. Avoid skipping meals.
2. Eat slowly and place your fork down between bites.
3. Completely chew your food.
4. Drink plenty of water.
5. Eat fresh fruit daily.
6. Don't forget the vegetables.
7. If you are a meat eater, choose lean cuts and discard any visible fat.

You're probably muttering to yourself right now that these are very obvious health recommendations. But do you drink at least eight glasses (1.5 liters) of water a day, which is the minimum suggested amount? Do you eat fresh fruit every day, or, if canned, fruits packed in their own juices? Do you make sure to have regularly scheduled meals each day at the same times?

For many of us, the answer to these questions is "no." Because we are dealing with the concept of success and the quest involved in reaching our goals, we are naturally dealing with time constraints. With our forward-moving agendas, we are inclined to overlook what, how much, and when we eat.

During your waking hours, don't skip any meals. Doing so wreaks havoc with your metabolism. For your optimum health and well being, you are better off eating between three and five small meals a day. Partaking in several meals is far healthier than overeating at one meal. Gorging is unhealthy behavior, whether it happens in the morning, afternoon, or night.

Fast Food for Thought

Sometimes, we simply don't lead nutritious lives. After all, it's a fast-food world. Dunkin' Donuts is always worth the trip. We grab sandwiches on the run, drop by McDonald's for an Egg McMuffin in the morning, a

Big Mac in the evening, and can't conceive of a world without pizza. However, there's more to convenience foods than meets the eye. While most are high in calories, saturated fats, and cholesterol, there are some healthy choices to be found amidst this dietary rubble. Here's a sampling of quickie foods and drinks that are considered good for you:

- Instant soups
- Fresh fruits
- Vegetables
- Yogurt
- Oatmeal
- Chicken or turkey sandwiches on wheat bread
- Bottled waters
- Skim milk
- Unsweetened fruit drinks
- Vegetable juices

The flip side to these good-for-you choices includes the less-than-stellar fast food selections. These are the very kinds of choices that thousands upon thousands of hungry souls make every day—with you maybe among them. These foods include the following:

- Hamburgers and cheeseburgers
- Sandwiches with processed meats
- High-fat condiments
- Fried chicken
- French fries
- Salted potato chips
- Chocolate bars
- Candies
- High-sugar fruit drinks
- Soda pop

The bottom line is that it's entirely up to you to make the most of your culinary time on earth. You can always eat healthier, if not downright healthy. You can devour deep-fried chicken served with French fries and coleslaw, and wash it down with a super-sized soda, or you can take a different route. Cafeterias sell fruit. On the road to Burger King or KFC, you probably pass plenty of stores that sell yogurts and granola bars. You can also find bottled waters in the same refrigerators that stock Hawaiian Punch and high-caffeine colas.

FACT

Did you know that for every pound you gain, you put extra stress on your knees? Maintaining a healthy diet and the proper weight means a lot to your quest for success—that is, if you want to make it on a good set of legs and avoid developing arthritis along the way.

Pound Foolish

The Battle of the Bulge is a fight that the majority of us wage at some points in our lives. Do you need proof? Dieting has spawned a multibillion-dollar industry unto itself—and why not? The extra weight that so many of us carry around greatly detracts from our health and our subsequent successes.

In Chapter 6, we stressed the importance of setting goals and seeing them through to their conclusions. This is how success happens. It's no state secret. Given that there are legions of us out there who have set a goal to lose weight, it makes sense to tackle the issue of weight loss right now in our general discussion of health, wellness, and success.

For many people, the road to success finds them running around like chickens with their heads cut off. A frenetic lifestyle, however, is hardly akin to exercising. Such fast-paced living often means we eat the wrong things at the wrong times. It's all too easy to get lost in a world of sugar, spice, and other foods that are not nearly that nice, certainly not as far as weight gain is concerned.

Being overweight is not recommended unless you are pursuing a career as a sumo wrestler. Excessive pounds on our bodies rob us of what we need to feel successful. One of life's great ironies is that we really do know the score. We just don't do what is required to change the score sometimes—in this case, that means shedding those pounds and keeping them off. Why? Because it's easier to stop in a restaurant than prepare a home-cooked meal. A bag of potato chips and a favorite television show are easy and more seductive than a banana and a good book. However, as we've said before, the success journey is one grounded in discipline, commitment, and a willingness to change.

Visit ✑ *www.caloriecontrol.org* for information on proper body weights and a whole lot more. This comprehensive site features all sorts of helpful calculators: a calorie count calculator that lets you evaluate all kinds of foods; a weight maintenance calculator; exercise calculator; and healthy weight calculator for both men and women, that requires you to simply enter your height.

Your Choice: Sedentary or Active?

Choices abound in our lives. Most of these are choices that, in many instances, we can't avoid making. You can certainly choose to be sedentary and sit in front of the television set for hours at a time, but you also should know that this choice of behavior slows down your metabolism and makes you more prone to overeating. It's a fact of life.

On the other hand, you can choose to lead a more active lifestyle. Your leisure hours need not be spent vegetating as a couch potato with a refrigerator stocked with goodies nearby. These are the kinds of basic life choices that are always available to us. Regardless of the situations we find ourselves in, there's always a better choice.

Nutritionists recommend that your daily diet consist of approximately 65 to 70 percent carbohydrates, 20 to 30 percent fat, and 10 to 15 percent protein. The ideal ratio of protein per kilogram of body weight is 1 to 1.2 grams. You can multiply your total weight in pounds by 2.2 to convert to kilograms. Remember that any additional protein in your regular diet is generally wasted.

The Food Diary

There are countless weight loss programs that you can join and gurus galore with weight loss advice available on tape, CD, and in books. Plenty of people are willing to take your money in exchange for telling you the secrets of good health. Of course, you could do what most of us do—attempt to lose weight on your own by watching what you eat.

An "Everything" Book

The best way to watch what we eat is to record everything we consume in a handy diary. Yes, *everything,* from the two slices of toast with orange marmalade you eat in the morning, to the pint of Chunky Monkey ice cream you devour before bedtime. A food diary's purpose is to make you fully aware of what you are eating. This information thus empowers you to make positive changes in your nutritional regimen.

Many dieticians recommend that their clients keep food diaries. The rationale behind this counsel is that it shows the diarists exactly how much—and what—they are eating at various times in their days and circumstances in their lives. In addition, the writing assignment in and of itself—documenting, contemplating, and evaluating eating habits—instills a valuable discipline.

In your quest for success, you must be self-aware. You have to know your strengths as well as your weaknesses. You have to *know*—that's the key to unlocking all sorts of doors. If you want to lose weight, eat healthier, and realize more successes down the road, it behooves you to know your calorie intake and what your overall diet is doing to your body and your mind.

Put It in Writing

In our discussion of time management in Chapter 8, you were asked to chart your every waking hour. You were asked to record your movements in writing because putting things in writing makes them more real. The same sound reasoning applies to keeping written food diaries. There are, in fact, food diaries that you can purchase. Of course, you can use any small notebook and accomplish the same objectives. Regardless of what you employ as your food diary, it is an inexpensive way to improve your diet, your overall health, and your energy level.

QUESTION?

What exactly should you put in a food diary?
List everything you eat and the time of consumption. Also keep scrupulous calorie and fat counts. Avoid estimating in a food diary. Be precise, and you'll maximize the very real benefits of keeping one.

People who keep food diaries regularly note patterns in their eating behaviors. Over time, food diaries enable you to locate the sources of weight gain. They permit you to identify and track the moods and events in your life that have any consequence for your eating habits.

When you chart what you eat every day, you learn a lot about yourself. You might see how emotional periods in your life affect your diet. A lot of us, when we're feeling down, find that our sweet tooth takes complete control. For others, it is just the opposite. A loss of appetite corresponds with the diminished zest for living.

A food diary affords you understanding of your behaviors and their connections to your diet. Watching television for several hours a day has an influence on the foods you choose to eat. The same is true of a lifestyle dedicated to partying—it affects your diet. Again, this discussion boils down to knowing yourself and equipping yourself with the wisdom to make the requisite changes to improve your life.

A comprehensive understanding of who you are—and what you want out of life—is a recurrent theme on the success journey. Self-improvement in any area of your life occurs only with self-awareness and a corresponding desire to make a change. The particulars involved in losing weight, and in eating right, fit neatly into the overall success model.

The Right Shape: Exercise

If good nutrition in your life is job number one, then regular exercise of some kind is job two. All you have to do to appreciate the importance of exercise in your life is recall how you feel after a workout. After engaging in almost any kind of exercise, you are likely to experience a natural high. Your body likes to go for a walk, or a bike ride, or a trip to the gym. It makes you feel good.

Exercise and Your Outlook

Fundamentally, an exercise regimen of any kind improves your outlook on life. If you've been paying attention, the quest for success requires just such a positive outlook—that is, if you want the quest to be fruitful.

Now we've established that exercise increases your productivity in all areas of your life, we know that it must be one of the keys to your achieving success in life. Who are your success role models? What kinds of physical shape are they in? Do they exercise regularly? Are they active individuals? In all likelihood, they are very active individuals, and not just in terms of achieving the obvious successes like job promotions, pay raises, purchasing nice homes, and winning awards. They are probably also involved in a lot of extracurricular activities beyond their careers.

So what are you waiting for? Start exercising! But do it wisely. Don't jump headfirst into anything so important without carefully considering your personal circumstances. If your lifestyle is sedentary and you are overweight, if you are middle-aged or older, or if you have existing medical problems, it would be unwise to run a marathon or play a game of tackle football right away. Consult your doctor before establishing any kind of exercise routine. At the very least, you should gradually introduce your body to the concept of exercise. The "getting to know you" program is the best way to go regarding exercise and your body.

Regular exercise improves your appearance, increases your stamina, and reduces your risks of all sorts of dreaded diseases. Regular exercise is also known to reduce your risk of heart disease by lowering LDL cholesterol levels—the bad cholesterol—and increasing HDL cholesterol levels—the good cholesterol.

CHAPTER 11: THERE'S NO SUCCESS WITHOUT GOOD HEALTH

Beware of Charlatans

Their names are legion: charlatans in the health and wellness sector. This really shouldn't surprise you, considering that the field is ripe for overblown claims and false promises. For example, there is one health "authority" who has written numerous books and who peddles a whole line of vitamins and supplements. He also entices his many fans to his fitness ranch for a week of mind and body enlightenment. What they get for their multiple thousands of dollars is a one-size-fits-all approach to health and wellness, not much different from the gym classes we all remember from high school.

This "all-knowing" Ph.D. has men and women in their sixties—some with ample guts, too—running around a track and gasping and panting along the way. He doesn't do any prescreening, health evaluations, or background checks on those who come to his ranch. This leap into exercising is not the way your fitness should ever be approached.

Again, you know yourself better than anybody else. You don't have to jog a mile on your very first day of exercising. Maybe a block is enough on day one, two blocks on day two, four on day three, and so on. Whatever kind of exercise you choose, start with a pattern that lasts only several minutes a day. Over time, make it your goal to exercise at least thirty minutes a day for three or four days a week.

Make your exercising part of a routine, and schedule it at the same time of the day, if at all possible. Wear comfortable and appropriate clothes and shoes. In addition, it's always beneficial to bring a friend along to make your exercise time more enjoyable and social.

The Exercise Spectrum

The beauty of exercising is that it makes no specific requirements. You don't have to be anywhere in particular to exercise. You don't need any specific props or equipment to exercise. You can be alone on exercise in a large group—it doesn't matter. You can exercise in a suit and tie or in your birthday suit, if that's your bag.

Remember that a long walk is exercise. Gardening and yard work are exercise, and so is housework. Of course, there are sports of all kinds and competitive exercising. Aerobic exercises are readily available to you, from power walking to jogging to swimming to bicycling. Let's also not forget old favorite at-home exercises, like sit-ups and pushups. Find the exercises that work for you and that complement your life circumstances and time constraints.

If the shoe fits, a good idea is to exercise with your family. A big part of being a success means cementing relations with our spouses and children. What better way to kill two birds with one stone than to plan exercises for the whole family that are both fun and healthy? Going to the movies as a family and wolfing down popcorn, candy, and rotisserie hotdogs covers the fun part, but it's not exactly healthy.

A Bicycle Trip

Many families ride bicycles together. In fact, bicycle riding is becoming an increasingly popular pastime. Bicycling embodies many positive characteristics. It is an activity that touches upon many of the facets that we've discussed in the context of being successful: forward movement, goal-setting, achieving inner peace, and, of course, exercising, health, and wellness.

Have you ever seen anybody riding his or her bicycle backwards? Probably not. Have you ever seen anybody achieving success and going in the wrong direction? Not likely. So we can say that bicycling is a fitting analogy to success, too.

Now don't expect to hop on a bicycle and ride your way to success. This isn't the Tour de France, and you're (probably) not Lance Armstrong. Nevertheless, bicycling is recreation that encourages you to establish goals that define how far and where you want to go. The more riding you do, the more ambitious your goals will become.

Bicycling increases your cardiovascular strength, not to mention the muscles in your legs. Most importantly, though, it builds up your overall confidence. For a lot of people, the prospect of riding a bicycle is nerve-wracking. Sharing a road with car traffic doesn't always sound appealing, but then again, achieving success on the road of life sometimes seems a little scary, too. However, the longer you travel on it, the less you fear its curves and obstacles.

FACT

Check out the National Multiple Sclerosis Society at *www.nationalmssociety.org* for their fundraising schedule of events. At *www.goodcyclist.org,* you'll find links to individual states and many scheduled bicycle tours. Here you will find locations, lengths of the tours, and whom to contact. The American Diabetes Association, the American Cancer Society, and the American Lung Association are among the many organizations that raise money with bicycling events.

Before long, you'll become a seasoned bicyclist taking long trips. You'll be visiting the next town and the town after that. Then you'll be ready to ride in a bicycle marathon for a good cause like multiple sclerosis. Bicycling and fundraising are popular allies today, and helping others by doing something that you love provides you with a very satisfied—and, yes, successful—feeling.

Staying Regular: Regular Checkups

We would be remiss in this discussion of health and success if we failed to stress the importance of regular visits to your doctor. As an exercise on your computer, do an Internet search on the words "regular checkup" and see what you come up with. Very likely, the results you'll get will link you to a whole range of sites and articles importuning you to see your doctor before, rather than after, you come down with a serious illness. In other words, practice preventive medicine.

Let's do a quick "virtual" Internet search right now, and see what happens. Hey, here's an article on seeking out prenatal care the moment you learn you are pregnant. There's a site that discusses regular checkups and screening tests and their effectiveness at preventing some of the more serious complications of diabetes. What's that over there? Senator John McCain credits regular exams with catching a skin lesion before it turned into a life-threatening cancer. There's even a hearing aid manufacturer advising users of its product to go for regular checkups. This virtual list goes on and on with a recurring theme: Regular checkups are valuable tools for maintaining good health.

ALERT!

Many of us substitute candy and other such sweets for our lunches, satisfying our appetites but denying ourselves any nutritional benefits. The long-term effects of this deleterious diet are poor health manifesting itself in obesity, inadequate muscle tone, lack of energy, and, eventually, more serious ailments.

Let's Get Physical

As part of your regular checkups, you should include routine but thorough physicals in the mix. Make sure you get your height, weight, and blood pressure periodically checked, but also have your eyes, ears, throat, skin, heart, lungs, and muscle reflexes tested too. Don't let your favorite sitcom characters be the only ones going for physicals and having their doctors whack their knees with a hammer.

How often have you learned of someone you know discovering during a routine physical that she had a lump, a blood disorder, an artery blockage, or something much worse? There are many times when these discoveries are lifesavers. Successful major league baseball manager Joe Torre, for instance, discovered he had prostate cancer during a routine physical, was immediately treated for the disease, and is now back in the swing of things.

It's surely one of humanity's great paradoxes that we often don't visit our doctors because we fear discoveries of terrible things. You know how it goes. You have this nagging pain in your stomach, and you've even spit up a little blood. You determine that it's not too bad and that you can live with it, and that it will pass. What's wrong with this picture?

In the recesses of your mind, you know that your symptoms could portend something serious. Your decision not to see your doctor is rooted in the possibility that he or she might find something, like a tumor. You opt to live with the pain and uncertainty today—and hope that it goes away tomorrow—rather than go to the doctor and be told that you have only six months to live.

Adults aged eighteen to sixty-four should have complete physicals every one to three years. At forty—or earlier, if there is a family history of cancer—men should have yearly prostate and colon cancer exams. Women should have annual mammograms and colon cancer exams. The over-sixty-five crowd should have annual physicals, and they should also be sure to get yearly flu shots.

From This Moment On . . .

From this day forward, why not resolve to act as successful men and women do. Successful individuals care about themselves. They don't risk their health and well being on unfounded fears of visiting their doctors, by pretending problems don't exist or that they will go away with inattention. When we are successful, *we care* and *we do.* This means that we are active, not reactive, in all areas of our lives, most especially when our very existence is at stake. Ⓔ

Chapter 12

Being Generous with Success

Successful people are positive and giving. They are generous with their financial resources but also with their time, know-how, and insights. A life of giving is one of the noblest forms of living. By being generous with all of your good fortune, you touch and better other people's lives while also strengthening your own.

Success Is Never Selfish

When you run down the list of people in your life whom you feel most fortunate to know (or to have known), what personality attributes do you most admire in them? High on the list is likely a generosity of spirit. Indeed, the individuals we admire are ordinarily people who have made positive differences in our own lives.

It's often easy to lose sight of the many aspects of the journey to success. As you well know from perusing the pages of this book, numerous ingredients go into making us successful or unsuccessful. We tend to focus on the "full speed ahead" actions required in reaching our goals and realizing our dreams. But how much thought do we give to the life rewards that are inherent in the act of giving of ourselves?

Giving Something Back

People of substantial means—those wealthy souls—want to "give something back" to society all the time. There are, in fact, many affluent philanthropists in our midst helping those less fortunate and aiding causes dear to their hearts, such as the arts. Some of these people even leap into the political fray to offer aid and comfort in making our world a better place—or so they claim.

For our purposes here, we will assume that the "give something back" gang's motives are pure and honorable. All of us should be interested in giving something back. We should want to enrich the lives of those around us. However, we shouldn't feel that we have to give of ourselves, nor should we calculatingly use our "generosity" for roundabout, ulterior personal motives.

ALERT!

Throughout your quest for success, keep your motives aboveboard at all times. If you use generosity as a payback tool—a tit-for-tat kind of thing—you won't garner the enriching benefits of giving freely. Do good deeds for good reasons only and never for the purpose of getting something back in return. This is successful behavior.

Generosity as Second Nature

The truly successful people in life give of themselves in untold ways. Much of the time, their generosity goes unnoticed and unheralded. For genuine giving is not broadcast on the national news or on the front pages of the newspaper. "Look at me and how generous I am" is not the cry of a successful and secure person. Rather, a successful spirit embraces generosity as a second nature, and the giving flows naturally and with humility.

The Joys of Giving

Former first lady Eleanor Roosevelt once said, "Since you get more joy out of giving to others, you should put a good deal of thought into the happiness that you are able to give." Mull over her words for a moment. Consider how they apply to your own circumstances and goals in life. To further assist you in this contemplative exercise, ponder the following questions:

1. What have you done recently that has helped others in some demonstrable way?

2. How did your unselfish actions make you feel? Describe your feelings in detail.

3. Specifically, what did you learn about yourself in the course of doing good for others? What did you learn about others?

4. Can you see the correlation between freely giving of yourself and your own personal success?

5. Do you have any ideas or plans for helping others (family, friends, neighbors, acquaintances, or even complete strangers) as you become increasingly successful?

As always, jot down your answers on a piece of paper. Thoughtfully reflect on whether or not you feel the "joy" in helping others that Eleanor Roosevelt referred to some years ago. If you feel little or no joy in being generous, ask yourself, "Why not?"

FACT

Popular self-help and motivational guru Tony Robbins has said, "Achieving goals by themselves will never make us happy in the long term: It's who you become, as you overcome the obstacles necessary to achieve your goals, that can give you the deepest sense and most long-lasting sense of fulfillment."

A Role Model of a First Lady

The life of Eleanor Roosevelt is an intriguing success case study in and of itself. Her life story was not always a happy one. She lived with an alcoholic, absentee father in her youth and an unfaithful, public husband throughout her adulthood. Born into wealth and privilege, she never wanted for any of life's material niceties. However, we all know that there's more to life—and to running with the baton of success—than living in nice homes, wearing expensive clothes and jewelry, and having food on the table every day. For Eleanor Roosevelt, her ultimate successes—her personal satisfaction and inner peace—were found in helping others.

President Harry Truman dubbed Eleanor the "First Lady of the World" because of all the work she did through the years for people who were less fortunate or the victims of discrimination. When Mrs. Roosevelt championed equal rights for women and for black Americans, it was courageous advocacy. In her time, attitudes were vastly different from what we consider normal now.

Eleanor Roosevelt worked for the American Red Cross as far back as World War I, when her husband, Franklin Delano Roosevelt, was assistant secretary of the U.S. Navy. She beseeched the federal government to compassionately assist war veterans who were suffering, mentally as well as physically, in the aftermath of that awful conflict. She got results for them while also filling a big void in her own life.

Eleanor Roosevelt continued to speak her mind and lend her voice to noble causes right up until her death. She found her niche in laboring to make the world a better and more humane place. Her generosity of spirit is what she will most be remembered for. In the end, she realized successes in the peculiar circumstances of her life. Because her material needs were provided for at birth, her quest was never for financial gain.

Instead, much of her life played itself out on a national stage in a social context. Nevertheless, Eleanor Roosevelt's long and varied life remains an intriguing model for us to consider as we embark on our quests for success and valiantly try to unearth what really makes us happy and content as human beings.

As you search for success, never forget that your goal goes beyond all the things that you acquire. Really what matters is what you do with them. Achieving success in life is never about personal excess or material gain. Ideally, success is a selfless journey. You realize the most personal satisfaction if you aim to simultaneously better yourself and those around you.

What Success Is and Isn't

Don't worry, it's not necessary that you fight for a particular social cause to be a success. You don't have to sign on with the Peace Corps and minister to the downtrodden in faraway places to earn a success merit badge. Success comes with no political philosophy attached to it. It is not a religious faith, either. Just tend to your little sliver of the world as best you can—that's both the success philosophy and the success religion in a nutshell.

The journey to success, as we never tire of repeating, is uniquely personal. It is in this journey that we figure out where we fit in life. When we make these amazing discoveries, and truly savor life's successes, it is only natural that we share our good fortunes with others.

The Generosity Spectrum

Our discussion of generosity may appear somewhat contradictory on the surface. On the one hand, we are telling you to establish bold goals and live out your dreams, which may include a mansion by the seashore, an expensive sports car, and a six-figure income. On the other hand, we are imploring you to be generous above all else and to de-emphasize materialism in your hunt for success. If you think about it, however, there is no contradiction. You can go after all life's material pleasures and want to live the good life and still be a thoroughly generous person.

Generosity is mostly about you—not other people. It's about your willingness and ability to connect with others. The most contented individuals are generous by nature in all aspects of their lives. Generosity, you see, spans a wide spectrum. Here is a brief list of some less obvious characteristics of generosity:

- Listening to others
- Accepting others for who they are
- Making time for others
- Letting certain life moments pass, without complaint or objection
- Saying "yes" instead of "no"

Listening Tours

Successful people are invariably very good listeners. Listening is the best learning tool there is. By listening to what others have to say along the road to success, you acquire knowledge and pick up skills that you otherwise wouldn't. As a matter of fact, in order to achieve success, you are going to have to do more listening than talking.

QUESTION?

What are the benefits of being a good listener?
They are incalculable. In your career, you acquire new skills and advance your knowledge. In your personal life, you strengthen relationships by hearing others out. You also bring unimaginable happiness into countless people's lives merely by listening to what they have to say.

What we are most interested in right now is applying your listening abilities to others who just want to talk—in other words, having you play the familiar role of the bartender from time to time on the success journey. Listening is a generous act. It will make you feel better about yourself and uplift others, too. If you've ever worked in a retail or service job in which you served the public, you know how tough it can be sometimes. You know then that there are customers who just want to talk and then talk some more.

Listening to a friend, or relative, or even a perfect stranger who needs an understanding and compassionate ear is a positive thing. You may writhe a little, and you may get antsy and impatient now and again, but reflect on what your listening means to these individuals. Again, you can realize all of your goals and dreams—and live the life that you want to lead—and still budget some of your time for all sorts of generous acts, such as listening. A little listening goes a long way toward making the world a better place, particularly your slice of it.

Accepting Others

If you don't learn to accept others for who they are, you are going to encounter a perpetually rough road on your way to success. You can bank on that. This is a crucial area and one where a generous spirit can greatly improve your lot in life.

Life: A Game of Leapfrog

Consider what it takes to really accept people with whom you really disagree, or who make lifestyle choices that make you uncomfortable or even angry. It's asking a great deal of you to overcome and move beyond your steadfast beliefs of the way things ought to be. However, when you leapfrog this hurdle and accept things outside of your normal parameters, you are expressing remarkable generosity.

In your quest for success, you should always be open to diversity of opinion and lifestyle choices. All through life, you will encounter people you don't much like, nor will you approve of the way everyone lives their lives. You must accept this fact of life and move forward.

Enlarge Your Worldview

Generosity of spirit is not merely the dispensing of assets or time; it is, most of all, an interior ride. There are so many of us living our lives with a diamond-hard worldview. For instance, you might well believe that every adult individual should be married, hold a secure job with good benefits to support a family, and build a retirement nest egg. In turn, you may look with disdain upon those who select different life paths. In this instance, generosity on your part would entail enlarging your worldview a bit. You might have to allow for people such as artists whose futures are less set in stone and who rely more on fortune and chance to make their ways.

Take Time to Make Time

It's that time again—to talk about time. It seems that we can't get enough of this subject. Those who give of their time are the most generous of souls. Writing out a fat check to a favorite charity is nice and necessary, but donating hours of your time to the same charity is even more generous. As we've stated earlier, you can reach your goals, wherever they may take you, and still give of yourself and give of your time.

FACT

Many parents miss out on the width and breadth of the experience of seeing their children grow up. In life's big picture, real and lasting success requires you to be there in both body and spirit when your kids are young. Know that when you choose to have a family, you also choose to make time for them and to put their needs above all other considerations.

Family Time

The "take time to make time" mantra looms especially large when you have a family of your own. Coaching little Eddie's Little League team may conflict with your fast and furious work day, but it will be time well spent if you can arrange your schedule to do it. Making time for others is not only a family affair. There are probably people in your life circles who want to see more of you, too—people who would love to talk to you and get your advice and opinions on matters great and small. Why not make a little time for them?

Benign Neglect

Life is chock-full of sadness and melancholy, which we often make more profound simply by neglect. The prime example of this is old age. All of us are destined to get old. In fact, we are careening in that very direction this very moment. Yet it's the elderly in society who are most often ignored and shunted aside.

What are the most common reasons given for not making the time to visit mom and dad, Aunt Agnes, or grandma? Oh, yes, it's awkward. It's uncomfortable. The old folks don't listen. They just don't understand the pressures of today's world. They've got some unpleasant physical habits. On and on, so the excuses go.

The unhappiest excuse of all for not making time for close relatives is that they are ill. Not wanting to see a member of your family because they are ailing is understandable on one level, but it is a poor excuse. Keep in mind that success encompasses a wide range of accomplishments. Not the least of these is a compassionate heart and understanding of what life is all about. Be generous with your time and tend to all aspects of your life, including the important people in it—come what may.

Don't permit the most vulnerable and lonely time—old age or ill health—of a friend or relative's life to be made more so by your fears of the future or your unwillingness to accept the realities of life itself. The quest for success is an integral part of the life cycle, not a separate part of it.

Letting Things Pass

There are times in all of our lives when it is best that we let certain things that are said or done to us just pass by. Generosity of spirit often asks us to go forward without complaint or objection. The sentiment, "What's done is done" is worth keeping in our back pockets all along life's journey.

Needless to say, there are life moments when complaints and objections are not only justifiable but also necessary. However, when you can say that your objections will achieve no positive results, then you should, by all means, desist from registering them. When you determine that your complaining will only make a situation worse, it's a better idea to remain silent and move forward.

A Most Generous Act

This exhibition of self-control is, in fact, a very generous act. This is especially true when you may well be entitled to an angry outburst, or, at the very least, to a well-earned complaint. To refrain from making yourself heard in such heated situations requires a truly giving spirit and a whole lot of willpower.

Go Quietly or Else

Certainly, you could make a big scene in an office meeting when you feel you are in the right. However, if you determine that it will scar your relations with your coworkers, you might opt to silence your anger. Achieving success always comes down to the choices we make. By being generous with yourself and with others, and by letting certain things just pass you by—when appropriate—you acquire many longstanding benefits. Confrontation has its place, but it also knows its place.

FACT

Winston Churchill said, "We make a living by what we get, but we make a life by what we give." And the Buddha said: "Thousands of candles can be lighted from a single candle, and the life of the candle will not be shortened. Happiness never decreases by being shared."

Saying "Yes" versus Saying "No"

What word do you think is easiest to utter: "yes" or "no"? They are both one-syllable words, so neither should get lodged in your throat. If you guessed "no," go to the head of the class. The impulse to say "no," while a benefit in myriad life situations—remember our discussion on time management—is still one of success's biggest obstacles. It will do you much more good to say "yes," and is much more likely to take you where you want to go.

As an exercise, recall recent situations in which someone asked you to do something, or posed a question seeking your approval, and you answered "no." Consider what the alternative answer—yes—would have meant in each one of the same circumstances. Here are a few examples to demonstrate the nature of questions that we are talking about:

- "Dad, can I go to the Destiny's Child concert?"
- "Ms. Fandel, would you be interested in volunteering to work a wheel at the church bazaar next month?"
- "Jim, would you consider mentoring Frank Kennedy?"
- "Would you go out on a blind date with Meg's best friend?"
- "Your mother called, and she wants to know if we can make it to Sunday dinner at her house?"
- "The new supervisor position is opening up, are you going to go for it?"

In completing this exercise, you may well conclude that your "no" responses were right in the first place. This sample is not aimed at converting "no" answers into "yes" answers. It's meant only to get you thinking about the consequences of your decisions, which is what we want to be doing every day throughout our respective quests for success.

Taking the Generosity Challenge

The message of this chapter is to be more generous in all aspects of your life—that is, to unleash your successful spirit wherever possible.

Be generous in the obvious circumstances of life, where generosity is called for, but also in the less-than-obvious, more complex situations that we encounter on our path to success.

It's now time for you to take the Generosity Challenge. You are ready for it. What follows are several suggestions that you can act on over the next few days, weeks, and months to test your generous spirit:

1. Leave a bigger tip at your favorite restaurant.
2. Buy your spouse a gift for no special reason.
3. Spend more time than usual visiting your parents or a close relative.
4. Give up your seat on the train or bus.
5. Volunteer to work a few hours a week at the local nursing home or hospital.
6. Allow a car into your lane in front of you that you wouldn't otherwise.
7. Call up an old friend whom you haven't spoken with in a while.
8. Help a colleague at work by staying a little later than you normally would.

Do any of these eight possibilities fit into your life circumstances? Many, if not all, probably do. So get to it. Be generous with all of your good fortune—your generosity is good for your health, and for the health of others. What's good for your health is good for your success. Remember, though, that generosity is not performance art. Never force it. It's got to flow willingly for it to qualify as generosity. Ⓔ

Chapter 13

E The Never-Ending Story of Learning

You should never tire of educating yourself; knowledge is power. In the current, dynamic world that we all call home, it is imperative that you equip yourself with the strongest life armor there is: an open mind and an unquenchable thirst for learning. Expand your knowledge base and grow your skills every day.

Knowledge Really Is Power

No doubt you've heard the old platitude "Knowledge is power" before, whether in school, at a motivational seminar, out of the mouth of your coach, at the office, or from a financial services outfit. No matter when or where you've heard the slogan, the sentiment expressed is as self-evident as it comes.

Knowledge really is power. All the information and advice dispensed in the previous chapters—and the information and advice still to come in subsequent chapters—is calculated to empower you with knowledge. Ostensibly, that's what all self-help books are supposed to do! Once you've gleaned and digested this mass of knowledge, it is then up to you to put it to work in your unique life circumstances and personal quest for success.

Bored of Education?

Don't ever let boredom worm its way in on your success journey, particularly where your continuing education is concerned. Your education did not end when you picked up your last diploma and hurled your graduation cap into the skies for that memorable flight. In the twenty-first century, in particular, the rapid advances in technology in all kinds of industries means that the learning curve is always there and is especially sharp. In other words, you have a lot to learn.

FACT

Upon graduation from the sixth grade of the Bronx's P.S. 7, circa 1974, a young, wide-eyed boy—armed with his trusty autograph book—approached a university professor, and the man whose lawn he also cut, for a signing. The educator gladly complied and wrote, "May your graduation be a beginning, not an end to learning." This is a sentiment that all of us should heed.

It Was Only Yesterday

Not too long ago in the scheme of things, the Internet was the province of selected highly educated scientists and academicians—nobody else. There was no software to speak of, and jobs did not require that you know how to work with cutting-edge computer programs. Plainly put, the knowledge and skills requirements for most forms of employment have changed rather dramatically.

We live in a new century, a new millennium, and a very vigorous Information Age. It's not going out on the limb to say that those of us who are saddled with the best and most up-to-date information are in the best positions to succeed. When computers first began flooding the marketplace, many people resisted the changes they brought. Individuals of all stripes declared their independence, refusing to get hustled into what they deemed the computer "fad" and vowing they would never permit themselves to be bewitched by those cold, impersonal machines. It wasn't just grandpa and his contemporaries on the shuffleboard courts who were talking this way. It was a wide range of people in various age groups.

Computers Are Here to Stay

When it became evident that the computer was here to stay, and—shockingly—that it could actually make our lives simpler and better in so many apparent ways, resistance crumbled like a powdered donut dunked in a piping hot cup of coffee. Soon grandpa was online and sending e-mails to his very computer literate grandchildren, with photo attachments and all. Remarkable!

In terms of change and technological evolution, there are several important points each of us should embrace:

1. Always keep an open mind.
2. Don't fight change; accept it and adapt to it.
3. View life's learning curve as perpetual.
4. Always seek out the latest, up-to-the-minute information.
5. Acquire knowledge and improve your skills every day of your life.

Open Minds Find Open Roads

Closed minds close doors. Open minds open doors. It's really as simple as that. When opportunity comes knocking, you don't ever want to slam the door in its face—even though that's what we so often do. Why, you ask, would anybody of sound mind close the door on a good opportunity? One reason that comes to mind is lack of preparation or readiness for the opportunity.

Roots and Wings

There are times in our lives when opportunities appear on the scene, but when we just aren't ready for them. We don't have the requisite knowledge or skills to meet the challenges. When we establish realistic goals and set out to achieve them, they are usually solidly rooted in our current knowledge and skills.

Our life goals, however, must also have wings. That is, they must anticipate that we will be wiser and more knowledgeable, with vastly improved skills, down the road. Success is just this kind of growth.

Accept the Times of Your Life

Accept the fact that there will be times in your life when you won't have what it takes, but that is through no fault of your own. At the age of twenty-two, for instance, there will certainly be career moves and interpersonal relationships you aren't ready for. That's just life—it doesn't mean you aren't moving forward and learning every single day. Realizing goals and dreams takes time and a lot of resolve on your part.

Opportunities abound in life, and you don't want to let them pass you by. By continually seeking out knowledge and acquiring new skills, you scrupulously position yourself to welcome opportunities into your life. You want to avoid missing any opportunities because of deficiencies in your knowledge or skills.

The opportunities you don't want to miss involve moments when you lack knowledge and skills that you could have had if you had made smarter and more determined decisions. This distinction is key. As mentioned, there are always going to be times in your life when apparent opportunities surface that you have to let pass. They simply are not right for you at that particular point in time. If, however, you commit yourself to expanding your knowledge base and growing your skills with no barriers, the right opportunities will eventually knock on your door at the right times.

Adapt to Change and Succeed

Embrace change, and adapt to it. In most instances, you have no choice anyway. When the blustery winds of change blow on in, there's no turning them off. Computers are here for the duration. So is cable television, and ATMs aren't going anywhere, either.

The following questions form a self-help exercise to see how you consider the notion of change and your reactions to it:

- Do you automatically view change as a threat to your way of life?
- Do you see change as a negative force?
- Do you regard change as a hindrance to your achieving success in life?

Change Is a Friend

Many of us have hostile initial reactions to the prospect of change. That kind of resistance seems to be an all-too-human trait. The poet Melvin B. Tolson wrote, "Since we live in a changing universe, why do men oppose change? . . . If a rock is in the way, the root of a tree will change its direction. The dumbest animals try to adapt themselves to changed conditions. Even a rat will change its tactics to get a piece of cheese."

Given that we are certainly smarter than the animals, why do we resist change as much as we do? Looking back over history, we find that we have been inclined to invent doomsday scenarios when we confront it. The telephone was going to talk us to death. The automobile would drive us into oblivion, and believe it or not, some people even considered indoor plumbing the ruination of society.

How can "change" level the employment playing field?
New technologies need to be learned and mastered virtually every day, and all of us start at square one, as it were. New computer programs are prime examples. Approach advancing technologies and innovations as opportunities, not roadblocks to your success.

Dance Partners: Success and Change

Look upon your quest for success and the need for change as partners that work together to help you move forward. We've noted more than once how achieving success in life amounts to lots of changes. You go from Point A to Point B, and you've changed. You go from Point B to Point C, and you've changed some more.

Never permit your resistance to change to impede your knowledge flow or preclude you from picking up new skills. Instead, you should consider change an opportunity because that's what it usually is. Look at change as a chance to get in on the ground floor of something new and exciting.

Life's Learning Curve

Life's learning curve gets sharper with each passing day, and this reality is often a double-edged sword. For one, there's so much for us to learn and absorb. Naturally, this can be rather intimidating, but, by the same token, the learning pool is deeper and more inviting than ever before. It is therefore always possible to strengthen our knowledge base and skill level.

Success in life corresponds with learning. Those people who think that they already know everything often stumble on their success journeys. They get hopelessly mired in their runaway pride. You are not going to advance in your career, and you will never start or succeed in a business of your own, unless you are firmly committed to perpetual learning. The same goes for finding a soul mate and raising a happy family. Learning as you go is key in all aspects of your life—personal and professional.

Practice Makes Perfect

Why is it that the best in any area—be it athletics or acting, business or cooking in kitchen—continually practice and finely hone their crafts? Certainly, there are some naturally gifted athletes, for instance, who don't need much practice to get it right. There are also some businesspeople who have the magic touch from the get-go. However, these are the exceptions to the rule.

The best and the brightest do what it takes to reach the heights in their professions and personal lives, and this usually entails a lot of hard work and discipline. If you want to be the best and successful in life, practice!

A basic rule of success tells us that a heaping helping of practice is the order of the day. As we set our goals, formulate plans, and spring into action, each of us will eventually learn that nobody is out there waiting to hand us our success. Success is never served on a silver platter. We have to earn it, and we should anticipate that at first it will be served on wax paper or maybe even in a paper bag.

Practice: The American Pastime

Practice on the road to success means starting small and thinking big. It means working to achieve incremental successes, which will inexorably lead to bigger and better things. As a living model of the importance of practice, let's trace the career of the average professional baseball player.

First, we invariably discover that he was swinging a bat and playing catch at the age of three or so. Then we notice that he played on a Little League team, starred in high school baseball, and was subsequently drafted into a rookie league. He then moved up to Class A professional ball, followed by Class AA, and Class AAA.

Finally, the big kahuna—he got the call to the major leagues and the major dollars that come with the honor. Of course, not all of us have what it takes to be a professional ballplayer and sign $20-million contracts to hit or pitch a baseball. However, the paths that we follow in our lives are similar.

FACT

We practice and sharpen our skills, whatever they are. We learn new skills as we progress in life, and, in due time, we find ourselves on a higher level. This growing process neatly builds upon itself.

Play Ball

Continuing with this baseball analogy, let's play ball with an interesting and edifying exercise. You are now going to consider where you are in your career—the rookie league, or have you made it to Class AAA?—and track your upward movements. First, you have to determine what you deem your Little League in career growth, as well as what knowledge and skills you had at that level. Then you identify what you specifically learned that let you move up to the next level of your career growth.

Life Position Table		
Life Position	**Job/Knowledge and Skill Level**	**Knowledge/Skills Learned**
Playing catch		
Little League		
High school team		
Rookie league		
Class A ball		
Class AA ball		
Class AAA ball		
Major leagues		
All-star team		
Hall of Fame		

By tracing your movements in this way, you'll be able to clearly see the power that your knowledge and skills have had in determining your life path. You'll understand more clearly why it's an absolutely necessity for you to keep learning all throughout your life.

This enlightening exercise can be replicated in your personal life, too. If you are happily married with a family of your own, you may well conclude that you've made it to the big leagues. Congratulations. Now it's time to make the all-star team!

Cutting-Edge Knowledge and Skills

When teenagers set out to look for jobs, they are often dismayed by the pay scale that confronts them. Minimum wage or thereabouts is what they regularly command in the job market. Why? Is it age discrimination?

No, it's simply the law of supply and demand at work. Unskilled workers are a dime a dozen in many places. Employers, therefore, look upon these workers as easily replaceable—the supply being greater than the demand. As the need for job skill increases, however, the supply of workers gets smaller. Hence, better wages are offered to attract more qualified help to meet the demand.

FACT

The modern workforce is stretched very thin in some parts of the country, particularly in retail and service jobs. Proving the old adage that "Good help is hard to find," McDonald's and the giant supermarkets are starting entry-level employees at $8.00 an hour and more in selected places. Smart businesspeople everywhere know, too, that "You get what you pay for."

Skills for a New Millennium

For the teenager getting a first job and for the middle-aged professional changing careers, it is critical to keep fully abreast of what's happening in the workplace and the wider world. Understand what skills are in high demand, and make sure that you have them. Don't let the technological revolution pass you by. Start mastering skills as early as possible in your success journey. Remember too that it's never too late to acquire new skills.

A Thing about Machines

How did your father react to his first VCR? Has he learned how to make use of the timer on that new-fangled machine yet? If he has, inform him that it's time he got rid of that obsolete VCR and bought a DVD player.

This amusing digression rings so true to life for many people. Indeed, it's illuminating to observe the older generations and their reactions to technological advances and innovations. Some members of the senior classes get with the program, while others resist it altogether.

Acquiring the knowledge and skills to participate in current events—like using a VCR or knowing how to surf the Internet—is a necessary plus and a success boon. Successful people don't know it all—nobody does—but they know a lot. They don't preclude learning or shy away from it. Very importantly, successful-minded individuals never leave the knowledge of new things or the mastery of particular skills to younger generations.

The law of supply and demand is something that you should consider as it relates to your knowledge and skills. It is obviously beneficial to your career and success to acquire knowledge and skills that are in short supply but great demand. If you have what society needs and wants, you have something valuable.

Every Day Is a Day of Learning

You really should make every day of your life a learning experience, and you don't have to go back to the classroom to accomplish this. You don't have to read a book a day, digest every page of your favorite newspapers, or attend all sorts of seminars—though these are all good ways of becoming knowledgeable and better informed.

For our present purposes, let's start with the basics inherent in adult learning. You've no doubt heard that experience is the best teacher. Here are a few lessons you might already have learned from Professor Experience:

- You learn about relationships by being in relationships.
- You learn how to manage people by managing them.
- You learn about human nature by interacting with human beings.
- You pick up skills by practicing and then mastering them.
- You achieve successes in life by gathering knowledge and applying what you know.

If you sincerely hope to be truly successful in life and to realize your dreams, you have to be learning every day of your life. This learning is not about filling up notebooks with facts and more facts. Rather, it's about understanding the game of life and how it's played. It's about being fully aware of the world that surrounds you and how you can best be part of it.

Open to Everything, Attached to Nothing

Along with your insatiable appetite for learning, be open to everything and attached to nothing. That is, never erect barriers to learning, and never let yourself get caught in a quagmire of stubbornness or nostalgia. Be open to acquiring skills in areas that you might ordinarily avoid. For instance, don't shy away from taking business management courses on the basis that you are not interested in pursuing a career in management or running your own business. That knowledge could still serve you well, regardless of your chosen path.

ALERT!

Understand cultural trends and values of the moment—the spirit of the times—and your unique role in the world. By knowing what is driving the present populace's likes, dislikes, and behaviors—and discerning why—you better position yourself to realize success.

The reality is that there is learning to be unearthed in the strangest places. In the prior example, a business management course could help you in your personal life—maybe in managing your personal finances, in dealing with people at your job, or even in bolstering your personal relationships at home. Business management lessons are as much about people and what makes them tick as they are about the minutia of running an office or business entity. There is so much interconnectivity in life that it always benefits you to forage far afield in your quest for learning and success.

Life Immersion

Yogi Berra, the common man's philosopher, once said, "You can observe a lot by watching." As usual, Yogi hit a homerun. In life, the learning tree is loaded with every imaginable kind of fruit, and none of it is forbidden.

It's no mystery why famous athletes have so much to say on the subjects of motivation and success. We can learn so much about ourselves, others, and life in general from playing games and testing our skills and resolves in competition. The same can be said about all sorts of activities and actions in life.

When you learn, you grow in all kinds of ways. You not only take on new challenges on the job and thrive in interpersonal relationships, but you are also better prepared to deal with all the little things in life. This ranges from the unsolicited phone call at dinnertime to a leaky pipe in your living room dripping on your expensive rug. Learning in life entails acquiring knowledge and skills to both do things and accept things.

The best advice is to create the optimum learning environment for yourself. Read a lot. Join groups and associations. Work with people. Understand and forgive them. Gather knowledge and new skills. In sum, set yourself to learn, move forward, learn some more, move forward again, and succeed.

Chapter 14

Success and Stress: The Battle of the Titans

We live in a world full of stress. At home, we struggle to make our interpersonal relationships work; at work, we fight office politics and other forces to do our best job and move up in the world; out in the world, we worry about the market, the economy, and all the subtleties of geopolitics that determine our quality of life. We have a lot on our plates as we set out after our uniquely personal visions of success.

Stressful Times

Modern-day life is a stress factory. The ultra-competitive, often unforgiving workplace of the new millennium produces stress like a factory production line. Raising a family—a stressful undertaking to begin with—is complicated even further by outside forces (such as the Internet, cable television, or negative Hollywood and sports role models), not to mention exorbitant higher education costs. Everyday life isn't what you'd call a "walk in the park" anymore.

That Was Then, This Is Now

From the homefront to the workplace, there's just a lot less "security" than there once was. In the 1950s and 1960s, for example, it wasn't unusual for an individual to enter the labor force as a wet-behind-the-ears hireling and stay with the very same company until retirement. Times have changed radically on this score.

QUESTION?

What exactly is "stress"?
Stress, like success, is not easily defined. Some describe it as the demands that are made upon our physical and emotional capacities in the varying aspects of our lives. Our ability to achieve success requires us to meet these demands and temper the stress associated with them.

Today's corporations are hardly renowned for exhibiting loyalty to their employees. To add insult to injury, the corporate bottom line is now joined at the hip with mergers and downsizing. The glacial relationship between management and employees manifests itself in job turnover rates. In other words, the corporate milieu generates tons of stress for all concerned, from those with corner offices on down to those crammed into makeshift cubicles.

In the current work environment, climbing up the career ladder as an employee of a single company is as rare as a manual typewriter in the office. On today's job scene, most career movements are simultaneously lateral and up. When you combine this fast and furious pace of job transition with the unavoidable scratching and climbing to get ahead—to succeed—you get a ready-made recipe for stress and stress-related illnesses.

FACT

The major causes of anxiety in the workplace—which can lead to stress—are poorly defined job roles, unrealistic expectations, lack of influence, conflicts with colleagues, boredom, and isolation. Work environments without support systems are breeding grounds for stress. If you feel that you are overworked, unappreciated, or bored silly, approach your superior and talk it out. If you can't get satisfaction, it's time to move on.

Stress Meets Success

In the previous chapters, the information covered also serves well as a kind of stress shock absorber. If you take those lessons to heart and apply them in both your personal and professional lives, you should be able to manage your stress. At the same time, you will be served well in your quest for success. Remember that it is the conscientious application of your learned lessons that will make a positive difference in your life.

For instance, if you maintain a high level of self-esteem, you automatically will feel less stressed out. If you nourish your spiritual well being, you will know less stress as a rule. If you practice sensible time management, stress is unlikely to get the best of you. Basically, if you believe in yourself and you take care of your physical and emotional needs, you will ward off the damaging effects of stress every time.

The Stress Symptoms

Setting out after success requires a lot of hard work. You've heard this line on every page of this book. However, it bears repeating that you have to fully dedicate yourself to the success mission, to crafting careful plans, and to seeing your life goals become reality. You've also got to look upon disappointments and failures as par for the life course. Learn from them, and you will move forward with more confidence than ever.

Down but Not Out

Count on it. From time to time, you are going to feel down. But what you have to avoid at all costs is being both down and "out." Do not ever permit yourself to let discouragement riddle your body and mind. We can't emphasize this enough: Successful people persevere in good times and in bad. They never say die.

Setting the Butterflies Free

We've all experienced butterflies in our stomachs at some points in our lives. When we faced an audience for a presentation, took driving lessons, or met the in-laws for the first time, we had that famous queasy feeling. Whether it's an oral presentation in high school to an office sales pitch, you know that anxiety and stress will always be around.

Beware of wearing your stress on your sleeve. Don't neglect your personal appearance. Keep yourself groomed from head to toe. Wash and comb your hair. And guys, be sure to trim your eyebrows and ear and nose hairs. Pay special heed to the clothes you wear. Make sure that they are clean and pressed and, of course, that they match.

Short-term stressful moments are commonplace. Nevertheless, we still want to manage them. We don't want to faint while giving that presentation at work, and we don't want to back into a telephone pole during our driving test. We have to survive these fight-or-flight moments in our lives when we are feeling stressed. We survive by fighting—not running away—and winning the battle.

Here are several battle plans for these common stress episodes in our lives:

1. Ask yourself, "What's the worst thing that can happen to me?" You'll find that in most life situations, the worst thing that can happen isn't so bad after all.
2. Practice simple breathing techniques. Breathe deeply in through your nose and out through your mouth. Repeat this process over and over.
3. Talk to yourself. Tell yourself that you have the situation under control and that you are up for the challenge. (It's recommended that you keep these conversations private, however.)
4. Look to the future. Don't dwell on the stressful moment as "the be all and end all." Think about tomorrow, next week, and next month, when the particular stressful snippet in your life will be history, and you'll still be standing and in the arena.
5. View stressful moments in your life, with the adrenaline pumping, as opportunities to overcome fears and better yourself as a person. Look at stress as something that's necessary for you to learn about yourself and your ability to overcome obstacles.

There are times, however, when stress takes on more serious ramifications than a nervous stomach or sweaty palms. There is cumulative stress—long-term stress—and this is something to guard against. If you can recognize the telltale indicators of stress buildup, you can deal with it before it becomes a full-blown crisis on your success journey. Here are some familiar early warning signs of stress buildup:

- Diminished attention span
- Headaches, back pain, skin eruptions, and other tension-related ailments
- Loss of appetite (or a noticeable change in eating habits)
- Feelings of lethargy and a general overtiredness
- Sexual dysfunction
- Insomnia and other sleep-related disorders
- Mood swings
- Indecisiveness
- Reliance on drugs and alcohol

The Ultimate Stress Buster

Now you know what to guard against as far as stress buildup is concerned, but what do you do if you or someone you know exhibits one or more of these symptoms? Depending on the severity of the symptoms, a visit to a doctor's office may well be in order. A complete physical can't hurt. Stress is often a precursor to depression, and when depression casts its debilitating pall, a visit to a qualified medical professional is absolutely necessary.

FACT

You can acquire fame, acclaim, and big money, but if these things are not complemented with real and deep satisfaction with your total life direction, they are all superficial accomplishments.

If, however, the problems are temporary and reversible (as most are), there's much that you can do on your own. We keep coming back to that definition of personal satisfaction as the linchpin of success. Why? Because unless you are content with your job or career and with your important interpersonal relationships, there can be no real success.

An Honest Day's Work

With this "personal satisfaction" reality reinforced again, let us now put in an honest day's work. Let's return to the workplace to explore some of the key factors that give rise to stress there. Once we've identified the various causes of anxiety and stress, we can then figure out how to change the ways they act upon us or remove them altogether from our life equations. Like it or not, your job or career is a reflection of you. In the world of success, you have to take delight in what you do, where you do it, and who are you doing it with.

When the word "stress" appears in the conversational hopper, "job" and "work" are invariably next on the tips of our tongues. For most of us, our jobs and career paths are laced with stressful moments. Finding success that melds with our unique personalities and dreams is hardly a cakewalk. It takes time, concerted effort, and perseverance.

Some jobs, for instance, place unrealistically high expectations on the employee. They expect perfection in an imperfect world. If you've ever worked under a boss who set fantastical expectations for the staff, you know how stressful it is. You find yourself trying to please a superior and company by doing the impossible. Ultimately, you realize that you can't do what is "required" of you. You naturally become overly apprehensive and dispirited, and your self-esteem takes a beating.

If perfection is a requirement for a job you are seeking, run for the hills. You don't want to work for a boss who expects perfection from you. Contrary to popular conventional wisdom, unrealistically high expectations do not make for more productive employees and better human beings. Recognize the difference between unrealistic and realistic expectations.

Powerlessness and Stress

There's probably no more deflating job position than one that lacks any semblance of authority. The hunt for success often finds us foraging around for places where we can make a difference. At work, what we want is to put our talents and abilities to work, all with the goal of making a difference.

It's easy to lose sight sometimes of human nature and the inborn desire all of us have for recognition. We should, of course, be humble en route to success. We should also want to help our fellow travelers along the way, too. However, we needn't shy away from longing to be acknowledged in some way, shape, or form for our various achievements—for a job well done, as it were.

This powerful human drive is why powerlessness on the job and stress go together as well as peanut butter with jelly. If you don't have much to do at work, or if you are doing menial tasks—when you have so much more to offer—you are naturally going to feel misused, angry, bored, and ultimately physically ill.

The Work That's Right for You

You have to make certain that your work suits your personality and special talents. If you find a job or career that balances you and your needs, you may in fact work very hard and feel stressed on occasion—but you'll return home every day with the satisfied feeling of having accomplished something meaningful and worthy of your potential. If, on the other hand, you end up in a job or career mismatch, you will likely find yourself in an unhappy situation that's an anxiety and stress producer.

A career or job in which you can leave your stamp on the finished product—whatever that happens to be—is the best possible stress buster. When you touch others in positive, substantive ways with your unique abilities, you automatically feel a sense of accomplishment and satisfaction. Personal satisfaction takes the place of stress in both body and mind.

Communication Is Key

On-the-job communication cuts down on stress—big time. Think about working in an environment with little or no communication. Everybody is on edge, not sure where they stand. Imagination—and, yes, paranoia—runs wild.

If you find yourself in a job where communication from the top is non-existent, it's up to you to fix the problem. That is, you must confront your mute or less-than-forthcoming superior and speak your mind about the communication vacuum. If you don't get any comfort in return, you have two choices: Stay put in a work environment that lacks communication channels, or move on to a more open, hospitable climate. The best course is to insist on communication. Start with yourself: Openly communicate in all aspects of your life, and demand the same in return.

War Is All Hell

We've saved the biggest on-the-job stress producer for last: conflict. Out-in-the-open, good old-fashioned warfare in the workplace is an inevitable part of the human condition. We fight with one another, particularly when money is involved and particularly on the front lines of business.

ALERT!

Be open and totally up front when communicating what's on your mind. Honesty is the best policy at work, and it will take you a long way as far as success is concerned. An up-front approach to conducting business will also knock stress on its proverbial bottom every time.

Going to work every day to do battle with your boss or a coworker is stressful. However, like anything else in life, you have the power to make just about any situation or set of circumstances better. That includes conflict at work. It's a lesson that successful people take to heart, both at home and on the job.

Follow these basic principles in dispatching conflict on the job, and you'll improve your situation and reduce your level of stress in the process:

1. Deal with conflict at its source. It is unwise and always counter productive to let things fester.
2. Before taking a dispute to a higher authority, first confront the person involved in the conflict.
3. Make absolutely certain that the problem is fully resolved to the complete satisfaction of all involved.

Home Is Where the Stress Is

The workday is over, and now it's time to go home. With any luck, you'll be able to relax and play a little. Work, as we've just chronicled, can be a very stressful place. After all, your job and career pays all of your bills, buys your home, and takes you on your vacations. It also determines whether you are going to comfortably retire at the age of sixty-five or whether it's going to be necessary for you to take that next job after retirement. Obviously, what you do for money cannot be separated from your home and family life.

Logically, if you are stressed out on the job, you will in all likelihood bring your stress home with you. Stress cannot be left in your desk drawer at the office. The things that generate stress at work are often the same things that occasion it at home: feelings of powerlessness in relationships, boredom, poor communication, and, of course, those many conflicts great and small.

The Stress Diary

You've read already about the food diary, an invaluable key to taking control of your eating habits and making that journey toward better health. There's also a stress diary, a technique some medical professionals recommend in order for us to learn more about ourselves and what's really eating us.

FACT

Through keeping a stress diary, some people discover that they work better with some stress in their lives, particularly on the job. Others determine that they perform well even under a tremendous amount of stress. Still others find out just the opposite. In any event, the stress diary empowers you with the knowledge to make positive life changes that are right for you.

Keeping a stress diary requires that you record the amount of stress that you feel at various points in your day, and, most importantly, during specific events. Since stress cannot be measured in the same way as calorie consumption, it's up to you to determine the potency of the stress in your life. You can use a number rating system (on a scale of one to ten, for instance, where ten means maximum stress).

The object of keeping a stress diary is to identify the sources of stress in your life and see how you handle yourself under their omnipresent thumbs. A stress diary enables you to pinpoint the levels of stress that you find acceptable, as well as the levels that reduce you to a bowl of quivering Jell-O. A working stress diary offers you a window into how stress affects you, how you can battle it, and how you can make it work in your favor.

The First Order of Stress Business

The first order of business in a stress diary is the accounting of your daily routine and the stress involved in your everyday activities. Take note of the ordinary occurrences in your life, such as sitting down to breakfast with the family, traveling to work, completing your various job tasks, grabbing a bite to eat at lunchtime, watching television at home, walking the dog, and so on. Record these events as they occur, jot down their times, and then describe how you feel. Finally, assign a stress grade to each one of these life episodes.

The Big Stress Events

In addition to your more established routine, pay special attention to the times when stressful situations and more unusual events encroach upon your life. Describe them in some detail, when and where they occurred, and then assign a stress grade. Next, ask yourself what made these particular circumstances or events exceptionally stressful.

Never downplay the importance of your diet in the war on stress. Eat less but better. See that your diet consists of lots of fresh fruits, vegetables, and whole grain cereals. Snack on nuts (without salt) instead of chocolate bars, ice cream, or candy. Eating right energizes you, and positive energy overpowers stress every time.

Your job is to analyze how you responded to these stressful moments in your life. Did you attack the causes of high stress promptly and with the requisite force? Did you render the high stress less likely to reappear in similar circumstances down the road? These are the important questions that you have to ask yourself. It is important for you to be candid in your answers.

The Stress Database

What you want out of all these observations of your stressful encounters in life is a database crammed with information provided by you about you. After several weeks of keeping a meticulous stress diary, you will be empowered to draw some important conclusions about your life, including what you can do to make it more efficient and less stressful. A stress diary will help you identify the chief sources of stress in your life, the circumstances that are the biggest stress carriers, and whether you are doing enough, or the right things, to vanquish stress's often crippling dark side.

Managing Stress Fundamentals

There are many ordinary things you can do to manage stress in your life. If you want to realize true success, you'd be a fool not to do everything in your power to keep stress from taking you down. Here are some basics of managing stress. These are actions you can initiate right now without any major upheavals in your life:

- Regulate your diet. Eat more fresh fruits, vegetables, and fiber, and cut down on your fat intake.
- Be active, and exercise as much as possible.
- Drink plenty of water. Take relaxing baths, too. In other words, wet both your whistle and everything on the outside as well.
- Feel your feelings. If you feel like crying, cry. If you feel like laughing, laugh. Don't hold back your emotions.
- Practice meditation or some other forms of reflective relaxation.
- Prioritize your life. Never lose sight of what's really important.
- Get enough sleep—at least eight hours a night if possible.

As you can see, your success depends in part on your making stress your friend. Stress happens. High-adrenaline and rapid heart rate moments belong on the success journey, but anxiety and fear do not.

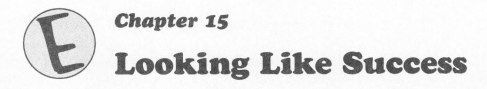

Chapter 15

Looking Like Success

There are lots of curves along the road to success, and one of the sharpest involves dressing for success. Your overall appearance on the journey to success matters a great deal in both your personal and professional lives. Success looks sharp and smells sweet.

Dressing for Success

The expression "Dress for success" has become something of a cliché. Trite or not, there is more than a whiff of truth infused in those three words. Unfortunately, the often inhospitable and generally banal corporate culture has poisoned the well of "dressing for success." The mere notion of wearing "power ties" and other such "success" apparel—to somehow advertise our worth as human beings—is a turn-off to many people, probably with good cause.

As we've mentioned on more than one occasion, success is definitely not about wearing expensive clothing and snappy jewelry. It's not about striking a pose to rise to the top of the heap in our chosen careers. Instead, it's a mostly interior journey driven by personal satisfaction and what truly makes us happy. If it makes you happy to dress to kill, go for it. Just be careful not to lose sight of the big picture of success.

Judgment Day

Like it or not, people are going to judge your appearance in countless life circumstances, and there will certainly be times when this judgment is unfair. However, there will also be occasions on which a negative judgment based on your dress and overall look is perfectly justified. Appearances can be deceiving, as we all know, but they can also be very revealing.

FACT

Sociological surveys of employers conclude that a powerful first impression is formed in the first seven seconds of a job interview— that is, before you even utter a word. The lesson of these findings is that judgment is often passed on us based solely on our appearances, not on our qualifications for the job we are seeking.

The Mangy Look versus Success

Strange as it may seem, some people pay no attention to how they look. They ignore even the basics of their appearances—often to their detriment. That is, they go on job interviews, show up for work, meet clients, or go out on dates looking and smelling like they spent the night in a refrigerator box or with the elephants at the zoo.

Unless you're in a rock band, the mangy look is not a career advancer. It doesn't do much to enhance your personal life, either. On top of everything else, looking rumpled doesn't do much for self-esteem. It doesn't help if we're setting out after success if we look like thirty-five cents. This is true no matter what paths we travel down and no matter what we want out of life.

When seeking a job, consider the old saying, "A picture is worth a thousand words." Your appearance and the way you present yourself are often as important as your qualifications to do the job. You want your appearance to create an aura of confidence and ability around you, not one of unstrung apathy.

New World in the Morning

When the rooster crows and you rise from another night's sleep, the rudiments of dress and personal hygiene take center stage. Start your new day with a morning shower. It'll not only clean the accumulation of dirt and grime off your body, but it will also wake you up—a worthy combination, if ever there was one. Never fear water, particularly in the morning.

The next item on the personal hygiene agenda is your fingernails. Make sure that they are clean and neatly trimmed before venturing out. Long, unsightly fingernails won't win you too many success points—or friends, for that matter.

Before you leave the house to make your way into the wider world, brush and floss your teeth as part of your daily routine, and don't forget to comb your hair. Make sure that it's neatly in place and pretty much going to stay that way for the rest of the day. If need be, a little hair spray or gel can go a long way. Remember that natural phenomenon known as the wind, which relishes playing games with your hair.

Scents and Sensibility

How do you go about telling a member of your family, a friend, or a coworker that she is exuding an unpleasant odor from her person? It's an uncomfortable quandary. Often, when we finally get up the courage to broach this touchy subject, we are received with a bristling hostility and are rebuffed in no uncertain terms. Of course, the irony of these situations is that our intentions are honorable—we just want to help.

Let that be a lesson to you. If somebody you know tells you that you have foul-smelling breath, for instance, don't shoot the messenger. Don't huff and puff. Consider that you may well have less than sweet-smelling breath, and set out to do something about it. This is what successful people do—they better themselves all the time!

ALERT!

There's an old saying that goes something like this: "He who corrects me, hands me a gold coin." In other words, regard constructive criticism or critical advice as a precious gift. Extract valuable lessons from it. Consider what you are hearing before you get furious and storm off into the night.

No Laughing Matter

Successful people are doers. They overcome obstacles all the time. They are ceaseless in seeking out self-improvement. If their body odor or bad breath is standing in their way, they rectify the problem. They don't let pride, embarrassment, or denial keep them in their malodorous states.

All levity aside, personal hygiene and proper dress are no laughing matters. A lot of very intelligent and charismatic people walk around disheveled and not tending to their appearance as they should. Their unkempt demeanors erect success roadblocks all the time.

Keep in mind that this discussion is not merely about going on job interviews and looking just right for interviewers. It's about finding true love, making friends, and garnering the respect of your neighbors, too. It's about life, your role in it, and how those inside your circle and outside of it, too, perceive you.

Job Applicant Grooming Checklist	
Item	Proper Grooming Protocol
Hair	Freshly washed, neatly trimmed, combed and/or styled
Facial Hair	Closely shaven, or mustache and beard meticulously trimmed
Teeth	Brushed and flossed
Breath	Clean smelling (avoid food, drinks, and habits that contribute to bad breath)
Fingernails	Trimmed, even, and clean
Body	Showered and deodorized
Perfumes/colognes	Preferably none at all, or used sparingly (no lingering odors)
Makeup	Use sparingly, if at all, and natural-looking shades only

The Cat Man

His name was Bill, and he worked as a chauffeur for an important corporate executive. Bill always presented himself as an urbane sophisticate, impeccably dressed in a navy-blue suit and natty chauffeur hat. The fly in the ointment of this seemingly perfect picture was that Bill, while regularly affecting a spiffy look, often reeked of cats.

Bill and his wife shared their house with a menagerie of pets—mostly of the feline variety—and the cats' natural odors wafted many places, including onto their various articles of clothing. Bill never tired of boasting how he kept his work suits in a fresh-smelling cedar closet. He was absolutely convinced that this cedar charm of his warded off the pungent animal bouquet that so freely roamed through his house. He was sadly mistaken.

Finally, Bill's long-suffering boss had smelled enough. He told Bill, in no uncertain terms, to do something about his odor problem, or else. Bill was shocked. He asked a friend if he ever detected an odor problem on him. His friend, who most certainly had smelled something foul, told Bill that he hadn't, which was an unhelpful and unkind untruth.

The moral of this story is threefold: Be honest, accept the truth, and, of course, groom yourself. Bill needed to know the truth to right an embarrassing problem in his life. His friend didn't do him any favors by skirting reality. Successful people need and want all the information they can get about themselves. The more we know, the farther we'll go.

First Impressions

It's the subject of eternal debate. Do first impressions really matter? Do they really tell you all you need to know about a person?

Let's make our investigation in an orderly fashion. The answer is "yes" to the former and "no" to the latter. However, it really doesn't matter whether you feel first impressions do or don't tell you what you need to know about an individual. On many occasions, someone will judge you by the first impression that you make. That's just the way it is, and whether these first impressions are accurate or fair is of no importance.

Beware of lingering. You don't want to leave your calling card in the form of too much perfume, cologne, or after-shave. When you leave a room, you want to leave with your perfume, cologne, or after-shave. Use common sense when applying any scents to your person.

Why First Impressions Matter

If you are on a job interview, that first impression might be the only impression that you get a chance to make. A first date is often a last date, too, courtesy of a less-than-charming first impression. Let's just say that first impressions are dangerous to overlook, and this is precisely why you must pay special attention to your dress and your overall appearance.

Professional versus Unprofessional Job Interview Basics	
Professional	**Unprofessional**
Clean and pressed clothes	Baggy, wrinkled clothes
Neat hair in place	Unruly hair in need of cutting or styling
Polished, shiny shoes	Dirty, scuffed shoes or boots
Long-sleeved shirts in a suit	Short-sleeved shirts in a suit
No flashy jewelry	Gold medallions, charms, ostentatious rings, costume jewelry
Men: sportcoat, shirt, tie, and coordinated dress pants	Khakis or jeans
Women: blouse and skirt	Low necklines, high hemlines

Food for Thought

The job interview is the prime example of when dress and appearance matter, an instance of how first impressions can really make or break you. Let's take another scenario. For instance, let's open up your dream restaurant. As a fledgling business owner, you certainly want to look your best when you greet your customers for the first time, don't you?

Of course you do. You also want to maintain your positive, pleasing appearance every single day of the week, because you always want to look attractive and attract customers. It will take more than meticulous grooming and stylish attire to win over a loyal following—good food and solid service go a long way in the restaurant business—but you can never afford to discount the power of proper appearances, anywhere and everywhere.

QUESTION?

What is the Rule of Twelve?
For those individuals who don't know where to draw the line on a job interview regarding what to wear, the Rule of Twelve simply says that no more than twelve articles of outerwear should be visible, counting everything from pants to jewelry to belts to socks.

Ambience

While we're still on the hungry subject of restaurants, we might as well talk about ambience. Successful restaurants usually look attractive. Their walls are decorated just right, and the lighting inside their dining rooms complements the food and mood. In other words, appearance matters all around. The lesson is to let it matter to you, too, whether you are a restaurant owner, a restaurant waiter, or someone with a completely different career who merely enjoys a good restaurant.

The Vision Thing

We've seen throughout this book that achieving success is a complex undertaking. Achieving success consists mostly of incremental moves forward that build inexorably, one upon another. The piecemeal nature of our progress explains why we can ill afford to create too many bad first impressions.

There will always be key moments in your life when you can't afford to fail or lose regard on what amounts to a technicality. You don't want to miss any golden opportunities because you forgot to wipe the sleep out of your eyes, wore a paisley shirt on a *Fortune* 500 company interview, or had plaque between your teeth on your dream date.

Most first impressions in life are visual. You are immediately judged by how you look. Before you open your mouth in any initial encounter, you are seen and not heard. Isn't it logical, then, to present the prettiest picture possible? You don't want to exhibit anything unsightly, or perversely memorable, to the person or people on whom you want to make a positive first impression.

FACT

Dress and appearance dictate first impressions in countless life episodes (dates, job interviews, and so on). When you look and smell good, you are ahead of the game in whatever game you are playing. Looks can kill—metaphorically speaking—so in terms of success, why not go for the kill?

Make a good first impression in your dress and collective appearance, and then worry about your second and third impressions. Poor second and third impressions can do damage to that positive first look, and they sometimes do. However, with all the sage counsel that you are gleaning from these pages, you should have what it takes to maintain that good impression from first look to last.

The Confidence Wardrobe

Dressing for success is not only about winning other people over to your side. It's also about winning over yourself. When you are neatly dressed and groomed, it not only enhances your appeal to others, it increases your own confidence and self-esteem, too.

Some people spend the preponderance of their lives in jeans and sneakers, or in housedresses and slippers. When they "dress up," they shock their family and friends, who are stunned to see their change in garb.

The Makeover

You have probably seen that long-time favorite of morning talk shows, known as "the makeover." The host and company parade out assorted frumps and nerds, and, with the help of beauticians and cosmetic artists, turn these ugly ducklings into veritable princes and princesses. Their accomplishments look like miracles.

Of course, these makeovers aren't any such things. It's within our powers for each of us to look the best that we possibly can—on any given day, at any given moment. It's not about always looking like a million bucks. Rather, the point is to decide what dress and appearance is right for us in any of the myriad situations that make up our lives.

Your Body Is Your Temple

In your personal quest for success, you always want to feel good about yourself and the progress that you are making. Start by feeling good about your body and how you look. It's your temple. How you groom and dress yourself along the way to success is important on a number of levels, and it will make a considerable difference—positive or negative—in your life. You make the call which way it will go when you choose your clothes, take your shower, and clip your fingernails.

ALERT!

Before going on a job interview, a date, or to a meeting with a client, you should avoid foods that contribute to unpleasant breath. Smoking and alcohol will do you no favors. Too much coffee will also leave its mark. Garlic is good for your health, but bad for your breath. Keep breath mints handy.

Case Clothes

If you walked into a four-star restaurant for a pricey meal, escorting a date on your arm, you would in all likelihood feel ill at ease if you were dressed in a T-shirt and a pair of shorts. Strangers would be looking at you and murmuring asides. You'd feel like a bumpkin in the royal court. On the other hand, if you were attired in neatly pressed dress clothes and shiny dress shoes, you'd feel quite differently. You wouldn't, for starters, feel so self-conscious, and you'd in turn feel more confident in the surroundings.

This scenario is not meant as a lesson in fine-dining protocol. It serves, however, as a lesson in fine-living protocol. We all want to convey a positive attitude and some strength of character as we go through life and attempt to make our dreams happen. We can't discount the importance of what we wear, the way we look, and how others perceive us.

One Size Doesn't Fit All

The lesson we all must learn is that the concept of dressing for success is open-ended. In some cases, such as the job interview, the rules are clear, and we've gone over those. For the most part, however, there is a tremendous amount of latitude in the dress-for-success business. You can dress for success in your own way.

When we speak about success, we are not talking about a one-size-fits-all formula, like "Wear Armani or fail." Our message is very much to the contrary. You could be a civil servant and be more successful than a corporate executive making seven figures. You could be a janitor and be more successful than a professional athlete making eight figures, and you could be flipping burgers in a greasy spoon and be more successful than a Hollywood actor making nine figures.

Success, as we've tried to make plain from the beginning of this book, is not merely an occupational game—although occupation and career play vital roles. It's more about living a life of real satisfaction, of genuine happiness and contentment. For example, if you are working in a surfer's hideaway in Honolulu, Hawaii, your choice of dress is going to be a tad different from someone else your age who works in an office building in downtown Boston. Just remember that dressing for success is more than a tired slogan. It's a way of life that you should adopt as your very own in your own life circumstances.

Chapter 16

Financial Planning Goes a Long Way

The success journey is multifaceted. While firmly grounded in the present, we who take this journey must also be fully cognizant that tomorrow takes shape courtesy of the choices we make today. Thoughtful financial planning in the here and now has positive consequences for all our tomorrows. When we prudently save and invest today, our futures automatically shine brighter.

Wealth Is Acquired over Time

Let's face it. Most of us aren't as fortunate as ol' Jed Clampett, who was out looking for some supper when he chanced upon more oil on his property than there is in the whole of Kuwait. The "black gold" and "Texas tea" made him a multimillionaire on the spot. We aren't likely to strike it rich by such a bizarre twist of fate.

Jed Clampett is the fictional patriarch of the *Beverly Hillbillies*. Nevertheless, unless you win the lottery, or author the next hot diet book, you are doubtless going to fashion your wealth over many years. This is the long and winding road that most of us will travel. It's an incremental approach to wealth accumulation.

What Was That Masked Investment?

In considering the right investment strategy for your future, be aware that the greatest opportunities are often shrouded. The next IBM could be right in front of you, and you might not even know it. For this reason, if for no other, you should diversify your investments.

Any financial advisor—also know as a financial planner—worth his or her salt will tell you that by diversifying your investments, you minimize your risk. In addition, by spreading out your assets among various types of investments, you also increase the likelihood that you will snare the next Microsoft or eBay. Wise financial planning teaches that the best way to avoid the investment lemons is to diversify and increase the chances that you also have some diamonds in your mix.

What Is Your Pleasure?

Investing in your future should be a carefully planned process that starts right now. Striving for success—in all aspects of our lives—is about investing in our futures. Thus, your financial planning should be the foundation that perfectly supports your unique personality and life circumstances. If you desire absolutely no risk, or very little risk, there are investments that fit this bill: savings accounts and money market funds that pay nominal interest rates, for instance. These aren't recommended methods for accumulating wealth, beyond the principal deposits themselves, but they are peace-of-mind places to rest your money.

If you are interested in a little more bang for your buck, you have plenty of viable alternatives that still come with very low risk: certificates of deposit (CDs), U.S. Treasury securities (bills, notes, and bonds), municipal bonds, and some individual retirement accounts (IRAs). There are also other investment vehicles with more overt and variable risks, like 401(k) plans, mutual funds, real estate, and, of course, common stocks.

Put a premium on feeling good about your investments. If you are losing sleep over any of them, get out! There are plenty of investment alternatives out there, and many of these options are secured. You shouldn't be sweating out your investments. If you are, they are wrong for you.

History Class

As an investor on the success journey, you should know that periods of economic uncertainty are very often the time for investing. The economic health of the country is dependent on the confidence of its people. Too often, we the people run away from our investments at the first sign of trouble or national malaise.

Consider the history of the stock market. It has always rebounded from its down periods. Logically, when the stock market has hit a low, there are plenty of investment opportunities to be found in those depressed stock prices. Similarly, when the real estate market is weak, there are investment opportunities, too. We've noted on more than one occasion how important seizing opportunities and sensible risk-taking are to achieving success. This counsel is never more true than in terms of investment.

In the investment arena, there are countless instances when opportunities come knocking. Don't ever feel guilty about seizing these moments. It is the risk-taking and discerning investor who time and again reverses national economic declines or crises of spirit. Such bold—but not irrational or extreme—actions benefit us all.

It's about Asset Allocation

First of all, any long-term investment strategy should be built upon an asset allocation model. This is a plan that assigns a proper balance to your portfolio of investments. Your asset allocation model weighs the choices that are right for you based on your present life circumstances and projected future. Among the many variables that go into constructing this model are your age, present job, career plans, family situation, and—of course—your specific goals. Here are some of the questions an asset allocation model addresses, as they pertain to your investments:

- What are the things you want out of life right now?
- What are the things you want in the short-term future?
- What are the things you want for your long-term future?

Goals Meet Investments

An entire chapter in this book, Chapter 6, is devoted to the magnitude of goals on the success journey. Whether you achieve real and lasting success largely rests on your ability to establish goals and then set action plans in motion to attain them. Your goals are unique to you and what you want out of life. Hence, your asset allocation model must be unique to you, too. For these doubly unique reasons, you need a financial advisor (if you don't feel you can handle it yourself) whom you can implicitly trust, and one with whom you establish a rapport. You need to be able to tell your financial advisor precisely what you want to extract from your investments and—more to the point—out of your life.

ALERT!

In the stock market crash of October, 1987, the Dow Jones Industrial Average fell 21.5 percent, but bonds rose 6.2 percent, and cash equivalents gained 0.6 percent. Such bumps in the road make a balanced portfolio crucial. A blended investment strategy is a shock absorber when one particular investment vehicle makes a wrong turn.

Regardless of what your personal asset allocation model resembles, there is a fundamental strategy that guides one and all. The strategy recognizes and doesn't flinch from the shaky reality that is the investment universe. Come again? Yes, asset allocation models fully appreciate that one invests with the winds of uncertainty always blowing. Thus, intelligent asset allocation models practice risk management above all else.

You don't have to be a financial planner or Wall Street executive to know that not all investments are alike or that they don't all behave in the same way. All of us have seen with our own eyes—and sometimes with our own dollars—that the various financial markets react differently to factors such as business cycle fluctuations, interest rate rises and falls, or military machinations halfway around the world. Entire industries and specific companies, likewise, often behave erratically, whether as the result of the aforementioned external factors or due to internal forces that are often hidden from the investing public.

The Balancing Act

An asset allocation model depends on balance as an integral part of its risk management approach. You don't ever want to concentrate all of your investments in a particular asset class (such as stocks), sector of the economy (for example, technology), or company (like WorldCom). The lessons of history, particularly recent history, teach us that throwing in with one investment type is not only risky, it's downright foolhardy.

Why Save and Invest?

The ultimate measuring stick of success is that little thing we call "personal satisfaction." Personal satisfaction means different things to different people. The big question for this particular chapter is this: Do we really need to save and invest to realize the warm and fuzzy feeling that accompanies personal satisfaction?

The short answer to the question is "Yes!" The vast majority of us would be well served by saving and investing when we can and what we can. You needn't be overly worried about your golden years when you pick up your college diploma, nor should you have to obsess about your financial future while trying at the same time to find the personal and professional life that is right for you. Nevertheless, at all points in your life, it is wise to consider the things you want and need. A house might be on this list, or a car, or your child's college education; these things, along with others, are what require you to save and invest. They are inextricably linked with your life goals.

FACT

Visit the American Savings Education Council at ✍*www.asec.org.* Among the council's many offerings, you'll find a link to "The Ballpark Estimate," a one-page worksheet that can help you calculate what you'll need to save and invest through the years— based on your earnings, Social Security, and other income sources—to retire comfortably. If you are concerned about properly funding your golden years, start crunching those numbers now.

Do you want to save money to buy a home? Do you need to save for your children's education? Are you hoping to retire comfortably? Do you want to help family members who might be in need? Thoughtfully examine your life priorities and your overall vision of success. When you finish figuring out the specific things that have a priority in your life, you'll have a keener understanding of what investment strategy will work best for you.

The Investment Playing Field

There are many investment vehicles for you to test drive. America is the land of opportunity on a whole host of fronts, not the least of which is opportunity for investment. What follows is a sampling of some of the more common savings and investment alternatives. Whether you act as your own financial planner, or you decide to put your trust in a professional, you'll at the very least have a rudimentary understanding of the width and breadth of your investment options.

There's No Accounting for Savings

A traditional savings account at a bank, or a money market fund with a brokerage firm, permits you to make withdrawals free of penalty. In addition, if your bank is a member of the Federal Deposit Insurance Corporation (FDIC), your deposit is insured up to $100,000. In other words, the basic savings account is a safe place to put your money. Shop around for the best interest rates—minimal as they are.

A good Web site for investor information is ✎ *www.investor.org*. Get the scoop on everything from investing fundamentals to tips on properly defining your investment objectives. A very informative Web site to check out is ✎ *www.investorwords.com*. There you'll find the definition for every investing term imaginable.

Certificates of Deposit

Certificates of deposit (CDs) are as simple to get as savings accounts. The difference between the two is that with a CD, you agree to both a fixed interest rate and a maturity date. Ordinarily, you'll get a better return on your deposit with a CD than a savings account. However, the catch is that if you cash the CD before it matures, you will be charged a stiff penalty. For example, let's say you invest $5,000 in a sixty-month CD at an interest rate of 5 percent. But after just twelve months, you decide you need to have your cash back in hand. Instead of paying you that 5 percent interest, your bank (or whatever other institution sold you your CD) will take a percentage of your original $5,000 as a penalty for failing to live up to your sixty-month agreement. Despite the consequences for early withdrawal, the CD has been dubbed the best investment for the individual who "must enjoy a good night's sleep."

U.S. Treasury Securities

Federal government securities (bills, notes, and bonds) are the investment of choice for the investor with a high net worth. These securities provide the dynamic duo of safety and liquidity. To put the icing on the cake, U.S. Treasury securities are free from state and local taxes. If held to maturity, these investment vehicles return their principal plus a fair rate of interest, which can be relied upon to be higher than the interest paid on savings accounts or CDs. Treasury securities are U.S. government debt obligations that are guaranteed to deliver as promised.

QUESTION?

Is investing in federal government debt obligations a good idea?
U.S. Treasury securities are backed up by the "full faith" of the government and pay a fair interest rate. Interestingly, when the federal government deficit spends, it sells securities to people looking for good investments to pay its bills. It sure beats taxing us!

Bond—Municipal Bond

Following on the heels of U.S. Treasury securities are municipal bonds. These are bonds issued by state, city, or local government agencies to finance civic operations or projects. Also known as "munis" (short for "municipals"), these issues are often free from federal, state, and local taxes, and they are generally considered safe investments. Nevertheless, when purchasing such bonds, a little due diligence is in order. Some governments are more respected and stable than others.

Individual Retirement Accounts

Individual Retirement Accounts (IRAs) are personal retirement funds. There are various types of IRAs, so be sure you find out which kind is right for you. Generally speaking, you can invest up to $2,000 every year into IRAs that are made up of mutual funds, stocks, bonds, and so on. Taxes are deferred on the money you invest. If you opt to withdraw money from your IRAs before you turn fifty-nine-and-a-half years old, you will be penalized by 10 percent.

It's Profit Sharing: 401(k) Plans

The 401(k) plan is a type of profit-sharing plan, and it is one of the most popular investment options of the day. In these plans, employees make tax-deferred contributions to an investment account. Employers often match contributions on a dollar or percentage basis (up to 25 percent of a company's annual payroll), and the monies are invested. Like IRAs, 401(k) holdings can be withdrawn after the age of fifty-nine and a half without penalty (and before that in some hardship cases).

Mutually Beneficial: Mutual Funds

If you are in the market for potentially higher returns on your investments, and you want to avoid the elevated risk of individual common stocks, mutual funds are a good option. Mutual funds reduce risk—although they don't eliminate it—by investing in an aggregate of stocks, bonds, and other securities. The funds work with a large pool of investors, which lowers the risk, and fund managers are in charge of selecting investments and maintaining rates of return.

FACT

Although mutual funds are generally considered to be a relatively safe way to invest in the financial markets, they do entail risk. Many mutual funds are heavily, or solely, concentrated in specific sectors of the economy. Government bond funds are decidedly less risky than any mutual funds.

Putting Stock in Your Investments

Putting your investment dollars in the stock market has the potential to get you the highest return of all. However, there's the flip side to this possible good fortune. Common stocks are, by their very nature, risky places to put your money. With that disclaimer out of the way, it should be said that any balanced and wise investment approach reduces this risk considerably. Therefore, investing in the stock market is a highly recommended avenue for building wealth.

Why are stocks considered the asset of choice for so many investors? When you purchase shares of common stock, you are buying into actual companies. You are investing in proportionate shares of real businesses and sharing in their earnings. Stocks are all about risk and reward and the volatility that comes with it. Volatility shoots stock prices up and up some more. (It takes stock prices down now and again, too.)

Real Estate Investment

It has become something of a cliché to say that real estate is a good investment. Generally speaking, it is. Land, after all, is a finite resource, and the population continues to grow. When we put two and two together, the law of supply and demand tells us that real estate values have only one way to go: up.

Also, when you consider what most people pay in rent these days, it's often more than the average mortgage payment on a home or condo—and mortgage interest is tax deductible, too. If you can afford the down payment and you qualify for a mortgage, purchasing a home is certainly worth considering.

Of course, investing in real estate isn't the perfect solution to your investing needs. With home ownership come the responsibilities of being a homeowner and all that can go wrong with a house. Also, depending on the location of your real estate holding, there's no guarantee that it'll appreciate in value. Many speculative real estate investments have bombed, and others that saw property values decline for all sorts of reasons (like a garbage incinerator being built in the neighborhood, and so on).

A veteran financial consultant and portfolio manager says, "There are very few get-rich-quick schemes that endure. Balance and moderation in investments over time are what gets us to the goal line. A sensible, conservative, balanced approach that respects an asset allocation model is what will win the day in investing. . . . Wealth is acquired over time."

Finding the Right Financial Advisor

The world is full of bad investment advisors. Some are ethically challenged; others are incompetent; on top of that, there's a miserable mixture of the two. That's the bad news. The good news is that there are also many respected and very astute financial advisors with well-earned solid reputations. These are the people who have not only delivered positive performance results over time, they have also established impeccable reputations for integrity by communicating openly and honestly with their clients. The very best financial advisors do more than invest their clients' money. They know their clients as individuals and tend to their individual needs.

ALERT!

When looking for a financial advisor, also called a financial planner, do not overlook the candidate's qualifications. Ask a prospective advisor if he or she is a certified financial planner. Find an individual with solid credentials in the areas that are most important to you, such as investments, insurance, or tax planning.

If you are in the market for a financial advisor, you have to locate one who's right for you. This, however, isn't a case where you should open the Yellow Pages and let your fingers do the walking. Nor is it time to throw yourself on the mercy of your friendly neighborhood banker, either. Rather, you have to carefully consider many factors before entrusting anyone with your hard-earned money. As you search for a financial advisor, here are several guidelines to help you make your choice:

1. Look for a person who will listen to you and empathize with your particular needs.
2. Above all else, make certain that the individual you select is trustworthy.
3. Financial advisors associated with respected investment firms are the cream of the crop.

4. Find out how your financial advisor is going to be paid for his or her services (for instance, by fees on a commission basis), and get it in writing.

5. You want a financial advisor who has an established track record of delivering positive results in concert with a positive reputation.

The Importance of Research

Before the Internet and cable television came along, the average individual's hands-on involvement in mutual funds and investing in the stock market was minimal. Investment research tools were limited. Necessary and timely investment information was available to financial planners and analysts but not to the average investor.

Times have changed. Now, many research and information tools are only a few clicks away on our computers. In addition, all-day cable television channels provide up-to-the-minute financial and investment information, and magazines and newspapers devoted to the average investors are available at nearby newsstands, too. In other words, there's no excuse anymore for ignorance on financial matters.

FACT

You can conduct background checks on potential financial advisors via the Securities and Exchange Commission (SEC), the National Association of Securities Dealers (NASD), and state documents. Find out if they have been investigated or have committed any ethical lapses in their field.

The Old College Try

If you are a new parent, or you plan on being one anytime soon, it's never too early to start saving for your child's college education. The average tuition at a public college is $25,000 per year; at a private college, it's $50,000 per year. Do the math. That's $100,000 to $200,000 for four years of higher education. That's at today's prices; we shudder to think what a college education will cost eighteen years from now.

Here's where a knowledgeable financial advisor comes in handy. You need one who works with you and your very specific needs. There are, for instance, education IRAs with maximum contributions of $2,000 a year. There are mutual funds that might be just what you are looking for. Ever hear of zero coupon bonds? However you decide to do it, make the commitment to save and invest for your child's education. Here are the basics:

- Start the process as early as possible.
- Examine all of your alternatives.
- Develop a sensible but aggressive investment strategy.
- Invest thoughtfully, and make adjustments as necessary.

Extreme Ops

Courtesy of the Internet and online trading, opportunities for the average person to invest in the stock market abound. The flip side to this ease of buying and selling shares of stock is that it's also an easy way to lose money. Keep in mind that investment is not gambling. Many day traders (who invest via their own computers) and plenty of others, too, play the financial markets as they do the casino tables.

On your quest for success, you should be careful to avoid such extreme behaviors. Nowhere is this more true than where your finances are concerned. For example, you shouldn't be playing in the futures or commodities markets with limited assets. These are very risky places to be—in fact, they make for downright dangerous investments on many occasions. You should tend to your financial bottom line with the same common sense, patience, and perseverance that you apply to all aspects of the success journey.

Chapter 17

Business Planning Can Make All the Difference

The idea of success and living the American dream is very often intertwined with starting a business. Who among us doesn't want to be our own boss? A steady stream of entrepreneurs opens up new businesses every day. What all of these fledgling businesspeople should have—but most of them don't—are business plans.

The American Dream

Entrepreneurs are called risk takers for good reason. We would like to know when we commit ourselves to building a business from the ground up—with all of our resourcefulness, sweat, and dollars—whether we can plan on sampling the sweet taste of success. However, that's not the way the business game is played—or the success game either, for that matter.

Ready, Set, Go

As you read these words, a virtual army of gung-ho Americans is poised to take the big plunge and invest both their time and money in a business of some kind. More than anything else, this valiant entrepreneurial spirit distinguishes America—and Americans—from the rest of the world. No country on the planet has ever offered its citizens a greater opportunity to succeed in business than the America of today.

It may therefore come as a shock for you to learn that the vast majority of these start-up businesses are destined to go the way of the common housefly. Most of them will spring to life, buzz around a bit, and then drop dead. The stark reality is that most new businesses aren't around to blow out the candles on their first anniversary cake.

The Secret of Our Success

The rather somber facts of business failures do little to dampen the spirits of a never-ending parade of eager businesspeople. While resilience isn't exactly unique to the Yankee character, it's a personality quirk that keeps the American free market alive with creativity and stability through good times and bad.

Why, you ask, does fate sentence so many new business ventures to such a speedy end? Just as there are countless reasons why people succeed in business, there are, similarly, a whole host of reasons why they fail. The father of evolutionary theory, Charles Darwin, may not have had the business scene foremost in his mind when he advanced the "survival of the fittest" concept in his famous theory. It is nevertheless very fitting in the highly competitive, dog-eat-dog world of business.

As a possible business player, it is imperative that you be as fit as a fiddle before entering the arena, and that you do everything humanly possible to avoid the popular pitfalls that do in so many businesses.

The Business Reality Puzzle

In business, success boils down to solid planning. That goes beyond the first good idea or a lifelong dream. It takes more than a stout heart and a heroic work ethic to succeed in business. An idea, a dream, and the most noble of work habits are laudable—and absolutely necessary companions on the success quest. However, these things are only pieces of the business reality puzzle. To triumph in the end, in a business of your own, you have to put all the pieces together.

Before starting a business in any field—and that means before borrowing money, signing a lease, or purchasing an inventory—you must first bombard yourself with questions. You have to cross-examine yourself with the aggressiveness and resolve of a Perry Mason. Ask yourself the tough questions:

- Is the current state of the economy conducive to my success?
- Is there a genuine demand for the product or service that I plan to offer?
- Will there be a steady demand for the same product or service tomorrow and the day after that?
- What's the competition like for my product or service?
- Do I have enough venture capital to get myself over the humps of the inevitable bumps along the road to building up my business?
- Am I temperamentally suited to interact with customers and fashion a loyal customer following?
- Am I compatible with my partner (if I have one)?
- How will my personal life obligations impact my business, and vice versa?
- Do I have a short-term and a long-term plan of where I want to be tomorrow, next year, and five years from now?

The Truth Mission

Before making any final and irrevocable decision to get the business ball rolling—that is, to leap from business notion to business reality—these questions and many others should not only be asked but also answered. Do so honestly, thoroughly, and to your complete and utter satisfaction. Don't set out to tell yourself what you want to hear, as so many people do. Embark on a truth mission like a veritable Columbo.

ALERT!

Before entering into any business venture, you should do a complete reality check. That is, take an objective, critical, and unemotional look at your business idea and its feasibility. This is most often accomplished with a researched and well-documented business plan.

If the truth turns out to be what you want to hear, then you are ready to rumble. If it's not, consider yourself fortunate to have narrowly escaped a disaster. Don't despair. You just avoided a ton of heartache and pain. Try again with another idea, a new notion.

Businesses of every size, shape, and form permanently close their doors every minute of every day. Sometimes it's an unfortunate twist of fate that does them in. If you open up a sandwich shop next to a bustling factory, for instance, you can count on a lunch crush of hungry hardhats to sustain your business. But if the factory unexpectedly shuts down, you've got some bad luck. A lot of folks lose their jobs, and you might see your dream downsized along with your customer base.

Most businesses visited by the grim reaper, however, are not the ill-fated victims of such misfortune. More often, their owners failed to do enough market research for the product or service that they were offering to the public. Or maybe these people were ill suited to roles requiring them to perform customer service and interact with vendors and employees. These are the people who didn't ask themselves the critical preliminary questions.

Due Diligence

Unprepared businesspeople start businesses that don't quite have what it takes. Be it poisonous partnerships, or contentious customer relationships, people who have trouble working with others bring down more than their fair share of businesses. Sometimes the business killer is an old-fashioned lack of knowledge and skills—incompetence. A barber who cuts hair like a butcher filets a steak, or a restaurateur who can't differentiate between chopped chuck and filet mignon, is destined for the entrepreneurial dumpster. Due diligence and the business discovery process comprise a wide range of issues, not the least of which is "Know thyself." You have to have a business plan.

What Is a Business Plan?

Business plans are not only for big shots and big companies, as so many people think. They are for anybody and everybody who is considering going into business. The fundamentals of getting an entrepreneurial venture off the ground are the same for big and small businesses alike. Succeeding in any kind of business amounts to doing several key things right.

QUESTION?

What are the five W's a business plan should address?
Just as would-be journalists are taught to address the five W's in their articles, business planners are to do the same in their presentations. They must answer the basic questions: who, what, where, when, and why. For good measure, throw in "how," too.

If you believe that there is a market for the product or service that you plan on offering to the buying public, you've completed step one. Now comes a little soul-searching on your part. Do you have what it takes to provide this product or service to the market (that is, the capital, marketing tools, personality, and so on)? If you believe that the answer is "yes," then you should put it in writing and devise a business plan. Show the world that you've done your homework and are ready for the challenge of starting and succeeding in a business of your own.

Business Planning Basics

A business plan presents a well-organized, cohesive vision of your company or idea. It is prepared logically and contains documentation—facts and figures to support your confidence in the undertaking. It serves as a handy tool for planning and anticipating eventualities. In other words, your business plan functions as your decision-making guide. It lays out what you expect to accomplish, and how exactly you are going to accomplish everything from beginning to end.

As obvious as this may sound, to succeed in business you have to make sound decisions based on the reality of your overall situation, not on your hopes and dreams. Of course, you can make your hopes and dreams become your reality. That's what we've been talking about throughout these pages. But it doesn't just happen with the waving of a magic wand.

The Business Plan Reality Check

A carefully considered business plan is your reality. The main reason that the majority of start-up businesses fail is that they are born in another reality—a false reality. In most businesses, the optimistic human spirit is willing. It's the marketplace reality—the flesh, so to speak—that is weak. To triumph in business, you have to match your dreams with your abilities, life circumstances, and what consumers want at a particular moment in time.

For many entrepreneurs, the most important reason for drawing up a business plan is to attract investors or lenders to their sides. Starting a business is never cheap, and there is often a need for some infusions of venture capital. A solid, well-crafted business plan can put money in your corner.

Preparing a thorough business plan compels you to think your idea through and see if it can pass muster in the real world. If it does, the business plan then serves as a valuable blueprint. It enables you to establish goals and objectives, as well as timetables from which you can evaluate your progress and success.

The Business Plan Foundation

Virtually anybody can write a business plan. An Internet search on "business plan" will inundate you with templates you can buy, workshops you can attend, courses you can take, and books you can read. With computer technology the way it is, you could turn out a nifty looking document, full of charts and colorful graphics, in no time flat.

However, keep in mind that business planning is not about the glitzy fluff. Nor can you simply insert any old numbers into the blanks to create sales projections and market figures. Many people design business plans that look really good but at heart are not any good at all. It's sort of like the Charlie the Tuna routine. Charlie fancied himself a talented, highly sophisticated tuna fish that he reasoned would be appealing to the brass at the Star-Kist tuna company. Again and again he had to be told: Star-Kist didn't want tunas with good taste, they wanted tunas that tasted good. Above all else, you need your business plan to taste good.

Here are the three key elements that all business plans should contain:

1. A detailed analysis of the product or service that you will be providing the public, along with a description of how it distinguishes itself from the competition.
2. An overview of your potential customer base, how you are going to attract them, and what you are going to do to keep them in the fold over time.
3. A full appreciation of your capital needs in both the short term and the long term, and an understanding of exactly what your investors or lenders expect you to deliver.

These three items address the most important business concerns: product and/or service, customers, and cash flow. If you can identify audiences for your product or service, effectively cater to them, and satisfy your investors or lenders in the short term, you can then work on strengthening your long-term prospects. Getting over the initial short-term hump is vital to the success of all businesses.

Business Planning Preliminaries

Before setting down to craft your "official" business plan—the one that you'll take to potential investors or lenders, if necessary—there are some essential preliminaries that you'd be wise to tackle. First, you should draft a personal vision. Look into your crystal ball and see the future that you anticipate being created as a result of your business endeavor. Remember that starting a business is a big life decision. It will have serious ramifications in all aspects of your life.

Vision Quest

Of course, we know that success as a whole, and business in particular, is not guaranteed to go as planned. Nevertheless, you should write down in detail exactly what you want out of starting your business. Why are you doing it? What benefits do you expect to derive from the undertaking?

Maybe it's as simple as financial security. Perhaps the challenge itself is what's driving you. Whatever your reasons are for taking the entrepreneurial leap, spell them out. It is, again, another helpful and cathartic writing exercise that makes what you are doing more real—more immediate.

Once you've envisioned the future that you expect and desire, you can then start setting goals and objectives and developing specific plans to make them real. Again, your personal vision has to be in the driver's seat. Your vision must be sharp and realistic. You cannot enter into a business, with all that it entails, without a firm conviction of where you—as a person with dreams, goals, and obligations—want to be tomorrow, next year, and even ten years from now.

FACT

A business plan is essentially a strategic vision, but before it takes shape with all of its particulars—budget, expense projections, revenue projections, and so on—a more personal vision should be laid out. That is, you need to figure out exactly what you want to get out of taking the business risk and what meaning you see it having for your future.

The S.W.O.T. Team

To help you work out your personal vision, there's something known as a S.W.O.T. analysis. This is a proven business tool that will enable you to measure your vision's feasibility in the bright light of day. A S.W.O.T. analysis examines the following:

- **S**trengths
- **W**eaknesses
- **O**pportunities
- **T**hreats

In a S.W.O.T. analysis, you first consider your strengths as an individual and what they will mean to you and your running of the particular business. Match your unique talents and abilities with what you want to accomplish in business. Then evaluate your overall track record in life. Does it all jibe with you in the role as businessperson? Finally, ask yourself if your present financial state and various financial and other obligations amount to strengths or weaknesses.

Follow this sober analysis of your strengths with one of your weaknesses. Explore areas that could have negative consequences for your business success. Address family concerns, lack of related experiences, and possible difficulties working with people in a business environment such as retail.

Next, locate the immediate opportunities and benefits inherent in starting the type of business you have chosen. Explore avenues that can bolster your business success, like working with a mentor in the industry or field you've chosen, or joining a small business network. Then contrast your various opportunities with potential threats to your long-term business success. These might include financial obligations, health concerns, and interpersonal relationship commitments that could be adversely affected by your building up and working a business.

Complete a S.W.O.T. analysis of your personal vision, identifying your strengths and weaknesses, as well as the opportunities and threats that you see in starting up and succeeding in business. Then do a S.W.O.T. analysis of your business idea itself, repeating the process of looking at strengths, weaknesses, opportunities, and threats.

Pilgrimage to M.E.C.A.

To properly perform a S.W.O.T. analysis of your prospective business, you should by all means complete a M.E.C.A. Another important acronym in the realm of business planning, M.E.C.A. stands for "market, environmental, and competitive assessment." In a comprehensive M.E.C.A., you determine your business's potential strengths, weaknesses, opportunities, and threats by venturing outside of you, and beyond your personality and life circumstances, onto the business playing field.

Among many things, a M.E.C.A. explores the current culture and societal trends that will have consequences for your business. It looks at the overall health of the economy and evaluates the health of the competition with reality-based, twenty-twenty vision. Once you've completed both your S.W.O.T. and M.E.C.A. analyses, you are ready to roll—to roll out your business plan, that is.

FACT

What's important is what's in your business plan. Sometimes looks can be important, too. Readability studies in *Eyewire Magazine* at ✍ *www.eyewire.com* have shown that adding a second ink color to any presentation increases retention of the written word. Similar studies have also revealed that two columns of text are easier on the eyes than are full pages.

The Business Plan in Action

Now it's crunch time. You've done your research, and you've performed an interior examination of yourself and an exterior one of the world you live in—the place where you intend to make your mark as a business success story. What remains is putting it all down in a document. These are things that you should absolutely know, or have at your disposal, as you sit down to write your business plan:

- Your audience
- Your competition
- Your resources
- Financial estimates and projections
- Documented proof of your claims

Basically, you want your business plan to prove to others and yourself that your idea is a sound one, that your business makes sense and, of course, that it will make money. A business plan is not a press release or an advertisement. It is not meant to be loaded with marketing mumbo jumbo and all the superlatives in the dictionary. Rather, research and lots of facts and figures should back it up.

Here are the nine key sections that make up a business plan:

1. *Executive summary.* Presents a one- to two-page abstract of the entire business plan.
2. *Table of contents.* Lists the sections of the business plan.
3. *The company.* Provides a thorough description of the company that you are starting.
4. *Market analysis.* Describes the industry and customer base of your chosen business.
5. *Marketing plans.* Reveals your advertising plans, and discusses how long you feel it will take to attract customers and generate sustained business.
6. *Business operations.* Presents an overview of exactly how your business will function.

7. *Funding.* Addresses the fundamental question of how much money you need to open your business.

8. *Financial data.* Presents quarter-by-quarter projections of profit and loss, and determines a break-even point.

9. *Appendices.* Concludes with pertinent materials that enhance the plan in some way.

Business Plan in Motion

Once you have your original plan in print, be sure that it's easily accessible on your computer's hard drive and a disk, because you are going to be revising it along the way to success. A business plan is a work in progress, as is the quest for success. It's not something that you devise to get investors in your tent and then file it away for posterity.

ALERT!

Make certain that your business plan is thorough and fact-based, particularly if you are seeking financial backing. However, this doesn't mean that it should be the size of federal budget legislation. Be succinct, and keep it in the twenty- to twenty-five-page range.

You should always be working on your business plan, revising and upgrading it as conditions warrant. Work with a business plan in starting your business (as previously laid out) and while making your business grow.

A Rich Lesson

One characteristic is found in all successful businesspeople. It's called perseverance. In the mid-1970s, with the ink still drying on his college diploma, Rich Covello opened up a business of his own on Manhattan's Upper East Side. Leasing a vacant storefront, he christened his new business the Mod Stop. It was a retail outlet featuring hip furniture and household decorative items that were all the rage in that groovy time. Rich did not bother to develop a business plan.

Nevertheless, the Mod Stop sold virtually every item in its diverse inventory, from unconventional chairs and couches to quirky bric-a-brac—and that's the business ultimate. Right? Yes, but let's go back to the business reality puzzle again. Remember that it's always got to be interlocking and complete, and only meticulous due diligence——and a thorough business plan—locates all of the pieces.

However, one day Rich and the depleted Mod Stop inventory were faced with a serious dilemma—not enough cash to replenish the store for another go around. Thus, the Mod Stop came—like so many businesses before and after it—to a not so mod stop. It descended into the ash heap of entrepreneurial history, just one of many businesses that run out of gas in under a calendar year.

Fortunately, failure can be a very powerful lesson, though sometimes a cruel and expensive one. In Rich's particular circumstances, he learned a fundamental business lesson while managing the Mod Stop. Nursing a serious—but hardly mortal—reality bite wound, he recognized that he didn't fully complete his homework. He understood that had he done a more scrupulous due diligence—and prepared a sound business plan—he would have anticipated the Mod Stop's inventory problems.

FACT

Bugsy Siegel may have had some short-term success living by his business maxim, "Shoot first and ask questions later," but in the big picture, if you want a bullet in the back of your business's head, that's the route to go. Ask questions—and lots of them—first! Then emerge ready for battle.

After the Mod Stop experience, Rich vowed never again to make the same mistakes. He would avoid getting blindsided by those "should have known this was going to happen" moments, the bane of the underprepared businessperson. True to his word, his next business venture—a mom-and-pop pet food business called the Pet Nosh—proved more successful. With a $7,000 investment, a partner named Joe, and a business plan, too, Pet Nosh grew in size to eight superstores, ultimately selling lock, stock, and barrel to retail giant Petco for $19 million. And here's a footnote: Rich is back in the pet food business again, with independent superstores called Pet Goods this time, and going head-to-head with the big kids on the block, Petco and PetSmart.

Chapter 18

A Mission Statement Is a Success Blueprint

I s success all about money and posses-
sions? Not by a long shot. Success is a
quest for self-fulfillment. It is a mission, if
you will, to be happy and contented in all
aspects of life, both personal and professional. Businesses (profit and nonprofit, big
and small), schools, and individuals, too,
work with mission statements. Do you have
a mission statement?

What's It All about . . . If Not Money?

There's nothing wrong with actually making money—and lots of it. We'd all be kidding ourselves if we didn't own up to the fact that, in many instances, money talks, and most of us are tuned in to its dulcet tones.

However, money—and the financial security that coexists with it—must come attached to a laundry list of other things in order for it to complete a picture of success. Many of us start businesses because we want to make money in them but also because we want to test ourselves by stretching our talents and abilities. We want to be our own bosses and control our own destinies. We want to sample from some of the many adventures and challenges that life has to offer.

FACT

The unmistakably successful people in business, and in other careers, are making money, but they are also enjoying their lives well beyond their blossoming bank accounts. Meanwhile, those individuals who are fixated solely on watering their money trees, while they may be bringing home the big bucks, are definitely missing out on much of what life has to offer.

Success and Freedom

Success in many ways is about freedom. In the grand scheme of things, our lives are remarkably short. Days turn into weeks and then months, and, before you know it, the years are piling up. One day, you look in the mirror and see a senior citizen staring back at you, and in your pile of mail is a Social Security check.

Let Freedom Ring

This mystery called time is precisely why the freedom to do the things that we want to do, and go places that we want to go, is so critical. There is also no denying that the power of money helps us do things and go places. When we have the financial wherewithal, we can purchase things that bring us pleasure. We can visit places that excite and enlighten us, and, most importantly, we can enjoy the company of family and friends without the worry and stress that often accompany an uncertain financial future.

Life: It's an Adventure

For many of us, the mere notion of success conjures up images of adventure. Maybe it's rock climbing that springs to mind, or traveling to faraway, exotic islands with pleasing climes. Adventure and starting a business of our own are joined at the hip. Simply stated, adventure is stepping outside of life's little box and doing the things that most people never do. It's fair to say that most people don't scale mountains of rocks, visit tropical isles, or ever start their own businesses.

It pays, in a manner of speaking, to have money in your pocket when you set out on any of life's adventures. Keep in mind, however, that in many instances, it's the adventure itself (a business, for example) that provides the financial gold strike that so many of us desire. That makes life complicated—as complicated as it is to seek success within its tricky confines. To help put your life in sharper focus, you should consider preparing a personal mission statement of your very own. Only you know what you want to do. Guided by a cohesive statement of your own goals, you will be better prepared to experience some of life's adventures.

QUESTION?

What is a mission statement?
A mission statement affirms a purpose. For a business entity, a mission statement answers the question of why it exists—its reason for being. A personal mission statement combines purpose with principles. It serves as a guide in all decisions and actions.

Mission Statement Fundamentals

Did you know that the Preservation Directorate at the Library of Congress has a mission statement? You probably didn't even know that there was such an entity. Well, there is, and they have a mission statement.

In part, the Preservation Directorate at the Library of Congress's mission statement reads as follows: "The mission of the Preservation Directorate at the Library of Congress is to assure long-term, uninterrupted content of the Library's collections, either in original or reformatted form. This mission is accomplished directly through the provision of conservation, binding and repair, reformatting, materials testing and staff user education; and indirectly through coordinating all Library-wide activities relating to the preservation and physical protection of Library material." The mission statement goes on, but you get the picture.

FACT

Mission statements are often part of a threesome. First comes a vision of what we hope to accomplish over time, then a mission to physically do something, and finally the strategic goals are presented—specific actions intended to carry out the mission and, if all goes well, make the vision a reality in the future.

Purpose Plus Principles Equal Action

The three chief ingredients that go into formulating a mission statement are purpose, principles, and actions. We stepped into the spiritual realm in Chapter 10, where we discussed at length the importance of being spiritually whole and of seeing life as more than just a catalog of decisions to make and tasks to undertake. A mission statement asks us in much the same way to venture beyond our regular routine and specific job roles. It asks us to affirm our purpose for living.

Much of what we've addressed throughout this book—and the success journey itself—is about defining a mission for ourselves. A mission statement is really our attempt to summarize the lessons we've learned and put them all together in a neat package. Most often associated with business enterprises and schools, mission statements are now finding their ways onto refrigerator doors and the corkboard next to the telephones, as well as right next to those self-affirmations we learned all about in Chapter 2.

You don't have to be a business or a university to have a purpose in life, do you? If you have a family of your own, you have a homemade purpose right there. Your purpose is, among other things, to love, teach, and care for your children. Every parent should have such a purpose for living, and the world would be quite a different place if all parents did.

A mission statement is not limited to any category of living. You may be a parent, but you are also many other things: a husband, a wife, a friend, a businessperson, a volunteer, a community leader, and so on. Your mission statement, and your purpose, should reflect all that you are and all that you want to be.

Principles in Action

To take your purpose in life a step further, a personal mission statement requires that you identify the principles that are most important to you. Remember the virtues and the virtuous behavior that we championed back in Chapter 2. If integrity is your foundation, then your mission statement will reflect this. When you combine purpose and the right principles, you create positive action—you get results that are your life story.

The Personal Mission Statement

When you formulate a personal mission statement, you are saying, in essence, that you want to take full control of your life. Your personal mission statement brings your life purpose and principles together to answer the following questions:

1. Who do I want to be?
2. What do I want to do?
3. What principles do I want to live by?
4. Who are the most important people in my life?
5. What legacy do I want to leave?

What Manner of Person?

As you ponder the questions concerning who you want to be, and what you want to be, you must also zero in on the most important roles and relationships—personal and professional—in your life and build your mission statement around them. That is, you have to grasp where you are in life and what you cherish most in it at the present time. With this reality emblazoned in your mind, you must consider where you think improvements could be made and where you want to be down the road.

There is no absolute right way to prepare a mission statement. However, the general rule of thumb is to summarize the actual "mission" part into one sharp sentence. For example, Iams, the pet food company, says, "Our mission is to enhance the well-being of dogs and cats by providing world-class quality foods and pet care products." Personal mission statements are often more verbose.

If we've said it once, we've said it a thousand times: The success journey is all about forward movement and self-improvement. It's a perpetual learning experience. Consequently, your personal mission statement is never final. You are not Moses, so it needn't be carved in stone. Your purpose, principles, and actions in life are not meant to be static.

It's to be expected that your personal mission statement will be different when you are twenty-two than, say, the one you write at the wise middle age of forty-two. As you grow older, you should whip up a more evolved document of whom you want to be and where you want to go. The success journey teaches us many things, and the answers to those five key questions may change somewhat—may even change dramatically, for a few of us.

A Change of Purpose

Beware of falling into the paralyzing belief that your stated purpose for living cannot change with time. As you know, the success journey is full of change and growth. If you are single and fresh out of college, you are going to see your purpose in life in a different light than you will when married and raising three kids.

So, approach the preparation of your personal mission statement in the same way that you view your quest for success. Look upon it as an opportunity for discovery—about yourself, what you can do, and where you can go. Don't slam any doors in your face. Seek out what life has to offer, without fear of failure or disapproval from people you know. Don't narrow your purpose in life. Don't reduce your mission in life to a pat saying from a bumper sticker or desk ornament. Let it shine in its dynamism and forward outlook, and let it evolve with time.

The Personal Mission Statement Model

Keep in mind that there is no fixed way to write a mission statement. Don't worry about putting it in iambic pentameter or anything like that. Your eighth-grade English teacher is never going to get to grade it. Your personal mission statement will be written by you and for you, and pleasing yourself is all that matters here.

FACT

A personal mission statement should serve as your life guide. Before you make any important decisions or set life goals, you should refer to it. You can take stock of your life on a regular basis by seeing if you are living up to the principles and the challenges that you established for yourself.

A Written Example

What follows is a sample personal mission statement to assist you in devising one for yourself:

I will valiantly strive to be a person of indisputable integrity. I will be honest and up-front in both my personal and professional lives. I will go to bed each and every night with a clear conscience, knowing that I treated others as I, myself, wish to be treated.

My word will always be my bond. I will be trustworthy in everything that I do. I will mean what I say, and say what I mean.

I will accept others in my inner circle of family, friends, and coworkers as unique individuals with singular talents and abilities.

I will expect to be treated the same way in return. I will appreciate the fact that life is full of distinct personalities who see and do things differently than I do.

I will never stop learning. I will view knowledge as a boundless frontier that I will explore until the day I die. I will dedicate my waking hours to bettering myself in every imaginable way possible, from understanding myself and human nature, to improving my skills, both interpersonal and technical.

I will teach others what I learn and learn from them in return. I will place no learning barriers in my path. I will not be deterred by setbacks. I will constantly move forward, making certain that I am in a better place tomorrow.

I will accept that I am an imperfect human being, and I will work at correcting my faults every single day of my life. I will accept that there are some things, however, that I cannot do.

I will work hard at my job for both my employer and for myself. I will strive to better myself as a worker commodity and as a human being. I will not attempt to advance my career at the expense of others but only through my own hard work and diligence.

I will be optimistic and will remove pessimistic thoughts from my life. I will not blame others for my faults or failures. I will not bear grudges.

I will be generous with my time and try to help others in need. I will be appreciative of those who help me in any way, shape, or form, and I will let them know it by acknowledging in some way their kindness or act of generosity.

I will make sure that I eat right and exercise on a regular basis. I will not permit myself to become sedentary or stale. I will put a high premium on my good health and well being.

I will take time each day for myself. I will relax and reflect on where I am in life, and where I want to be tomorrow, and the day after that. I will take stock of how my decisions and actions are impacting both others and myself.

I will strive always to lead a good life. I will seek inner peace and contentment. I will touch other people only in positive ways and leave a legacy that I can be proud of.

Living the Mission Statement

Don't worry too much if you are not living up to the letter of your personal mission statement. There are enough stressful factors in life without you having to fret over missing your mark now and then. Your mission statement is a reflection of who you want to be and what you want to do with your life. If you are on a mission of any kind, it means you want to get somewhere. It doesn't mean that you are already there.

If you are finding it difficult to grasp what exactly a personal mission statement is, think about it as your life compass. A personal mission statement should be your moral and ethical guide as you go through life. It should be relevant to all aspects of your life.

Mission statements are invaluable on the success journey because the journey itself is about setting goals, formulating plans, and setting them in motion to fulfill your dreams. Your personal mission statement is your life beacon. It sets high standards that you hope to meet, but you might not always quite reach your mark.

The Business Mission Statement

Business mission statements are ubiquitous. Burger King has one, and so does Microsoft. Nonprofit organizations have them, too, from the Big Brothers/Big Sisters of America to the American Red Cross. Schools from the primary level on up to universities have mission statements that spell out what they want to accomplish. There are many organizations dedicated to many different things.

Beyond the Bottom Line

When you prepare a mission statement for your business ask yourself, first, what is the business's chief purpose? Why did you choose the particular business, and what need are you trying to fill? Of course you want to make money and grow your business, but beyond dollars and cents, there usually is a larger reason or reasons for a business's existence.

FACT

A good example of a mission statement comes from the Gwinnett County Public Schools in Georgia. It says, "The mission of the Gwinnett Public Schools is to pursue excellence in academic knowledge, skills, and behavior for each student, resulting in measured improvement against local, national, and world-class standards."

Successful entrepreneurs usually have a guiding mission, so to speak. They build their businesses, and ultimately reap the monetary rewards, by fulfilling their missions. Purpose and mission strengthen business entities because they answer the central questions that allow businesses to thrive and succeed. Mission statements give businesses depth beyond maximizing bottom lines and making profits.

Three Questions to Ask

When you prepare a business mission statement, ask yourself three questions:

1. What needs or opportunities am I in business to address?
2. What actions am I taking to address these needs or opportunities?
3. What are my guiding principles in conducting business?

These three questions go to the heart and soul of what you and your business are all about. You identify why you are in business, what you are going to do to succeed in it, and how you will conduct yourself along the way. If you know your mission—one, two, three—you certainly increase the odds of your success.

Chapter 19

Giving Yourself a Hand

The quest for success is not a solitary journey, and none of us can do it alone. We need assistance all along the way from our inner circle of family, friends, and career network. There are countless sources of support to tap, including hired help ranging from personal coaches to professional counselors, hypnotherapists to motivational gurus.

Personal Coaches

Why do you suppose talk radio shrinks are so popular these days? How did an obscure therapist named Dr. Phil McGraw become a national sensation and a best-selling author? Why do you think people are plunking down $125 per hour and more to rap with "life coaches"?

The answer to all three of these questions is the same. We live in very pressure-filled times, and because of the stress that so many of us absorb on a daily basis, in both our personal and professional lives, we seek guidance whenever and wherever we can get it. Sometimes we find it in the strangest of places: on the radio, television, and even over the telephone chatting with a coach.

FACT

Informal career coaching and mentoring has been around since the dawn of time. A more formal brand of coaching debuted on the business stage in the mid-1980s. It grew exponentially in the early 1990s, as dot-com companies sprouted up all over. When numerous young and inexperienced entrepreneurs found themselves in leadership positions—and without a clue on how to lead—the industry of business coaching found it had arrived.

As a matter of fact, coaching and mentoring have taken the corporate world by storm, with many companies replacing their old-style managerial hierarchy with a support system. With this change, directive-style managers (taskmasters) are going the way of tyrannosaurus rex and the dodo bird, and coaches and mentors are taking their place. In addition, coaches are also coming from the outside to troubleshoot problems in a wide range of areas. In general, however, coaches are asked to focus on issues of leadership, career advancement, and all kinds of success-related concerns.

Throw out the Lifeline

The notion of coaching is no longer reserved to the sports field. It is no longer the sole province of people wearing whistles around their necks and presiding over exercise regimens of four-count jumping jacks, squat thrusts, and running in place. Coaching has found its way into the office milieu. More importantly, perhaps, individuals are now enlisting personal coaches—life coaches, as they are sometimes called—to help them get what they want out of life, reach their goals, and realize their dreams.

If you are considering hiring a personal coach, be aware that unlike professional therapists, coaches do not need accreditation of any kind. Make sure that your prospective personal coach backs up the talk and assurances with real accomplishments—a proven track record of helping people realize their ambitions.

Coaching Moments

If you feel that an objective outsider could help jumpstart or improve your lot in life in any way, this is a personal coaching moment. If you want career advice from an individual of accomplishment, this is a personal coaching moment. If you are considering starting a business, and are as nervous as a turkey at Thanksgiving, this is a personal coaching moment.

An ever-increasing number of coaches are waiting by their phones for your call. Tracking down a personal coach, however, isn't like looking for an exterminator in the Yellow Pages. You don't just place a call to AAA Personal Coaching Services, agree to terms, and sign your name on the dotted line.

First of all, you won't find many personal coaches in the Yellow Pages. If you feel that one-on-one coaching could positively benefit you in some demonstrable way, research who's available, and find someone who specializes in the area of particular concern to you. Talk to people who have coaches of their own or know others who do.

If you are starting a business and want to talk to a personal coach—a business coach—about your undertaking, find one who's already walked the path you are about to venture down. Identify a successful businessperson who is simultaneously a personal coach and/or small business consultant. Not all coaches are created equal, and the fact that anybody and his mother can call themselves a coach merely adds to the uncertainty of picking a winner. You want to get what you pay for, and good coaches don't come cheap.

QUESTION?

Where do you find personal coaches?
Not likely in the Yellow Pages under "P" or "C." Most personal coaches don't advertise their services. It's positive word of mouth from satisfied clients that brings them business. Ask around. Get a referral from a friend or coworker if you can.

The Power of Personal Coaches

A coach of your very own could well make a positive difference in your life. The catch is that you have to enter into the right marriage of coach and client. Most important, the relationship must be voluntary. If somebody's pushing you to hire a personal coach against your will, don't do it. This is your decision and yours alone. Hiring a personal coach is not only a very important life decision, it's also a highly expensive one. You also have to be completely compatible with your personal coach—on the same page, as it were.

If you haven't figured it out by now, you are unique. An individual is truly unique; there isn't anybody quite like you on Planet Earth. You want certain things out of life that your neighbor doesn't. Your notion of success is probably at odds with your own brother's, and mom and dad's quest for success was very likely a different shade than yours is today. The moral of this little digression is that if you want a personal coach for guidance, you must locate an individual who complements your needs. You need someone who understands where you are in life and where you want to go.

Personal Coach Moments

In your quest for success, you are more than likely going to encounter some rough roads. That's just the way life is. There are even times when you might actually find yourself in need of a serious helping hand—somebody to help pick yourself up and point you in the right direction again.

Here is a sampling of the most common life circumstances that lead people to a personal coach's door (or telephone, in most instances):

- Need to improve marketable skills
- Insatiable appetite for a higher income
- Boredom and frustration on the job
- Personal problems at home
- Financial difficulties
- Major job change
- Desire for a career change

When seeking a personal coach, be sure to select someone who is the right fit for you. If you need a coach to help get a business off the ground, for instance, find a successful businessperson with a track record of success in business, and not a one-size-fits-all bag of coaching wind.

Personal coaches work one-on-one with their clients to assist them in overcoming all kinds of problems and life crises. They help their clients focus on exactly where they are in their lives and what actions they must take to keep moving forward. By nature, coaches are positive and solution oriented. They work closely with their clients in both formulating goals and monitoring the progress they've made in realizing them.

The Personal Coach Interview

When selecting a personal coach, take pains to prepare yourself for a good interview. You have to make certain that you find a suitable match. Your needs and personality must be in complete accord with the coach's life experiences and approach. This is common sense.

Most personal coaches offer a free, no-obligation consultation. Before signing any agreement, you can use this opportunity to get a good feel for whether this relationship is right for you and whether it will benefit you. Use this initial consultation to ask your prospective coach questions of immediate concern to you.

FACT

Your personal coach is your mentor and is there to give you objective feedback. She is not hired to tell you what you want to hear but what you need to hear to improve your life situation. A personal coach serves as a constant support system in your life by being both honest and reassuring.

Hiring a Personal Coach

There are several key things that you should absolutely know about a coach before signing any contract. You don't want to regret hiring a coach, and you don't want to find yourself down the road in the awkward position of trying to extricate yourself from an adverse relationship. You certainly don't want to be on the receiving end of bad advice. Let's face it—not all counsel is worth its weight in gold. Personal coaches are a fallible lot, with some more unreliable than others. However, the one thing they have in common is that they charge a tidy fee.

In your initial consultation with a personal coach, gather this essential information before you consider establishing a relationship:

- Fees schedule
- Background and credentials
- List of references
- Memberships in professional associations
- Style and approach

Style and Approach Matters

Don't overlook investigating the style of a coach. This does not mean finding out whether he or she is up on the latest fashions; rather, it means learning how your coach is going to treat you as a client. There are coaches who are decidedly more aggressive in their ways than others. Some prove to be very demanding counselors who will expect that you produce results for them.

When you set goals and timetables, taskmaster coaches will hold your feet to the fire if you don't deliver as promised. This "tough love" approach works wonders for some people, but is counterproductive for other more sensitive and thin-skinned personalities. Some of us require that periodic "kick in the can" and want to be chastised when we go astray or slacken off.

Although you don't have to be accredited in any way to call yourself a coach, there are organizations, such as the International Coach Federation and others, that abide by coaching codes of ethics. Ask any coach that you are considering working with if he or she is aware of these ethics and abides by them.

It's all about philosophy. Drill sergeants in the armed forces often gain the respect of their soldiers, despite the fact that they run and rag them pretty hard. We are not suggesting here that your personal coach would in any way behave like a marine drill sergeant in boot camp. Nevertheless, there are widely differing coaching approaches that you should know about. There's the rougher side of the street, where you are going to be held to unrelenting performance standards, and then there are the nurturers. This is the more common personal coaching stance and the one that we most often associate with one-on-one coaching.

The Nurturers

Whether your personal coach is authoritarian by nature, or a nurturer, he or she should support you. Whatever approach they use, all coaches should aim to help you realize your goals and succeed in life. This doesn't mean that coaches are personal cheerleaders, on the sidelines encouraging their clients' every move. Support and encouragement entail a lot more than yelling "Go team go!" It means talking things out, contemplating decisions together, monitoring progress, and offering prudent advice, for a start.

The nurturing personal coach approach works well for most people. This is true provided the nurturing doesn't degenerate into the equivalent of giving a child a peanut butter sandwich and a piece of celery for lunch. Nurturing means being there and imparting valuable lessons to clients all along the way. It means empowering individuals to make the changes in their lives that are right for them and their futures. The nurturing philosophy believes in the old adage, "You can catch more flies with honey than with vinegar."

ALERT!

There is a difference between personal coaches and consultants. Ordinarily, personal coaches work with their clients over the long term. Consultants usually offer short-term counsel, provide advice and instruction, and then let their clients solve their problems on their own. Personal coaches monitor their clients' progress and check in with them regularly.

Where There Is Self Self-Doubt . . .

Personal coaches work with clients in areas of their lives that will determine their success. If you take the leap and hire a personal coach, you obviously want to upgrade select areas of your life that you feel require a boost or overhaul. Personal coaches can be life coaches, business coaches, fitness coaches, relationship coaches, or a combination of any of these. Coaching options are available if you are experiencing problems or self-doubt in these areas:

1. Job and career
2. Personal finance and investment
3. Personal growth and self-esteem
4. Relationship betterment
5. Health and wellness
6. Personal organization
7. Management and leadership

Professional Hand Helps Sometimes

You've already heard the biggest complaint about the personal coaching phenomenon. It's that personal coaches do not have to be licensed to claim the designation. Most aren't. This naturally permits charlatans to wander around more freely in the coaching realm, without anybody's being able to challenge their right to do business.

Professional therapists, in particular, have been known to gripe about how even well-meaning coaches sometimes tread in areas that they have no business being in. A coach may have clients suffering from depression, or some other clinical disorder, who may truly require the help of a trained and licensed professional. There is some validity in this concern.

Depending on the particular fields the personal coaches are practicing in, some of their clients may have problems beyond their ken, and the coach could be doing more harm than good dispensing advice to those people. If, however, the coaching counsel centers on goal-setting, career advice, and business-related issues, there is no such ethical dilemma.

When Therapy Is Right for You?

There are times in our lives when we may feel desperate—subsumed by disheartening events, or trapped by ill-fated circumstances. Talking it out with family members and friends sometimes isn't enough to make us feel better. To get us past our troubles, a professional therapist may be just what the doctor ordered.

If you are in the market for professional help, visit ✑*www.4therapy. com.* This sprawling site is designed to equip you with all the necessary tools to locate a therapist near you and right for you. If you have a problem (like addiction, anxiety disorders, chronic fatigue, divorce, identity issues, self-esteem, or stress management), they've got a therapist.

Therapists and therapy have helped many people reach their life goals by giving them the confidence to overcome all sorts of obstacles. Individuals have been diagnosed with medical conditions that they were unaware of, treated, and had their lives wholly transformed. Ideally, qualified therapists' goals are to equip their patients with the capacities to feel better about themselves and more personally satisfied—the success essentials.

Emotion in Motion

There isn't one of us who doesn't suffer emotional pain on occasion. When, however, this emotional torment becomes a long-term thing, it affects our abilities to live normal lives and feel any sense of contentment. Whether it's melancholia, grief, or some fear that is running rampant, a professional therapist could help right things. By addressing the fundamental reasons for the pain, and offering solutions to relieving the crippling symptoms, therapists help countless individuals get on with their lives.

You Are Getting Sleepy: Hypnotherapy

Another helping hand for hire is hypnotherapy. Many people visit hypnotherapists regularly, and they do so to realize successes in their lives. They visit hypnotherapists to help them quit smoking, to shed pounds, to get a better night's sleep, to deal with pregnancies, to relieve pain, to fight alcoholism and drug dependency, and to get over fears of all kinds—including the all-encompassing fear of success.

Hypnotherapy is really a form of coaching. If you enlist the services of a hypnotherapist, you are doing so to better yourself. Whether you are battling the bottle or fear taking a plane trip, you have some problems that you want to overcome—problems that are impeding you in finding true inner peace and personal fulfillment.

FACT

Hypnotherapy is proving effective in helping many individuals improve their lives and their chances of realizing success. Ever-growing numbers of people are employing hypnotherapists—or self-hypnosis devices like audiotapes, CDs, and books—to help them stop smoking, lose weight, reduce stress, fight addictions, raise self-esteem, and overcome phobias or bad habits.

An Unconscious Mind

A personal coach deals with the conscious mind and doesn't attempt to put you under a spell or have you crow like a chicken. It's all out in the open. It's about attitudes, actions, and making the necessary changes to improve your life.

In a somewhat different realm, hypnosis explores the unconscious mind. We've all got an unconscious mind of our own that can function as either a trusty friend or bedeviling enemy. The main objective of hypnotherapy is to bring the unconscious mind into proper alignment with the conscious mind. When this happens, the results can be pretty amazing.

Hypnotherapy: Is It for You?

Hypnotherapy is rooted in self-improvement. You can go to a hypnotist, purchase self-hypnosis audiotapes or CDs, or get your hands on a pair of hypnotic glasses that give you a relaxing light show. Whatever route you choose is about tapping into your unconscious.

It is fair to say that many people—and you may be one of them—are skeptical about the benefits of hypnosis and hypnotherapy. When we conjure up images in our minds of hypnosis, we think about getting lulled to sleep by a swinging stopwatch, and then being asked to strip to our underwear and sing embarrassing songs. Of course, this is not what hypnotherapy is like.

Just as enlisting the services of a personal coach has got to be right for you, the same thinking applies to visiting a hypnotherapist. The medical consensus is that anybody with normal brain function is a candidate for hypnosis, and since hypnotherapy is not like its Hollywood depictions, you might want to consider it. Hypnosis is fundamentally a state of deep relaxation of both mind and body.

A Suggestion

Hypnotherapy takes this deeply relaxed state—that, by the way, we are all capable of reaching—and acts as a tour guide of sorts. The hypnotherapist "suggests" things to the patient that the patient will more readily remember and absorb because of the deep state of relaxation that he or she is in. This is the bridging of the unconscious state with the conscious state.

If, for example, you need help in boosting your confidence level to make a bold career move, hypnosis could lend a helping hand. A qualified hypnotherapist could instill in you a new confidence by the power of suggestion. This would be accomplished by spelling out the key life changes that you need—and, very importantly, want—while you are hypnotized.

The chief requirement that an individual seeking hypnotherapy must possess is an open mind coupled with a conscious desire to change. Since hypnosis requires a strong level of concentration, you have to be a willing client, or you won't achieve positive results.

Sources Unlimited

How is that an inoffensive parable about mice looking for their next meal has sold over a million copies? The book, *Who Moved My Cheese?*, by Dr. Spencer Johnson, has received rave reviews from scores of people. It has helped many who have found a couple of rodents' mundane predicaments relevant to their own lives. There are various testimonials from individuals who have called the book "life changing."

Again, in the quest for success, you locate sources of succor in all kinds of places. The sky's the limit. There is knowledge and inspiration in books, on audiotapes and CDs, and at seminars and workshops. *Who Moved My Cheese?* may not get you to move your cheese, so to say, but another book might.

"Success binges" of people who buy all sorts of books and cassette packages on the subject of self-improvement and achieving success are not unusual. However, as is often the case, these individuals emerge from their success orgies feeling more disillusioned and despairing than ever. That's because success is not a crash course; it's a journey, and an incremental one at that.

Success sources—the various helping hands—run the gamut. It's good to read books on self-improvement topics. It's beneficial to listen to inspirational audiotapes, too. Meditation is a plus, if you can manage it in some way, and there's a lot you can learn at workshops and seminars. Just remember that these are learning aids on the success journey. ⓔ

Chapter 20

The Success Lessons of History

History is life's ultimate lesson laboratory, and all of us would be well advised to explore the lives of the individuals who have achieved notable successes. This does not necessarily mean patterning our lives after theirs, but it is a worthwhile goal to appreciate the personality characteristics, life decisions, and actions that were in the vanguard of their good fortunes.

Success: Read All about It

It's always good to reflect on the lives of those individuals—past and present—who have realized exceptional accomplishments in their lives. Better still, read autobiographies, biographies, memoirs, and anything else that you can get your hands on about people you admire. Learn valuable lessons from both their successes and failures.

There are edifying and uplifting rags-to-riches stories to educate and inspire us. There are illuminating accounts of bold leaders who made positive differences in people's lives (Susan B. Anthony, Winston Churchill, and Dr. Martin Luther King, Jr., for example). There are the lives of altruists of all stripes to delve into, individuals who gave much more than they ever received—Mother Teresa comes to mind. In fact, history is filled with one story after another of individuals from all backgrounds, from the celebrated to the obscure, overcoming seemingly insurmountable odds to find successes and happiness in life.

FACT

Two years before she achieved fame and fortune by turning over letters on the game show *Wheel of Fortune*, the comely Vanna White was a contestant on another game show, *The Price Is Right,* in which she didn't win a thing. In life, you never know what's around the corner. It benefits all of us to approach these corners with anticipation and confidence.

As members of the human family, we instinctively seek out guidance from others. Beginning in infancy and continuing all throughout adulthood, we look to our role models to point us in all the right directions and keep us out of harm's way. The motivational gurus, whom we've discussed briefly, inspire people with their life stories. You know how it goes. They've confronted the most intractable of life's hurdles, called home life's deepest and darkest valleys, and yet somehow managed to turn their lives around completely.

Are We Historical Copycats?

"If I can do it, you can, too!" True or false? If you read accounts of historical personages, or attend a guru's self-help seminars, don't expect to emerge capable of duplicating the successes you hear about item by item. Understand that the quest for success is never about replication. It's a deeply individual journey on which you establish your life goals—your purpose and vision. Essentially, you write the script that will lead you to attaining your goals with a positive attitude and forward-moving actions. No plagiarizing other people's stories is allowed!

Creating a Little History of Our Own

Let us, however, learn what we can from others, both past and present. To grow as human beings, we need to recognize the personality traits that are typically found in successful individuals. We need, too, to appreciate the kinds of attitudes, choices, and behaviors that have long fueled the successful among us in finding compatible life partners and raising healthy and happy families, in building successful businesses and careers, and, of course, in discovering inner peace and true contentment in life. By identifying the patterns in successful people's lives and applying them to our own particular life circumstances and unique personalities, we are simultaneously learning the lessons of history and creating a little history of our own.

QUESTION?

What is history's most important success lesson?
The most important lesson that history teaches us is that we must persevere if we wish to succeed. "Never give up" and "If at first you don't succeed—try, try again" are the tried and true sayings to live by.

Titanic Endeavor

Let's suppose, for example, that your career goal is to be a successful actor. There's a lot you need to know about being a smash hit in a very competitive industry. After all, half the waiters and waitresses in New York City and Los Angeles are aspiring actors and actresses. But don't expect to become the next Leonardo DiCaprio by reading a quickly written biography. Instead, seek success in the business by being the next *you*— that's right, *you*. Learn the things that others in the profession have done to break into show business, to get their first big breaks, and to realize some sustained successes. Acquire what knowledge you can from the lessons of history in this particular field, and then chart your own course.

A History of Perseverance

This great nation of ours could not have been founded without the perseverance of our forefathers. The settlers, who boldly opened new frontiers, accomplished their great feat with a mother lode of—you guessed it—perseverance. The great medical and scientific breakthroughs of the past centuries were realized, again, with much perseverance and supreme dedication.

The Wonderful World of Disney

Did you know that popular culture icon Walt Disney was fired from a job at an advertising agency because the top brass there concluded that he had "a singular lack of drawing ability"? If you've ever been to Disney World or Disneyland, or if you've ever seen a Walt Disney film (and who hasn't?), you would have to conclude that the big shots who sent Disney packing were poor judges of artistic talent. There are countless Walt Disney-type tales in the annals of history. Some, however, never make it into the history books. That's because unlike Disney, those people opted not to persevere after getting knocked for a loop.

FACT

Often, when we experience failures in life, the setbacks make us give up on our hopes and dreams. But when we throw in the towel, we don't have any way of knowing how close we are to realizing success. This tendency to give up is really the sorriest of all human stories.

The reality is that many of us take discouraging words, setbacks, or outright failures, as mortal blows. Walt Disney could just as easily have said: "My bosses are right. I'll try my hand at some other more secure line of work." Fortunately for generations of kids, Disney didn't extinguish his dream. You might want to reflect on this Walt Disney example the next time you meet Mickey Mouse or Snow White and the Seven Dwarfs, or on your next visit to one of the Disney stores in any mall.

A Trump Card

It's no stretch to say that he's not the most likeable guy in town. But he's certainly a well-known personality and a paradigm of perseverance. His name is Donald Trump, and it's a name synonymous with wealth and power. "The names sells," says Trump.

However, Donald Trump wasn't born into great wealth. It's certainly true that he had an innate eye for business, courtesy of his entrepreneurial father, Fred, as well as an affinity for "recognizing a good deal," as he likes to say. Indeed, Trump has recognized more than a few along the way, and he has made a megafortune in the process.

In 1990, however, Donald Trump's billion-dollar empire faced financial ruin. He was forced into bankruptcy, owing banks more than $2 billion in loans that he could not afford to repay. Even though he had to hand over the preponderance of his assets to creditors as part of the bankruptcy settlement, Trump still managed to rebuild his crumbling empire in less than a decade. In short order, he was back in the penthouse again, so to speak, closing more deals and building more buildings. He even added the title of "author" to his impressive portfolio of achievements. Of the books he has written, one chronicles his return from the financial depths, *The Art of the Comeback*.

Trump says that "Anybody who thinks my story is anywhere over is sadly mistaken." Anybody who knows "The Donald," as he is sometimes called, would probably concur. Whether you love him or loathe him, you can't deny that he's accomplished a great deal by persevering. This is a lesson of history and success that none of us must ever forget, no matter where we are in life or where we want to go.

ALERT!

Isaac Fleischman, longtime director of the U.S. Patent Office, once remarked, "During times of economic decline when unemployment increases, so does the number of patents. Dark days often force us to become more ingenious, to monitor and modify the ways we reached failure and reshape them into a new pattern of success."

The Winning Edge

We are a sports-obsessed society, and very little can keep us away from the playing fields, courts, and rinks that dot the landscape. We are also drawn to our television sets to root, root, root for the old home team. Sports and athletics are thus ideal analogies for achieving success in life. The fact that we find ourselves so enraptured by athletes, athletics, competition, and winning makes the sports analogy come alive as no other.

When we look at athletes and competitive sports, for instance, we encounter similarities with what it takes to be successful in all aspects of our lives. Some of us are born with athletic talents. For most of us, however, we determine whether we succeed or fail in our attempts to be competitive in sports. The outcome is largely the result of our determination, discipline, or lack thereof, to better ourselves. The same sound logic applies to our successes in interpersonal relationships, career advancements—you name it.

A Rose by Any Other Name

You are probably aware of the trials and tribulations of baseball legend Pete Rose. You might not, however, be acquainted with baseball talent scouts' initial assessment of young Pete Rose—he seemed to have mediocre skills at best in the categories that counted. He wasn't fleet of foot. He didn't hit for power, nor was he a standout defensive player at any particular position.

The rest is history. What Rose lacked in obvious athletic acumen, he made up for in determination and work ethic. Between the game's white lines, Pete Rose proved to the world what positive attitude and drive could accomplish. He was aptly nicknamed "Charlie Hustle."

Unfortunately for Pete Rose, his willingness to give 110 percent and his patented love for the game didn't extend to other aspects of his life—those beyond the job. His utter unscrupulousness in his personal life landed him in jail for a spell, and he has been tossed out of the Major League Baseball Hall of Fame for a longer spell (life, as it stands now). Sadly, this baseball giant, who was a hero to so many, is today a living example—but the wrong example. Pete Rose needed to take his winning edge athletic traits home with him, which he never did.

FACT

In their book, *The Eight Traits of Champion Golfers,* authors Deborah Graham and Jon Stabler identify some key attributes of the successful golfer. They list eight: focus, abstract thinking, emotional stability, dominance, tough-mindedness, self-assurance, self-sufficiency, and optimum arousal. The authors conclude that peak performers have "an expectation of success."

Success is always open to redemption and second chances. Rose, however, has passed up many opportunities to redeem himself and own up to the errors of his past. He continues to live in a world of denial, blaming others for his past travails and wallowing in self-pity. These are not the qualities of a successful person, despite that person's prodigious athletic accomplishments.

Cold Lessons

Considered the greatest player the sport has ever known, Wayne Gretzky—known as the "Great Gretzky"—is the antithesis of Pete Rose in many ways. Gretzky translated his heroics on the ice into a solid reputation in the other areas of his life, where he has also made his name. That is, Wayne Gretzky made the transition between success in the world of sports and in life as gracefully and effortlessly as he played the game of hockey.

At ✑ *www.sportpsych.org,* Dr. Jack J. Lesyk lists the nine mental skills of successful athletes. Among them, Dr. Lesyk cites the athlete's ability to choose and maintain a positive attitude, set high realistic goals, and manage anxiety effectively. Dr. Lesyk advances the case that the very qualities that make for successful athletes also make for successful human beings in the game of life.

Love What You Do

Just how exactly did Wayne Gretzky become the greatest professional hockey player to ever lace up a pair of skates? Was he blessed at birth with talent to shoot that puck and score that goal? Or was it that he practiced and practiced his craft until he got it right? Or could the secret be that he just loved what he was doing?

Whatever the reasons for why Gretzky was so great at playing hockey, there's no getting around the fact that he, from the tender age of two, had a thing for the game. He wanted to play and play some more, so much so that his father built him an ice rink in the backyard of the Gretzky family home.

Wayne's father, Walter Gretzky, said: "Everyone thinks I made that rink so that Wayne could get rich and famous. It was pure self-defense. I was tired of freezing to death from taking him to the park every night." Wayne wasn't forced at parental gunpoint to play hockey. Quite the contrary. In fact, looking back on his childhood and hockey fascination, Gretzky professed: "You know, if I thought I was practicing, I probably wouldn't have done it. I just loved to play."

A characteristic often found in successful people is a love and passion for what they do. Maybe they love politics and pressing the flesh, or it's the thrill of closing a sale. Some people get a charge from driving an eighteen-wheeler across the country. Passion comes from sources as straightforward and ennobling as raising a family and seeing the children grow up to be happy and successful at what they love to do. The bottom line is that much of our success is rooted in commitment to what we are doing and pleasure in doing it. Success is never about proving our worth to others or rising to the top of the heap in our careers for vanity's sake. It isn't about besting others, either, by buying the biggest and most expensive house on the block or demanding the highest salary in the office. Success is pride in our accomplishments for positive, uplifting reasons.

FACT

If you want a crash course in the lessons of history, stop by Sybervision at ✍ *www.4iq.com.* There you'll find opportunities aplenty to purchase audiotape titles such as *The World's 100 Greatest People, The World's Greatest Thinkers,* and many others. The audiotapes include philosophers, composers, explorers, military leaders, political leaders, artists, and more.

The Ultimate History Test

Throughout your formative years, all through your schooling and right smack dab into your adult years, you've met a lot of people. Some of the people have been long dead and buried, encountered only through history books, and others you've known in the present, as living parts of your own life. In this eclectic mixture of past and present, you've studied the lives of individuals who shaped the world for both good and ill. You've probably seen people crossing your own life path who also made a difference. On this varied roster of the renowned and the ordinary, you likely admired some of these individuals for their accomplishments—their successes—above and beyond the others.

Let's take a little history test—a fun test. This isn't an exam that comes with a grade attached to it. Rather, it's designed as an exercise with the purpose of finding out what you most respect in other human beings—that is, the personality traits, attitudes, behaviors, and achievements that strike you as worth admiring and, perhaps, using as a pattern for your own life.

In this exercise, you make a list of the five to ten people—living or dead, famous or not—you regard most highly. The list could include of historical figures from the past, famous people from the present, family members, friends, or coworkers—there are no restrictions. You are then to identify the particular characteristics that, in your opinion, make them stand out from the crowd. In completing this assignment, carefully consider the virtues and visions and anything else that, in your estimation, makes these individuals special. To help you, here are several personality traits and attitudes that successful people regularly exhibit. In fact, we've addressed each one at some point in the book:

- Integrity
- Self-esteem
- Confidence
- Passion
- Compassion
- Purpose
- Discipline
- Courage
- Resilience
- Direction

Whether personal or professional, mentors are our own private history tutors—they are people who have been there and done that, and their experience can really help us out. These people can help us make our own treks down similar roads less lonely and less fraught with life's landmines.

Once you've cataloged the five to ten people you most admire, past and present, and you have identified the personal characteristics that you feel really make them shine, your next step is to chronicle which of their particular decisions and actions won you over. Lastly, you have to connect all the dots—examine their personalities, behaviors, and the larger picture of their lasting accomplishments. How did their personalities, coupled with their life choices, set the stage for their admirable successes?

My Ten Most Admired People			
Name	Personal Characteristics	Decisions/Actions	Accomplishments
1.			
2.			
3.			
4.			
5.			
6.			
7.			
8.			
9.			
10.			

Once you complete this exercise, you've in essence created a valuable document that says a lot about the people on your list but that tells much more about you. The things you hold dear in others are also the things you want for yourself. Perhaps you are working on acquiring more of the personality traits of successful people. Whatever position you are in right now, the exercise you've just completed will equip you with a higher understanding of yourself.

History's Supreme Success Lessons

Regardless of whom we admire from the present or from the past, there are some very fundamental success lessons—and personality attributes—that we can smoothly pluck from the annals of time. Just as we identified "perseverance" as a major highlight in the big picture of success, there are other traits that we should acknowledge for their critical importance in making an individual into a success.

FACT

We must never forget that studying history is more than just memorizing facts and dates. Just as much, it means learning from past mistakes and the consequences that followed them, as well as finding out what makes humanity tick. This is vital to our goal of becoming successful in our lives.

A Life of Purpose

Successful people, by and large, lead lives of purpose. Take the life of Ronald Reagan, fortieth president of the United States. Reagan had unwavering core beliefs and principles. Whether you agreed with them or not, his success in political life against great odds came in large part from a life of purpose and commitment. As president, Reagan was a staunch believer in freedom, and he abhorred the totalitarian forces in the world that aimed to reduce individual freedoms to ashes (and with them all individual quests for success).

When Ronald Reagan announced his candidacy for governor of California in 1966, it was considered something of a joke. After all, he was a Hollywood actor whose best acting days were already behind him. The incumbent governor, Edmund "Pat" Brown, salivated at the prospect of running against an aging actor. Reagan defeated him in a landslide.

In 1980, after a couple of unsuccessful tries for his party's presidential nomination, Reagan was again considered yesterday's news. Seeking re-election, President Jimmy Carter deemed Reagan his preferred opponent—the most beatable. After all, Reagan was sixty-nine years old and a relic of the past, or so it seemed. Reagan beat Carter in another landslide, never wavering from his core message—his life's purpose.

During the Reagan presidency, the Communist stranglehold in Eastern Europe was broken. The world will not soon forget the image of an idealistic and forward-looking American president standing at the Berlin Wall (the ugliest, most conspicuous symbol of oppression), and demanding that Mikhail Gorbachev "Tear down this wall!" That was in 1987, midway through Reagan's second term. In November of 1989, the wall was at long last torn down to the ground, along—eventually—with the ideology that built it.

The Network Stars

Its history is richer and deeper than that of the CBS television network, and, without question, its appeal is even more titillating than the FOX network. It's called the SUCCESS network. Throughout history, successful people have employed networking and mentoring to better their own lives. Very often in our own lives, we can credit key people—coaches, mentors, friends, and so on—for having taught us particular things and for paving the ways for our own successes in life, be they personal or professional.

ALERT!

Do you have someone in your life who can "show you the ropes"? If you don't, you should. Powerful networking on both the personal and the professional level plays an important role on the success journey. Coaches, mentors, and other confidants can give you an edge by offering encouragement, sound counsel, and by opening key life doors.

No matter what our personal lives resemble, what professions we are in, or what career paths we would like to tread, it is important to know people whom we respect and with whom we can interact in the same life circles. Our successes often depend upon it. First-time parents, for instance, have long found that talking with more experienced parents helps them enormously in their own parenting. This makes perfect sense. Those people who have lived with a newborn baby, survived the "terrible twos," the "tween" years, and the teen rebellion, have a lot of knowledge to pass on.

There is no better place than in a chapter devoted to the lessons of history to underscore again the importance of networking and mentoring to the success journey. After all, this chapter's chief message is that there is so much to learn from what's gone before us, and that really is what networking is all about.

Curiosity, Vision, and the Work Ethic

Did you know that Thomas Alva Edison patented 1,093 inventions in his lifetime? He is, of course, best known for inventing the incandescent light bulb. However, Edison was quite prolific as a scientist and inventor. He created the first electric generator, the phonograph, and the modern battery, to name just a few of his inventions. Edison was also instrumental in upgrading the telephone, telegraph, and the stock ticker among many other things.

Did you know that Edison was partially deaf for all of his adult life? A bout with scarlet fever at the age of twelve left him hearing impaired. This personal misfortune could have left him feeling sorry for himself, and he could very easily have cast aside all his dreams. Edison, however, remained optimistic and determined throughout his life. He even credited his hearing disability with increasing the focus that he felt was required for a scientist and inventor.

Let your successes unfold and build over time. Remember that Madonna worked at a Dunkin' Donuts in New York's Times Square before achieving fame and fortune, and both Al Pacino and Sylvester Stallone were movie theater ushers before they hit it big as actors.

Thomas Edison's curiosity, vision, and work ethic revolutionized the world for the better. You don't have to transform the world on that scale to earn your success diploma; you merely have to change your little slice of it in a positive way. Your curiosity about the ways of the wider world can help you make those changes for the better if you match it with a vision of where you want to go and a corresponding work ethic to get you there.

The lessons of history are many and varied. A single chapter of a book can only dip its rhetorical toes into the vast ocean that is history. As for achieving success in life, history tells us that if we understand ourselves, define a life purpose, and go after it with gusto, we will in all likelihood succeed in some way. There are no certainties in life, but those of us who believe in ourselves and our missions—whatever they happen to be—raise the odds considerably that we will know some success— perhaps even a kind of success that will belong in the history books yet to be written. Ⓔ

Chapter 21

Success in a Brave New World

Endings are always beginnings, just like the end of this book is merely the beginning of your more insightful success journey. In this new millennium, chock-full of new challenges and new concerns, you are now properly outfitted with the wisdom and understanding to embark on your personal quest for success with discipline and confidence.

Plan Your Future, but Live in the Present

We've devoted one chapter after another to such important subjects as career planning, financial planning, business planning, goals and planning, and so on. You name it, and we've talked about planning for it. This perpetual counsel on painstaking planning is offered with an attentive eye on your future—that is, your future happiness and well-being.

Despite the spirited emphasis we've placed on planning as a way to achieve success, we must nevertheless always be mindful of keeping our feet firmly planted in the present. While preparing for our futures is an integral part of our current living, we can't ever let such conscientious preparations for tomorrow rob us of the personal satisfaction and inner peace that we deserve in the here and now. Plan, plan, plan, but also live, live, live.

A New Millennium, a New Focus

For the first time in recorded history, opinion surveys reveal that we, the current working generations, do not think that our children and earthly heirs will have more opportunity and better lives than we presently know. In other words, we think things are getting worse, and we don't expect them to get any better. When we combine the rising cost of living with a frigid corporate job climate, and then add to the mix the omnipresent threats to domestic security, life as a whole does appear much less hospitable than it was only a few short decades ago.

FACT

E.W. Howe wrote, "Every successful person I have heard of has done the best he could with the conditions as he found them, and not waited until next year for better." The great humanitarian, Albert Schweitzer, said, "Man must cease attributing his problems to his environment, and learn again to exercise his will, his personal responsibility."

The realities of our times cannot help but transform our quests for success in some very fundamental ways. To effect all of the scrupulous planning that is such an imperative part of the success journey, and to achieve our goals and live out our dreams, we need to feel confident and secure about where society is and where it's headed.

Can We Be Optimistic about the Future?

Can we strike out after successes in life with the same level of optimism that previous generations did? Or should we view our hopes and dreams in the dim light of the new reality in the new millennium? The answers to these questions are at once simple and complex.

First of all, let us unhesitatingly accept the fact that there are many larger societal issues completely out of our control. Certainly, we need to be more vigilant living in this new reality. The rules of daily life have changed quite a bit over the past few years, but change has always been part of an active history. We can't let change—even rapid change—render us impotent. There is nothing more deflating to our psyches than surrendering to unknown forces—to fears—and giving up hope.

ALERT!

Take a fear inventory of yourself. Ask yourself this basic question: What am I afraid of at this very moment? Then initiate specific, corrective actions that are completely at odds with your fears. When you confront your fears head on—whatever they happen to be—you invariably conquer them.

If we want to be truly successful in life, we have to be optimistic. We must always be on alert for creeping pessimism so we can nip it in the bud before it rears its gloomy head. Regardless of what the general consensus is on overall life in the twenty-first century, we must always believe that better days are coming. Without this firm conviction, there really is no hope.

A Better Tomorrow

Does this optimistic advice amount to a sugar-coated version of reality? Not at all. It really boils down to our belief that we can always improve our straits—now and in the future. We must maintain our faith that the present day isn't half-bad, and tomorrow is not as bad as it seems.

Consider what life was like for millions of people during the Great Depression. It was the darkest economic period in American history. Nevertheless, the majority of the population believed that things would improve. President Roosevelt served as the country's reassuring mentor, offering hope and prescriptive medicine for a recovery of spirit. It is true that many people's beliefs were grounded in the conviction, "It can't get any worse than it is now," but this wasn't the whole story. There was an ingrained American spirit of optimism that survived even the Great Depression, and it lives on in the new millennium.

Life: It's What You Make of It

Life is always what you make of it. Regardless of where you live, or what your life circumstances are, success is ordinarily an option. It really is! This hopeful nugget of fact is as American as apple pie, and no security-alert Code Orange, corporate rightsizing or wrong sizing, or astronomical college tuition bill is going to alter this truth.

To counter some of the cold hard facts of living and working in the twenty-first century, take full advantage of the boundless wealth of career-related information on the Internet and in libraries. Join professional associations in your career field. Stay informed about what's happening in your industry and in the overall economy as well.

Success Roadblocks

There are some very common roadblocks to success, as we've chronicled throughout the book. When, however, you are self-aware, and keenly in tune with your attitude and actions—and, of course, their ramifications—you can navigate around those obstacles, or you can find alternate paths to success. When you fully understand what your attitudes and actions mean to your success, you are in a much stronger position than if you are pursuing success like a game of blind man's bluff.

Energy Crisis

Just as your car won't start without gas in its tank, you won't realize success without a source of energy in your tank—the tank that fuels your human engine. It's easy for us to become complacent in life and to accept second best. Quite often what separates the successful among us from the unsuccessful are our levels of energy. Typically, these are converted into the two key elements on the success journey: perseverance and discipline.

FACT

People in the industrialized world—that's us—watch an average of three hours of television per day. This is approximately half of our leisure time, a greater portion than we devote to any other activity, save work and sleep. Television has its place, but consider this. If you make it to the ripe old age of seventy-five, you've spent nine full years of your life just watching television.

Many of us enjoy relaxing in front of our television sets watching reruns of *Gunsmoke* and the *Beverly Hillbillies* or our favorite sporting events. However, hours upon hours of watching television, and other such leisure activities, can become very counterproductive.

The modern world has introduced the Internet into our lives in a big way. Like any other technological breakthrough or advance, the Internet has both its good side and its bad. The good side is that the Internet is a source of a tremendous amount of information, and it is all at our fingertips—just a few clicks away.

The bad side is that Web surfers sometimes get lost at sea. A little personal pleasure and entertainment on the Internet goes a long way, but spending every moment of your spare time (and not-so-spare time), in the pursuit of what really adds up to nothing, does not enhance your chances at succeeding in life. Don't permit lethargy and wasted time to hold you back.

QUESTION?

Is the Internet helpful or hurtful to the success journey?
It's up to you to determine whether the Internet is going to better your chances at achieving success. It's an infinite source of information that's there to be tapped. It's also the king of time wasters, when used only as a source of frivolity and distraction.

This Is Your Life

No matter how you slice it, your life is yours and nobody else's. You are the one who is ultimately responsible for what happens within its broad confines. Ultimately, the life decisions that you make about which roads to travel will determine whether you ever find happiness and contentment.

It is essential to your success that you assume responsibility for all of your actions. Stop blaming others for your problems. Renowned hockey coach Fred Shero once said, "I believe that a man may make mistakes, but he can't be considered a failure until he blames others for his mistakes." These are the words to ponder as you go through life blaming your parents for damaging your self-esteem or your cruel superiors at work for holding you back in your career.

Success: It's an Incremental Journey

We've made numerous references in these pages to the fact that we achieve success via an incremental journey. Success itself doesn't occur in one big bang, and it doesn't happen overnight. Contrary to popular mythology, there are very few "overnight successes." Smaller successes, building one upon another, are more commonplace. Then one day we turn around, and in our wake we see a string of accomplishments. In the grand scheme of things, they may look rather trifling, but upon reflection we find that they are very significant.

A Success Story

What follows is a genuine blueprint of a business partnership's success timeline. It chronicles what they considered big accomplishments and giant steps forward in their entrepreneurial evolution. It's a real-life sketch of the way success is achieved step by step, and how accomplishments that looked big—really big—yesterday can look so infinitesimal today. It is often the case, believe it or not, that what looked big yesterday was big, both yesterday and today. None of today's successes would be happening without those past accomplishments. Here is how this small business unfolded, along with several of the key milestones that were noted along the way:

1. Two guys purchase a mom-and-pop retail store—their American dream.
2. The store makes its first sale, with its owners tallying up sales on an adding machine and referring to a tax chart taped to the countertop.
3. The owners purchase a used van from a police surplus auction to assist them in making home deliveries, which they had been doing out of the trunks of their cars.
4. The partnership leases warehouse space and starts an ancillary wholesale business.
5. A second retail store is added to the mix. That's two retail stores and one wholesale operation.
6. This second retail store eventually grosses over $1,000,000 in sales (approximately $20,000 per week), a major achievement.

FACT

Longtime owner of independent pet food superstores, Richard Covello, started in the business by taking Ben Franklin's maxim "A penny saved is a penny earned" to heart. Covello would personally leave his original store to call information from a pay phone, knowing that it was a freebie on the outside but would be charged to his bill if he called from within his place of business.

This incremental timeline's larger point is that each one of these accomplishments was a cork-popping event. Buying a clunker of a van at an auction was exciting and big news when it happened. It was an indication that the business was forward moving and dynamic. When the very same business eventually consisted of eight superstores, and was bought out lock, stock, and barrel by a retail giant for $19 million, the purchase of the business's first van may have seemed like an insignificant piece of trivia, but it wasn't. For that old, sky-blue van with protruding brake lights on its roof was an important cog in the success machine, a consequential footnote in the success story.

Putting Things in Perspective

Everything that we accomplish in life must be put in the proper perspective. Whether we run our own businesses, or forge our own careers working for others, we have to remember to stop now and again. We need to take time to appreciate our accomplishments as they occur. There really are no small accomplishments in life, only small individuals who don't realize that life really is about waking up and smelling the coffee in the morning, the flowers in the afternoon, and the burning logs in the hearth at night.

The Family Plan

While we are still on the subject of incremental successes, we would be remiss if we didn't delve into our personal lives. The same logic that applies to career and business also applies to interpersonal relationships and family life. Success in entering into relationships that click, and in raising healthy and happy families, is likewise an incremental journey, with successes building one by one.

Celebrating small accomplishments in marriage and family is recommended behavior. When little Remy comes home from kindergarten with an original piece of artwork, this is an accomplishment worth celebrating, even if it's not quite Metropolitan Museum of Art caliber. Recognizing and living the wonders of the moment—particularly when watching children grow up—is one of the most rewarding aspects of the success journey. Don't let any of these moments, the important times of your life, pass you by.

Putting It All on Paper

On the success journey, we are going to have to present our credentials from time to time. While businesspeople prepare business plans to attract investors and lenders to their sides, as well as to plot their future entrepreneurial courses, the rest of us write resumes. Resumes are records of what we've done and what we can do in the future.

Looking for help in writing your resume? Check out *www.provenresumes.com*. There you will find resume writing services, workshop opportunities, and loads of career-specific resume tips. Whether you are looking for a job in retail, a restaurant, a nonprofit organization, an engineering firm, or anything in between, you'll surely find a helpful hint or two.

Don't ever overlook the importance of preparing your resume. Take the necessary time and effort to make it glow. Don't forget to document any of your relevant accomplishments. This doesn't mean that you should pad your resume with extraneous stuff or silly hyperbole. Make your resume stand out as the ultimate reflection of you. Make it a focused piece of paper free of any spelling, grammatical, and typographical errors.

In addition, you should be sure to tailor your resume to fit the job you are seeking. Place special emphasis on the skills and experiences in your life that are applicable to the position you want. Make certain to include all the fundamental elements that go into a functional resume, including the following:

- Objective
- Education
- Experience
- Skills
- Activities
- References

Remember that there is no single, absolutely correct way to prepare a resume. If you make it a positive reflection of who you are and where you want to go, you will increase your chances of getting that good job. Don't ever undersell yourself, but also be mindful not to promote yourself like an infomercial on the Home Shopping Network.

A Golf Analogy

In writing about the subject of success, authors never tire of finding analogies. After all, the meaning of success and all that it entails is wide-open space. So, in keeping with the wide-open spaces and green fields that often demarcate "success," it's time to make one last analogy. This time, let's talk about the sport of golf.

Golf is a game normally associated with success. After all, we can safely say that many of its players are—how shall we put it—financially secure. Playing eighteen holes of golf takes some time and can cost a few bucks, too. However, golf is not only a game for the rich and famous or for retirees with a lot of free time on their hands. It's a game that is increasingly luring average, everyday men and women onto its greens. The game erects few barriers. It is gender neutral, and you can even play golf—and play it well—with a not-so-perfect physique.

ALERT!

Many new golfers practice the more "glamorous" long-range shots, while neglecting the short game shots—putts, which account for more than half the game shots. Similarly, some individuals on the road to success focus their energies on "striking it rich" at the expense of mastering the basics required in getting there.

Play It Again

The keys to playing and succeeding in the game of golf are discipline and confidence. Sound familiar? The game is mastered by playing it, practicing, playing it again, and practicing some more. Isn't the game of life played in the same fashion? We acquire valuable life lessons as we go along. We stumble on occasion, but we also learn from our mistakes.

The game of golf requires you to pace yourself, set goals, and plan. You don't just show up on the golf course and whack balls into the stratosphere. There's much more to the game than hitting for distance, just as there is so much more to success than shooting for the moon and stars.

Seasoned golfers say that self-doubt is their greatest enemy on the course. Self-doubt spreads quickly, often insidiously, into every aspect of the game. On the success journey, too, there is no greater adversary than self-doubt. When we stop believing in ourselves, the game is over. You had better believe in yourself because if you don't, nobody else will. If you don't believe that success is within your grasp, you won't succeed.

Poetic Justice

There is a definition of success that you may find resonant: "To laugh often and much; to win the respect of intelligent people, and the affection of children; to earn the appreciation of honest critics and endure the betrayal of false friends; to appreciate beauty, to find the best in others; to leave the world a bit better, whether by a healthy child, a garden patch, or a redeemed social condition; to know even one life has breathed easier because you have lived. That is to have succeeded." Ⓔ

Appendices

Appendix A

Resources

Appendix B

Glossary of Terms

Appendix A
Resources

Books

The Emperors of Chocolate, by Joel Glenn Brenner (Broadway Books: 2000).

How to Win Friends and Influence People, by Dale Carnegie (Pocket Books: 1998).

The Seven Habits of Highly Effective People, Stephen R. Covey (Simon & Schuster: 1990).

Winning with the P & G 99, by Charles L. Decker (Pocket Books: 1998).

This Is Your Life, Not a Dress Rehearsal, by Jim Donovan (Bovan: 1998).

Ten Secrets for Success and Inner Peace, by Wayne W. Dyer (Hay House: 2002).

The Magic Lamp, by Keith Ellis (Three Rivers Press: 1998).

Cultivating Inner Peace, by Paul R. Fleischman (Putnam: 1997).

Leadership, by Rudolph W. Giuliani (Miramax: 2002).

What Color Is Your Diet?, by David Heber (Regan: 2001).

Get a Financial Life, by Beth Kobliner (Fireside: 2000).

Pathfinder, by Nicholas Lore (Fireside: 1998).

Your Road Map for Success, by John C. Maxwell (Nelson: 2002).

Time Management from the Inside Out, by Julie Morgenstern (Henry Holt: 2000).

Success Is Not an Accident, by Tommy Newberry (Looking Glass Books: 1999).

The 100 Simple Secrets of Successful People, by David Niven (HarperCollins: 2002).

What No One Ever Tells You About Starting Your Own Business, by Jan Norman (Upstart: 1999).

The Nine Steps to Financial Freedom, by Suze Orman (Three Rivers Press: 2000).

The Road Less Traveled, by M. Scott Peck (Touchtone Books: 1998).

Staples for Success, by Thomas G. Stemberg (Knowledge Exchange: 1996).

Joe Torre's Ground Rules for Winners, by Joe Torre and Henry Dreher (Hyperion: 2000).

Create a Life That Tickles Your Soul, by Suzanne Willis Zoglio (Tower Hill Press: 2000).

Web Sites
Business Plan Writing

www.bplans.com

Career Planning

www.careerbuilder.com

www.collegegrad.com

www.mapping-your-future.org

www.monster.com

Goal-Setting

www.topachievement.com

Health and Wellness

www.activekarma.com

www.goodcyclist.org

Investing

www.asec.org

www.fool.com

www.investoreducation.org

www.investorwords.com

Reference

www.4therapy.com

Resume Writing

www.provenresumes.com

www.10minuteresume.com

Time Management

www.mindtools.com

Glossary of Terms

asset allocation model: An investment strategy that practices risk management as it weighs the choices that are right for you, based on your current life circumstances and projected future.

business plan: A strategic vision of a potential business that identifies audience, competition, and available resources.

business reality puzzle: A business idea combined with an objective, critical examination of whether a possible entrepreneurial endeavor is a sound one with a chance to succeed.

coaching and mentoring: A support system that is usually found in the corporate world, as well as in other places, in which coaches or mentors help clients to overcome a variety of life obstacles.

confidence: A genuine feeling of self-assurance and freedom from uncertainty.

dress for success: A term that embodies "striking the right pose" in dress and overall appearance to realize your life goals in both your personal and professional lives.

fear of success: The irrational fear of forward-moving changes in your life that bring with them higher expectations, demands on your time, and other "negative" consequences.

five brushstrokes of success: Virtue, confidence, dedication, consistency, and happiness.

food diary: A daily recording of everything that you eat and drink, along with calorie counts, the purpose of which is to instill a valuable nutritional discipline.

Generosity Challenge: A variety of possible actions—in all areas of your life—designed to spur your capacities for giving.

generosity of spirit: Unconditional willingness to give of your time, know-how, and insight.

goals: The particulars in life that we desire in both our personal and professional lives, and which we formally set out to make reality.

Golden Rule: The timeless philosophy of treating others the way we want to be treated.

hypegiaphobia: The fear of responsibility.

hypnotherapy: A self-help option that endeavors to tap into the power of the unconscious mind.

inner peace: A deep feeling of contentment with who you are and what you are doing with your life.

intuition: An accurate feel for another person, or a particular life situation, that assists you in your decision-making.

M.E.C.A.: Market, Environmental, and Competitive Assessment; a tool for assessing the viability of a potential business by exploring factors such as the health of the economy and societal trends.

mission statement: An affirmation of purpose, be it an individual life purpose or reason for a business entity's existence.

networking: The beneficial associations that we establish through the years in both our personal and professional lives.

optimism: A dynamic, empowering, and invaluable outlook that focuses on possibilities and opportunities in all life situations.

outcome goals: Established objectives that define a very specific result, such as winning a certain competition or achieving a certain goal.

performance goals: Established objectives to meet certain levels of accomplishment, not based on competing with others.

perseverance complex: An indispensable personality trait that permits us to keep moving forward despite life's many obstacles.

personal fulfillment/satisfaction: The quality of being content with your lot in life; the quintessential measure of success.

personal/life coaches: People who work with clients one-on-one to assist them in overcoming a variety of life obstacles.

personal spirituality: The interior paths that all of us—in our unique ways—travel to unearth the true meaning of life.

positive associations: Interpersonal and professional relationships that strengthen our lives in innumerable ways.

positive thinking: Approaching interpersonal encounters and life moments from the best possible angle.

self-actualization: The process of becoming in *actuality* what we are *potentially* as human beings.

self-affirmations: Compliments and encouraging words that we give ourselves, whether orally or in the form of notes and messages to ourselves.

self-awareness: The capacity to know yourself and ramifications of your behavior.

self-control: The virtue of knowing what you want and don't want, right from wrong: not giving in to the dark side.

self-esteem: Confidence in your talents and abilities in all areas of your life.

stress: Demands made upon your physical and emotional capacities.

stress diary: A written record of the amounts of stress that you feel at various points of your day, with special emphasis placed on specific events.

success: The realization of your life goals coupled with an abiding and deep sense of personal satisfaction and inner peace.

S.W.O.T.: A business technique that explores strengths, weaknesses, opportunities, and threats to a potential entrepreneurial undertaking.

time management: Developing an awareness of how your time is spent in order to determine how all your time can best be invested.

Type A personality: An aggressive, impatient, highly competitive individual with an unrelenting desire to be active.

Type B personality: A relaxed, reflective individual who tends to roll with life's punches with little fanfare.

values: A variety of beliefs that we hold dear to our hearts.

virtues: Deeply ingrained positive and ethical attitudes or behaviors, absolutely essential to achieving success.

Index

intuition and, 134
laughter for, 137
personal nature of, 129–30
playing and, 136
reasons for, 128–30
relaxation and, 135–36
revering life and, 131
tough times and, 130, 131, 132–33
as ultimate pick-me-up, 132–34
Stabler, John, 259
Stallone, Sylvester, 266
Stocks, 211–12, 215
Stress, 179–90
    causes, 109, 181, 190
    communication alleviating, 186
    conflict and, 186–87
    defined, 180, 282
    diet and, 189
    high expectations and, 185
    at home, 187–88
    managing/relieving, 109, 181,
        182–83, 184–87, 189–90
    medical attention for, 184
    personal appearance and, 182
    powerlessness and, 185
    self-esteem and, 181
    symptoms, 181–82
    time management and, 108–9
    weight and, 144
    at work, 180–81, 184–87
Stress diary, 188–90
    benefits of, 188–89
    daily routine in, 189
    defined, 282
    entries in, 189
    identifying stress causes, 189–90
Success
    defined, xi, xii, 277, 282
    golf analogy, 276–77
    incremental journey of, 272–74
    selflessness of, 159
    wealth vs., 26, 61, 231, 232
Support groups, 124–25. *See also*
    Personal coaches; Professional help
Supportive relationships, 35–36
S.W.O.T. analysis
    for business plans, 225–26

defined, 225, 282
for personal life, 226

T, U, V

Talents
    career complementing, 10–11
    creative impulse and, 48–49
    early development, 6–7
    expressing, 6, 7
    finding, 6–8
    risk-taking and, 7
    self-actualization and, 7–10
    self-awareness and, 48–49
Technology, 168–69, 175–76, 271–72
Television, 271
Therapy, 249–50. *See also*
    Hypnotherapy
Thoreau, Henry David, 121
Time management, 101–13
    awareness, 102
    beginning now, 112–13
    chart, 103
    in college, 104–5
    defined, 106, 282
    delegating and, 107
    home, family and, 110–12, 162–63
    interruptions and, 108
    multitasking and, 110
    mystery of time and, 112–13
    overextending and, 107
    planning and, 107–8
    priorities, 104–5, 109–10, 111–12
    procrastination and, 106–7
    responsibility and, 102–3
    saying "no" and, 109–10
    stress and, 108–9
    time wasters, 105–9
Tolson, Melvin B., 171
Trump, Donald, 257
Type A personality, 64–65, 282
Type B personality, 64–65, 282
U.S. Treasury securities, 209–10
Virtue(s), 18–23
    compassion as, 21–22
    courage as, 21

defined, 19–20, 282
fairness as, 22
generosity as. *See* Generosity of
    spirit
Golden Rule, 43, 122–24, 281
honesty as, 20
learning, 19
list of, 19
overview, 18–19
self-control as, 22–23
supreme importance of, 18–19

W, Y

Wealth, success vs., 26, 61, 231, 232
Web sites, 280
    health, wellness, 145, 151, 249, 280
    historical reference, 261
    investing, 208, 209, 280
    job-seeking, 69, 280
    writing resumes, 275, 280
White, Vanna, 254
Work. *See* Career
World stage, 17
"Yes" vs. "no" answers, 165

THE EVERYTHING® GET RICH BOOK

By Jennifer Lane, CFP, with Bill Lane

Trade paperback
$14.95 ($22.95 CAN)
1-58062-670-X, 320 pages

The Everything® Get Rich Book provides you with professional, insider information on how to multiply your savings. Full of practical tips on making money, saving money, and protecting assets, it shows you how to avoid accruing debt, manage your spending to increase savings, and plan in advance for a luxurious retirement. Featuring comprehensive information on setting goals, building a plan, investing, managing a portfolio, and filing taxes, The Everything® Get Rich Book will have you building your wealth in no time!

OTHER *EVERYTHING*® BOOKS BY ADAMS MEDIA

BUSINESS

Everything® **Business Planning Book**
Everything® **Coaching and Mentoring Book**
Everything® **Fundraising Book**
Everything® **Home-Based Business Book**
Everything® **Leadership Book**
Everything® **Managing People Book**
Everything® **Network Marketing Book**
Everything® **Online Business Book**
Everything® **Project Management Book**
Everything® **Selling Book**
Everything® **Start Your Own Business Book**
Everything® **Time Management Book**

COMPUTERS

Everything® **Build Your Own Home Page Book**

Everything® **Computer Book**
Everything® **Internet Book**
Everything® **Microsoft® Word 2000 Book**

COOKBOOKS

Everything® **Barbecue Cookbook**
Everything® **Bartender's Book, $9.95**
Everything® **Chinese Cookbook**
Everything® **Chocolate Cookbook**
Everything® **Cookbook**
Everything® **Dessert Cookbook**
Everything® **Diabetes Cookbook**
Everything® **Low-Carb Cookbook**
Everything® **Low-Fat High-Flavor Cookbook**
Everything® **Mediterranean Cookbook**
Everything® **Mexican Cookbook**
Everything® **One-Pot Cookbook**
Everything® **Pasta Book**

Everything® **Quick Meals Cookbook**
Everything® **Slow Cooker Cookbook**
Everything® **Soup Cookbook**
Everything® **Thai Cookbook**
Everything® **Vegetarian Cookbook**
Everything® **Wine Book**

HEALTH

Everything® **Anti-Aging Book**
Everything® **Diabetes Book**
Everything® **Dieting Book**
Everything® **Herbal Remedies Book**
Everything® **Hypnosis Book**
Everything® **Menopause Book**
Everything® **Nutrition Book**
Everything® **Reflexology Book**
Everything® **Stress Management Book**
Everything®**Vitamins, Minerals, and Nutritional Supplements Book**

All Everything® books are priced at $12.95 or $14.95, unless otherwise stated. Prices subject to change without notice.
Canadian prices range from $11.95–$31.95, and are subject to change without notice.

HISTORY

Everything® **American History Book**
Everything® **Civil War Book**
Everything® **Irish History & Heritage Book**
Everything® **Mafia Book**
Everything® **World War II Book**

HOBBIES & GAMES

Everything® **Bridge Book**
Everything® **Candlemaking Book**
Everything® **Casino Gambling Book**
Everything® **Chess Basics Book**
Everything® **Collectibles Book**
Everything® **Crossword and Puzzle Book**
Everything® **Digital Photography Book**
Everything® **Family Tree Book**
Everything® **Games Book**
Everything® **Knitting Book**
Everything® **Magic Book**
Everything® **Motorcycle Book**
Everything® **Online Genealogy Book**
Everything® **Photography Book**
Everything® **Pool & Billiards Book**
Everything® **Quilting Book**
Everything® **Scrapbooking Book**
Everything® **Soapmaking Book**

HOME IMPROVEMENT

Everything® **Feng Shui Book**
Everything® **Gardening Book**
Everything® **Home Decorating Book**
Everything® **Landscaping Book**
Everything® **Lawn Care Book**
Everything® **Organize Your Home Book**

KIDS' STORY BOOKS

Everything® **Bedtime Story Book**
Everything® **Bible Stories Book**
Everything® **Fairy Tales Book**
Everything® **Mother Goose Book**

EVERYTHING® *KIDS'* BOOKS

All titles are $6.95
Everything® **Kids' Baseball Book, 2nd Ed.** ($10.95 CAN)
Everything® **Kids' Bugs Book** ($10.95 CAN)
Everything® **Kids' Christmas Puzzle & Activity Book** ($10.95 CAN)
Everything® **Kids' Cookbook** ($10.95 CAN)
Everything® **Kids' Halloween Puzzle & Activity Book** ($10.95 CAN)
Everything® **Kids' Joke Book** ($10.95 CAN)
Everything® **Kids' Math Puzzles Book** ($10.95 CAN)
Everything® **Kids' Mazes Book** ($10.95 CAN)
Everything® **Kids' Money Book** ($11.95 CAN)
Everything® **Kids' Monsters Book** ($10.95 CAN)
Everything® **Kids' Nature Book** ($11.95 CAN)
Everything® **Kids' Puzzle Book** ($10.95 CAN)
Everything® **Kids' Science Experiments Book** ($10.95 CAN)
Everything® **Kids' Soccer Book** ($10.95 CAN)
Everything® **Kids' Travel Activity Book** ($10.95 CAN)

LANGUAGE

Everything® **Learning French Book**
Everything® **Learning German Book**
Everything® **Learning Italian Book**
Everything® **Learning Latin Book**
Everything® **Learning Spanish Book**
Everything® **Sign Language Book**

MUSIC

Everything® **Drums Book (with CD),** $19.95 ($31.95 CAN)
Everything® **Guitar Book**
Everything® **Playing Piano and Keyboards Book**

Everything® **Rock & Blues Guitar Book (with CD), $19.95** ($31.95 CAN)
Everything® **Songwriting Book**

NEW AGE

Everything® **Astrology Book**
Everything® **Divining the Future Book**
Everything® **Dreams Book**
Everything® **Ghost Book**
Everything® **Meditation Book**
Everything® **Numerology Book**
Everything® **Palmistry Book**
Everything® **Psychic Book**
Everything® **Spells & Charms Book**
Everything® **Tarot Book**
Everything® **Wicca and Witchcraft Book**

PARENTING

Everything® **Baby Names Book**
Everything® **Baby Shower Book**
Everything® **Baby's First Food Book**
Everything® **Baby's First Year Book**
Everything® **Breastfeeding Book**
Everything® **Father-to-Be Book**
Everything® **Get Ready for Baby Book**
Everything® **Homeschooling Book**
Everything® **Parent's Guide to Positive Discipline**
Everything® **Potty Training Book, $9.95** ($15.95 CAN)
Everything® **Pregnancy Book, 2nd Ed.**
Everything® **Pregnancy Fitness Book**
Everything® **Pregnancy Organizer, $15.00** ($22.95 CAN)
Everything® **Toddler Book**
Everything® **Tween Book**

PERSONAL FINANCE

Everything® **Budgeting Book**
Everything® **Get Out of Debt Book**
Everything® **Get Rich Book**
Everything® **Homebuying Book, 2nd Ed.**
Everything® **Homeselling Book**

All Everything® books are priced at $12.95 or $14.95, unless otherwise stated. Prices subject to change without notice.
Canadian prices range from $11.95–$31.95, and are subject to change without notice.

Everything® **Investing Book**
Everything® **Money Book**
Everything® **Mutual Funds Book**
Everything® **Online Investing Book**
Everything® **Personal Finance Book**
Everything® **Personal Finance in Your 20s & 30s Book**
Everything® **Wills & Estate Planning Book**

PETS

Everything® **Cat Book**
Everything® **Dog Book**
Everything® **Dog Training and Tricks Book**
Everything® **Horse Book**
Everything® **Puppy Book**
Everything® **Tropical Fish Book**

REFERENCE

Everything® **Astronomy Book**
Everything® **Car Care Book**
Everything® **Christmas Book, $15.00 ($21.95 CAN)**
Everything® **Classical Mythology Book**
Everything® **Einstein Book**
Everything® **Etiquette Book**
Everything® **Great Thinkers Book**
Everything® **Philosophy Book**
Everything® **Shakespeare Book**
Everything® **Tall Tales, Legends, & Other Outrageous Lies Book**
Everything® **Toasts Book**
Everything® **Trivia Book**
Everything® **Weather Book**

RELIGION

Everything® **Angels Book**
Everything® **Buddhism Book**
Everything® **Catholicism Book**
Everything® **Jewish History & Heritage Book**
Everything® **Judaism Book**

Everything® **Prayer Book**
Everything® **Saints Book**
Everything® **Understanding Islam Book**
Everything® **World's Religions Book**
Everything® **Zen Book**

SCHOOL & CAREERS

Everything® **After College Book**
Everything® **College Survival Book**
Everything® **Cover Letter Book**
Everything® **Get-a-Job Book**
Everything® **Hot Careers Book**
Everything® **Job Interview Book**
Everything® **Online Job Search Book**
Everything® **Resume Book, 2nd Ed.**
Everything® **Study Book**

SELF-HELP

Everything® **Dating Book**
Everything® **Divorce Book**
Everything® **Great Marriage Book**
Everything® **Great Sex Book**
Everything® **Romance Book**
Everything® **Self-Esteem Book**
Everything® **Success Book**

SPORTS & FITNESS

Everything® **Bicycle Book**
Everything® **Body Shaping Book**
Everything® **Fishing Book**
Everything® **Fly-Fishing Book**
Everything® **Golf Book**
Everything® **Golf Instruction Book**
Everything® **Pilates Book**
Everything® **Running Book**
Everything® **Sailing Book, 2nd Ed.**
Everything® **T'ai Chi and QiGong Book**
Everything® **Total Fitness Book**
Everything® **Weight Training Book**
Everything® **Yoga Book**

TRAVEL

Everything® **Guide to Las Vegas**

Everything® **Guide to New England**
Everything® **Guide to New York City**
Everything® **Guide to Washington D.C.**
Everything® **Travel Guide to The Disneyland Resort®, California Adventure®, Universal Studios®, and the Anaheim Area**
Everything® **Travel Guide to the Walt Disney World Resort®, Universal Studios®, and Greater Orlando, 3rd Ed.**

WEDDINGS

Everything® **Bachelorette Party Book**
Everything® **Bridesmaid Book**
Everything® **Creative Wedding Ideas Book**
Everything® **Jewish Wedding Book**
Everything® **Wedding Book, 2nd Ed.**
Everything® **Wedding Checklist, $7.95 ($11.95 CAN)**
Everything® **Wedding Etiquette Book, $7.95 ($11.95 CAN)**
Everything® **Wedding Organizer, $15.00 ($22.95 CAN)**
Everything® **Wedding Shower Book, $7.95 ($12.95 CAN)**
Everything® **Wedding Vows Book, $7.95 ($11.95 CAN)**
Everything® **Weddings on a Budget Book, $9.95 ($15.95 CAN)**

WRITING

Everything® **Creative Writing Book**
Everything® **Get Published Book**
Everything® **Grammar and Style Book**
Everything® **Grant Writing Book**
Everything® **Guide to Writing Children's Books**
Everything® **Screenwriting Book**
Everything® **Writing Well Book**

Available wherever books are sold!
To order, call 800-872-5627, or visit us at everything.com